The Life and  Henry Gassaway Davis

1823-1916

Charles M. Pepper

Alpha Editions

This edition published in 2020

ISBN : 9789354012082

Design and Setting By
Alpha Editions
email - alphaedis@gmail.com

THE LIFE AND TIMES
OF
HENRY GASSAWAY DAVIS
1823—1916

BY

CHARLES M. PEPPER

Disce ut semper victurus; vive ut eras moriturus
Work as if you were to live forever; live as if
you were to die to-morrow

NEW YORK
THE CENTURY CO.
1920

PREFACE

The pages that follow are the record of a remarkable life, a life written in deeds. Henry Gassaway Davis for three-quarters of a century was absorbed in the healthy activities in which a constructive mind naturally found expression. The romance of railway building, the development of natural resources, the creation of industrial communities, all of which marked definite stages in the progress of the country, were one phase of his character. Public service, political leadership, citizenship in its highest sense, were another aspect. Generations that came and went left him pursuing his course with unabated energy.

The source material for this work existed in a mass of contemporary documents relating to public affairs, in newspapers and periodicals extending through more than half a century, and in a large volume of letters and private papers. The thanks of the author are due to the family for the access to these papers and for their assistance in many ways. Personal association in the later years of his career afforded insight into his character and the motives which governed his business enterprises and his support of international projects such as the Pan-American Railway. All this material has been studied with a view to exhibiting his life and times as a whole. In a career which covered so long and so eventful a period and which embraced so many and varied activities the most that can be done is to exhibit it in outline.

PREFACE

Perhaps the reader in following this history will understand why the life of Henry Gassaway Davis is worthy of permanent record. His broadly human sympathies endeared him to his fellow-countrymen, but there was more than this to enlist their enduring interest. His was a many-sided character. In his early struggles against adversity, in his qualities of initiative, in his individuality and self-confidence, in the sentiment which centered in the region that owed so much to him for the development of its resources, in his habit of looking forward, in his abiding faith in the institutions of his country, in his willingness to do his part as a citizen and his readiness to accept political responsibilities, people saw in him the Distinctive American. Such was Henry Gassaway Davis throughout his long and honorable and useful life. It is as such that these pages seek to record him.

C. M. P.

Washington, January, 1920.

CONTENTS

CHAPTER I

PAGE

ANCESTRY AND YOUTH 3

CHAPTER II

PIONEER RAILWAY DAYS 17

CHAPTER III

EARLY PUBLIC LIFE 34

CONTENTS

missionary's illuminating letter—Filial sentiment given expression in church edifice—Family affection exemplified in a memorial hospital—Failure of plans for girls' industrial school—Realization of similar idea in Child's Shelter—Mr. Davis's deep personal interest in the homeless little ones—Belief in organized Christianity—Substantial support of Young Men's Christian Association—Eulogy of its methods

CHAPTER XV

Deeply rooted affections of Mr. Davis—Sentiment for the ancestral home Goodfellowship—Recalling the children of Caleb Davis and Louisa Brown—The four brothers—The tie between Henry and Thomas—A brother's tribute—Friendship for his cousin, Arthur P. Gorman—Warm eulogy of Senator Elkins, his son-in-law—Children of Henry G. Davis and Kate Bantz —Marriages, births, and deaths—Loss of eldest son at sea—Fifty years of ideal married life—Death of Mrs. Davis—The final resting-place

CHAPTER XVI

Colleagues in the Senate—Thurman, the sturdy oak of Democracy—Schurz and Sherman—Windom as Senator and Secretary of the Treasury—Blaine's friendship—Bayard's esteem—Qualities in common with Allison—Vice-Presidents Wheeler and Hendricks—Benjamin Harrison's personality—Porfirio Diaz and Mexico—A page from contemporary history—The Cuban War—W. W. Corcoran, the philanthropist—Andrew Carnegie—Railway men and events—The great strike of 1877—John W. Garrett as a board of directors—Annual dinners to railway presidents—Estimate of George B. Roberts and A. J. Cassatt—George F. Baer—Presentation of urn to Mr. Davis—Daniel Willard and the younger generation of contemporaries

CHAPTER XVII

Gleanings from many contemporaries—Political history unfolded in correspondence—Senator Thurman's expectations in the famous Ohio campaign of 1875—George H. Pendleton on factional politics—Many communications from William Windom—Hopes and fears in the tragedy of Garfield's life—Comment from Paris on parties and candidates in 1884—European travel—Indignation over Blaine caricatures—Lines from Samuel J. Randall and Augustus H. Garland—West Virginia correspondents—Appreciation from the two Goffs—W. L. Wilson's ambition

LIST OF ILLUSTRATIONS

THE LIFE AND TIMES
OF
HENRY GASSAWAY DAVIS

THE LIFE AND TIMES
OF
HENRY GASSAWAY DAVIS

CHAPTER I

ANCESTRY AND YOUTH

Leaves from Maryland's colonial history—Two ancient worthies—The Davises and the Browns—Memories of Goodfellowship estate—Parents of Henry Gassaway Davis—Baltimore at the time of his birth—The child who saw Charles Carroll lay the corner-stone of the first railway—Epochal events—Baltimore and Ohio's test of Peter Cooper's engine—Effect of family reverses on a care-free lad—Earning money at the stone quarry—Plantation steward for Governor Howard—Beginning of his railroad career.

MARYLAND'S early history is principally a record of the Calverts, Lord Barons of Baltimore, and the families that settled in their Province. On the Rent Rolls of the several Lord Barons of Baltimore appear the names of the forbears of the Davises and the Browns, to be followed later by those identical names. These families and their descendants bore their part in the transition of the Province from a semi-feudal proprietary possession to a democratic colony. The Davises were of Welsh extraction; the Browns were of Scotch-Irish blood. Two ancient worthies figure in the family records. One was Colonel Nicholas Greenberry, with whom the Davises were kin;

3

the other was Colonel Nicholas Gassaway, a progenitor of the Browns.

Colonel Nicholas Greenberry was Deputy Governor of the Province in 1692, and from the documentary history of that period he appears to have filled various positions of responsibility, for the list of the official titles he bore is a long one.   From one document is disclosed that, Henry Jowles, Esquire, "Chiefe Judge in Chancery," etc., being afflicted with gout and other indispositions of body, and unable to attend to the duties of his office, Colonel Nicholas Greenberry was one of three persons assigned to sit as Judge in Chancery pending this indisposition of the Chiefe Judge.

The Great Seal of William and Mary, under date of March 2, 1695, attests this appointment. Colonel Greenberry performed various other functions, and, in the troublous times which vexed the Lord Baltimore of that day, his name is frequently mentioned, sometimes as a supporter of the Lord Baron, and sometimes as a leader of the popular element.

Colonel Nicholas Gassaway arrived in the Province about 1650, and at once began to take an active part in its affairs.   He was a Captain in the Indian Wars, later with the rank of Major, a Commissioner of Peace, Member of the Quorum, and in 1690 a member of the Committee of Twenty which was formed to govern Maryland.   Captain Thomas Gassaway, his son, was High Sheriff of Anne Arundel County from 1711 to 1714; and a son of this Gassaway, John by name, appears in 1740 as one of the principal gentlemen belonging to the Ancient South River Club, "conveying for and in consideration of the sum of Eighty Pounds" a half acre of land on which the club-house was erected.

Colonel Nicholas Gassaway, the father of John, died

in 1730. The minutes of the club meeting held on February 14, 1750, show that Henry Gassaway was chairman. Three years later the minutes disclose that by resolution Mr. John Gassaway was directed to provide a large punch-bowl; so it is clear that the Gassaways continued to be among the leading gentlemen of the Club.

In the direct line Henry Gassaway Davis was descended from Thomas Davis, a gentleman of the City of London, of an ancient Welsh family that had settled in Shropshire. Thomas Davis arrived in Maryland late in 1688, as a factor for several large mercantile establishments in London. He had a son Robert, who had a son Eli, and Eli had a son John, who was married to Sarah Randall. An only son was born of this union, Caleb Davis. Nathan Randall, the brother of Sarah, was a large landowner, and in his will he made his sister's son the sole heir to a tract of land known as Goodfellowship, some two hundred and fifty acres in extent, as recorded in the deed.

This land appears to have been from time to time a common possession on both sides of the family, probably due to intermarriage between the Davises and the Browns. It is certain that the Browns were large landowners, and a considerable tract was patented to them early in the seventeenth century. This patent extended over a considerable section of the hills and valleys that afterward came to be known as Anne Arundel County. Some of it was included in the purchases of Thomas Browne (the family had not then dropped the final vowel), who must have been a landowner with a sense of humor, since the several tracts patented to him are indicated as Browne's Folly, Browne's Chance, Browne's Adventure, and Browne's Increase. The name of

Joshua Brown is entered in the Debt Book of Anne Arundel County from 1750 to 1756 as paying Lord Baltimore quit-rent on one hundred acres of the Goodfellowship tract. Later it appears from the records that John Riggs Brown was the owner of this part of Goodfellowship.

John Riggs Brown was born in October, 1775, the second son of the Revolutionary patriot, Captain Samuel Brown. In December, 1799, he was wedded to Sarah Gassaway, the daughter of Brice J. Gassaway and Katherine Warfield. Brice J. Gassaway was the son of Nicholas Gassaway and a brother of Captain John Henry Gassaway and of Lieutenant Nicholas Gassaway, officers of the Maryland Line, and direct descendants of the original Colonel Nicholas Gassaway.

The Browns occupied and cultivated Goodfellowship. On a gentle eminence sloping down into the glades, a rectangular stone house had been built some time after 1650. There were the outbuildings of the complete plantation, the granary, the milk-house, the barns, which went to make up the estate of a landed proprietor of those days. Part of the stone house still stands, though later occupants covered it with concrete and enlarged it by a frame addition. The old chimney is there, and the mantelpiece and a few other reminders of the solid house furnishings of olden days. The milk-house remains. The granary, transformed in the course of centuries into a big barn, stood until 1918, when it was torn down to make room for a building better suited to the needs of modern farming.

The issue of the marriage of John Riggs Brown and Sarah Gassaway was a large family, principally girls. At Goodfellowship, on the tenth day of March, 1799, was born Louisa Warfield Brown, the mother of Henry

G. Davis. There also was born her sister, Elizabeth A. Brown, the mother of Arthur P. Gorman.

Caleb Davis was born near Baltimore in March, 1792, the only son of John Davis, also an only son, and of Sarah Randall. He was early left an orphan, and was given a home by an aunt. When the British expedition of Lord Ross sailed up the Potomac and destroyed the Capitol at Washington, Caleb Davis was one of those who volunteered for the defense of Baltimore, and he served during the remainder of the War of 1812.

In April, 1815, Caleb Davis married Sarah Rowles, who died in 1819, leaving him one son, Nathan R. Davis, who died in boyhood. Caleb Davis did not long remain widowed. The family Bible records that he was married to Louisa Warfield Brown on the ninth day of March, 1819, by the Reverend Mr. Linthecomb. Of this union six children were born, John B., Elizabeth, Henry Gassaway, Eliza Ann, Thomas B., and William R. The child that was named Henry Gassaway was born in Baltimore on November 16, 1823.

Caleb Davis, at this time, was an enterprising and adventurous young merchant, living part of the time in Baltimore and part of the time in Anne Arundel County at the little settlement among the hills that was known as Woodstock. C. Keenan's Baltimore City Directory for 1822 and 1823 designates him as "Caleb Davis, grocery and feed store, 283 Western Row, Baltimore Street, d. w., Paca, W. side S. of Baltimore." Later entries up to 1827 add to his lines of business, but apparently he remained in the same neighborhood. It was from near there that Barnes and Williamson's stages left five times daily for Washington.

Baltimore at this time was the third city in the Union and had sixty-five thousand inhabitants. It was a port of varied nationalities and vied with New York in the number of its great merchants. Foreign governments maintained consuls there, and the Patapsco was filled with the ships of many countries. But it was still a city in the making, with little outward evidence of the magnificent metropolis it was to become. When Lafayette visited it in 1824, the year following the birth of Henry G. Davis, the Washington Monument, which was to give it the name of the Monumental City, was off in Howard's Woods, still surrounded by scaffolding.

John H. B. Latrobe, who was identified with the history of Baltimore for more than half a century, said that on the left from the Fort to Federal Hill the only building was the town powder-house, while on the right it was no better. Far off in the distance, where the Philadelphia turnpike crossed Loudenslager Hill, there were some houses. Beyond the Fort and within the harbor proper, were the pungies, or small boats used for the transport of wheat, oysters, and wood.

This was the actual view; but the Baltimore merchants, and even the politicians of that day, had visions of the commerce of the future which its situation on the Chesapeake assured it. Yet they had become disquieted because of signs that this commerce might be lost to them. The cause of their uneasiness was the building of the Erie Canal. It was feared, and with reason, that this waterway would divert to New York the trade from over the mountains which the city had previously held. Another artificial waterway to serve the interests of Baltimore was the natural thought, and this thought bore fruition in the project of the Chesapeake and Ohio Canal.

There were men in Baltimore at that day who, while not doubting the Canal project, believed that better means could be developed for holding the traffic of the great West. They had heard of George Stephenson's engine, and some of them, the Thomases among others, had even gone so far as to have Evan Thomas visit England and examine the Manchester Railway in operation. A railroad to the Western waters thereafter became the leading idea of P. E. Thomas, and with his associates he mapped out a great national route to the Mississippi which would not only serve to fetch the coal from the mountains to the sea, but also would transport the agricultural products from beyond the Ohio to the Chesapeake Bay section of the Atlantic coast.

The Baltimore and Ohio Company was the first chartered and fully organized company in the United States for the construction of an extended line of railroad. It was distinctively a Baltimore enterprise. Its early difficulties and the resourcefulness of the men who projected and carried it through—even to their extravagance, as it was then considered, in offering Louis McLane a salary of four thousand dollars to tempt him from the presidency of a New York bank to assume the responsibilities of the railway—are part of the history of the development of the country through transportation enterprise. They are referred to here because they concern the subject of this biography; for, as a child, Henry Gassaway Davis lived in the midst of those epochal events.

On July 4, 1828, Caleb Davis took his entire family to witness a great event. All the substantial citizens of Baltimore were there with their families, and the unsubstantial ones also. This event was the laying of the "first stone," the corner-stone, of what came to be historic Camden Station, at the southwest line of the city, for the new railway project, and the address by the surviving signer of the Declaration of Independence,

Charles Carroll of Carrollton. "I consider this," said the venerable signer, "among the most important acts of my life, second only to my signing the Declaration of Independence, if even it be second to that."

A child of five years was held on his father's shoulder while this memorable address was made. Probably there were many other children of the same age who were held in the same way, but this one lived to recall it after more than eighty years. As he recited the circumstance, the impress left on his mind was that of "a big crowd of people and a very old man making a speech"; but the recollection was distinct, and the child, Henry G. Davis, always had a good memory for faces and places.

Caleb Davis, as a venturesome merchant alive to new opportunities, saw what the building of the railway would mean to the Western Shore through which it was to pass. The line was to run along the narrow valley of the Patapsco to Ellicott Mills, and then, following the course of the river, through Anne Arundel County and beyond to Frederick. This would mean increase in land values and contracts for enterprising men. He moved his family back to the farm, and began to put up houses and to develop some small factories.

The laying of the first stone of the railway line was truly an epochal event, but Henry G. Davis, a child of five, was not likely to appreciate its eventfulness, although it was to have much to do with his career. Another epochal event about which he heard his elders talk, and concerning which he preserved some recollections, was the test of motive power. When the Baltimore and Ohio project was undertaken, the feasibility of steam, or rather its superiority to animal power, had not been fully tested. The line, or rather a double line, was built to Relay, and from there on to Ellicott Mills, which was fourteen miles from Baltimore City. When the first division was opened in 1830, horse and mule power were employed. Evan Thomas built a car rigged with sails, which was fittingly called the "Eolus," and this was tested and declared to be a success on windy days, but it hardly could be considered seriously as permanent motive power.

There was to be a real test between steam power and animal power. Peter Cooper, afterward to become known for his business success and his great philanthropies, had devised an engine which he was confident would solve the problems of the curves and grades that made the engines employed on the Liverpool and Manchester Railroad unsuitable for use in the United States. He was a stockholder in the railroad company, and that may have had something to do with the readiness of the directors to let him try his little boiler and engine. In the summer of 1830 he made a trial trip from Baltimore to Ellicott Mills and back at a speed of fifteen miles an hour, and the first journey by steam in America was declared to be a success.

Yet even then the old fogies did not yield readily. The stage proprietors asked for a test, and they were given it on the parallel tracks. A car drawn by a powerful gray horse, and another propelled by the little steam engine, started simultaneously. For a while steam seemed to be winning; but an accident to the band that drove the pulley of the steam engine put it out of use, and the horse got into Baltimore first, to the delight of the stage owners and the chagrin of the champions of steam power.

But the feasibility of steam had been demonstrated, and Peter Cooper's boiler and engine were accepted by the Baltimore and Ohio managers as the basic idea for motive power on the railway that was to surmount the Alleghanies. They developed his ideas with their own mechanics and engineers, and thereafter the physical progress of the Baltimore and Ohio Railway was steady and uniform, although attended with many difficulties and taxing the energies of the resourceful men who were at the head of the enterprise. In the meantime, Ross Winans was giving the road the benefit of his inventions, and at the same time gaining the experience which caused the Czar of Russia to intrust to him the construction of the Russian railways.

It was not within the recollection of Henry G. Davis in his later years that these portentous developments made a deep impression on his mind. He was a care-free lad, with a love for out-of-doors and a real liking for farming, which was the principal industry of this agricultural region, although the water-power of the Patapsco provided for the flour mills at Ellicott, and also for cotton and woolen mills. With other boys of his own age he roamed the forest and fished in the creeks.

One of his boyhood friends was John Hambleton, who lived across the Patapsco in Baltimore County, and who afterward became the head of the banking firm that bore his name, and a director in the railways built by Henry G. Davis. 'Possum hunts with young Hambleton were among the boyhood sports which he was wont to recall. There was also Beale Cavey, a farmer's boy with whom he played and worked in the fields to earn a little money. Many years afterward, whenever Mr. Davis returned to Goodfellowship, he would hunt up Beale Cavey; and after he had gone, the old man would tell how they had worked at planting corn in order to obtain spending money, a quarter of a dollar representing the maximum of their expectations.

All this time Caleb Davis was prospering, or seemed to be prospering; for his family lived in comfort, if not in luxury, and had all that their wealthy neighbors had. They lived in the lavish manner of the times—the family carriage with outrider, ponies for the boys, and generous hospitality. But the conditions were not so favorable as they seemed. The effort of Caleb Davis to build a little town was not a financial success. Like other enterprising men of the day, among whom was Peter Gorman, the father of Arthur Pue Gorman, he had taken contracts for grading sections of the Baltimore and Ohio Railway, which was pushing the line on to Frederick. Some of those contractors made money; others lost. Among the latter was Caleb Davis, who also had gone on the bonds of some of his fellow contractors. The shadows that lengthened into the panic of 1837 were already stretching across the country, and the region in which the greatest enterprise had been shown, due to the railway construction, was the first to feel the gathering financial gloom. Caleb Davis found that he had undertaken too much. He might have maintained himself alone, but those for whom he had indorsed went to wreck and the whole burden was thrown on him.

When the crash came it was complete. All of Caleb Davis's property was sold to meet his debts. Thomas, the younger brother of Henry, used to recount how the calamity affected their childhood. His recollection was of the sale of the ponies to the neighborhood butcher, and of the anguish caused him by the butcher boy riding by on his pony and making faces at him. Henry took the loss of his pony with the stoicism befitting an elder brother.

The business failure was rendered more acute by the mental infirmity that overtook Caleb Davis. He was not only left incapable of affording any means of support for the family, but himself became an object of care. In these distressing circumstances the Scotch-Irish will power and mental force of his wife showed itself. There were four sons and a daughter to care for and to bring up in a way that would be worthy of their race and name. Mrs. Davis did not shrink from the task before her. Her little household was at once remodeled. She herself opened a school for girls, or, as it was called in those days, a seminary for young ladies. She also contributed by her own physical labor to the maintenance of the household, and even found time to teach the growing children.

Henry G. Davis was then in his fourteenth year. There were no free schools in Maryland in those days, and it had not been considered necessary to provide for his systematic instruction. Supplementing the home teaching, he had received perhaps a year's actual schooling. He had not been known as a studious lad, and possibly the prospect of breaking off his education did not then look to him as it looked in later years, when he was overcoming the disadvantages of his lack of earlier facilities. Whatever the boy's feeling, there was no remedy. His great love for his mother and his natural inclination to do his part in supporting the family caused him to seek employment.

Matthew G. Emery, a New Englander, was at that time working one of the Woodstock quarries. Years afterward he became a leading capitalist of Washington and mayor of the capital city while Lincoln was President. When Henry G. Davis had become a United States Senator and a railway builder, Emery told the circumstances of the boy's first employment. One day a husky lad came to him and asked for work. There was need of a water-boy to supply the men. Emery at once put him on the job. Before the day had passed he noticed the willingness and the alertness of the lad, who was everywhere when needed, anticipating the thirsty men in their call for water. This was the characteristic that years afterward found expression in his various business enterprises. This employment lasted for some time. Three quarters of a century afterward Mr. Davis spoke of it reminiscently as the first money he had earned.

When there was no more work in the quarry he took odd jobs on neighboring farms. One of the beautiful estates on the Western Shore is known as Waverly. It is not far from Goodfellowship. In the '30's it was one of the finest plantations in all the region, not even second to Carroll's Manor, on which it bordered. The proprietor, to whom it had descended from colonial times, was former Governor Howard, after whom the county that in 1851 was carved out of Anne Arundel was named.

Governor Howard knew the Davises, and he knew the Browns better. They had been neighbors for a long time. He sympathized with the misfortunes that had overtaken the family. One day he reined his horse in front of the cottage in which they were living, and said to the mother: "Let Henry come with me. I want a good boy on my place and I know he will suit me."

Young Davis therefore went to Waverly to live. His duties were steadily extended until he was virtually superintendent of the plantation. Three times each week he rode into Baltimore with the garden truck that found its market there. He doled out the stores for the slaves, and he had a steward's responsibility for the accounts, while he also had much to do with the actual farm cultivation. The change in the family circumstances, while hurtful to his pride, never caused him to lose his self-respect; but there were some of his former companions that bore historic names who chose to take note of it in boyish ways. Where formerly there had been free intercourse, the young steward was now given a cool nod of recognition. Long years afterward the bearer of one of those historic names came to Senator Henry G. Davis to ask his aid in securing some humble government employment. Family reverses in middle age had done for him what they had done for Davis in boyhood. A place was found for him by his boyhood companion.

In his position with Governor Howard the young steward was able to contribute substantially to the support of his mother and the younger children, and even to save something for himself, although the amount could not have been large. He continued as superintendent at Waverly until his twentieth year. Then came the change that was to mold his whole future and open to him the gates of opportunity. This change was what, in these days, is succinctly called "railroading."

Reproduction of daguerreotype of Mr. Davis and his mother

CHAPTER II

PIONEER RAILWAY DAYS

A brakeman on the Baltimore and Ohio—Crude methods of early days—Reasons for Davis's promotion—Washington in the '40's—Famous passengers—Henry Clay's friendship—The conductor's courtship and marriage—Duties as station agent at Piedmont—Crossing the crest of the Alleghanies—Leaving the railroad service for business—General merchandising—Coal and lumber enterprises—Establishing a bank—Civil War conditions—Supplies for the railway under difficulties—Contractor Davis's interview with Lincoln—Extensive land purchases after the war.

RAILWAY building in the second quarter of the nineteenth century was a pioneer chapter in national development. Naturally, the incidents connected with it affected the local communities through which the Baltimore and Ohio line passed. It also opened opportunities for employment, although the modest scale on which the construction was carried forward did not call for a large number of men. And there were even doubters and those who preferred to stay on the farm or in other employments. Railway operation in itself was crude.

It was not possible that Henry G. Davis, living in the district through which the Baltimore and Ohio was pushing its lines, should belong to the class that saw no future in railway work. The Washington branch of the railroad was opened in midsummer of 1835. The line to Frederick had been opened nearly four years earlier, and in the boyhood of young Davis it was pushing on toward Cumberland and the Alleghanies. The greater part of the traffic was over the Frederick line, which passed near to Waverly and Goodfellowship.

From this circumstance the young steward of Governor Howard's plantation came to know the men who managed the railway. One of these was Dr. Woodside, the superintendent, who was a friend of the Davis family. When the railway reached Cumberland there was a demand for more men, and Dr. Woodside, who had noted young Davis's interest, offered him a place as brakeman. This was in 1842, when he was in his twentieth year.

In the early '40's a brakeman was a person of marked responsibility in the operation of a railway. There were no automatic couplings, no air-brakes, no system of telegraph signals. Physical strength and mental judgment were prime qualifications for the brakeman. Young Davis had both. He was six feet tall, all muscle and bone, and weighed probably one hundred and seventy-five pounds. He had an iron grip. In the colloquial railway language of the day, the "armstrong" brakeman was the essential thing, since the train had to be stopped by forcing the frictional shoes against the wheels by sheer manual power. Many years afterward, when he was a railway president, Mr. Davis was wont to recall some of the incidents of this early railroading experience.

"We coupled our freight-cars with bars about eighteen inches long, wrought with a hole in each end," he said. "These were held by bolts, one dropping down through the bumper of each car. Passenger-cars were coupled with bars of similar shape, but made of wood and having iron ends. The wood was used so that in case one car should overturn the coupling would snap and leave the other cars upon the track. The Baltimore and Ohio track in those days was built by first laying end to end stone sills about as far apart as the gage of the rails. Over the sills were laid cross-ties, and on top of these, parallel to the sills, there were laid lengthwise pieces of yellow pine six inches wide and of about the same thickness, which held the rails. These were flat strips of iron about an inch thick and two and a half inches wide. There were no means of communicating with the train after it started on its run. Everything had to be done by the arbitrary schedule of instructions, and this was a pretty tedious business. It took all day to go a distance that afterward only required three or four hours."

When young Davis became a brakeman the daily traffic requirements of the railroad were adequately supplied by three freight trains. These were run in sections a few minutes apart—and rear-end collisions were ordinary incidents of railway operation. One day the usual rear-end collision caused a very bad wreck. While it was being cleared away a passenger train drew up. Here is the rest of the story as it was told by Thomas Swann, who was then president of the company:

"Before I took young Davis from the freights, one of our directors had been on a train that was brought to a halt by a wreck on the line between Baltimore and Frederick. He came to me and commended the energy and intelligence shown by a young man in removing the obstructions. Everyone on the train, he said, seemed to look to him for direction in clearing away the wreck. I thought that this would be a good man with whom to begin the experiment of promotion from the ranks, so I sent for him."

When young Davis appeared in President Swann's office he made a very favorable impression, although, as he afterward stated, he was somewhat overawed.

Years later the two men were to meet in public life under conditions somewhat reversed, the younger as a Senator and the elder as a Representative in Congress. The promotion, though not sought, was agreeable to young Davis, and while he continued to be associated with the Baltimore and Ohio Railroad, both as an employee and a contractor, he enjoyed the good will of President Swann.

While serving as conductor of the freight train, he had a wider field for his qualities of initiative. He showed them in many ways, and it was not long before he had become supervisor of the road between Baltimore and Cumberland, a position somewhat similar to division superintendent of the present day. At that period no one had thought of running night trains, or else no one had been willing to attempt the hazardous experiment, although there was much loss of time in the schedule through laying them up from dark to daylight. Davis suggested to his superiors that the trains could be run during the night as well as during the day. He was given the authority to make the experiment, with what misgivings was known only to the officials themselves.

Supervisor Davis had made his plans, and he did not intrust carrying them out to anyone else. The first night train was to be run from Cumberland to Baltimore. A curious crowd, which included the skeptics and the scoffers, gathered at Cumberland when it was to start. The comment was not encouraging. One man was especially anxious lest harm come to the train crew. "You may run into a cow and throw the train," he said. It is not certain that Supervisor Davis knew of George Stephenson's experience with the parliamentary committee which asked him what would happen if his train should run into a cow, and received the reply that it would be a bad thing for the cow, but a similar answer on his part would have been natural under the circumstances. A more serious suggestion was that the engineer would not be able to see far enough ahead to keep from running against stones that rolled down from the mountains, for this was not an uncommon incident.

The train moved off in charge of young Davis, despite the misgivings of the crowd. Frequently it would be stopped or would proceed at a snail's pace, while a brakeman walked ahead with a lantern; but, in spite of the obstacles that were met, it reached its destination in safety. Supervisor Davis had solved the problem of running trains at night, removing what was then thought to be an important obstacle in railroading. So far as the chronicles of railway operation disclose, he was the first man to run night trains.

Mr. Davis served as a passenger as well as a freight conductor. This gave him the opportunity of meeting many noted public men both in Washington and on the line. He was accustomed to stay over in Washington, and in later years would recall some of the incidents of that period, particularly during Polk's administration. The national capital was then a muddy village, with Pennsylvania Avenue as the main thoroughfare, and with a few hotels and boarding-houses, where the majority of the Congressmen lived, at the foot of the Capitol. On the south side of the Avenue, farther up toward the White House, between Twelfth and Thirteenth streets, the only building was a two-story brick known as Hancock's. This was the place that for three quarters of a century was celebrated for the excellent food and a certain punch that could be had there.

Teetotalers were very rare among public men in those

days, and Mr. Davis sometimes told the story of seeing Daniel Webster at Hancock's partaking of the famous punch.   On the following day he was one of those who were fortunate enough to shoulder his way into the Senate chamber to hear the great debate that was then going on, with Clay, Calhoun, and Webster as the giant figures.   It was on the series of measures known as "Clay's Compromise."   The speech that Davis heard Webster make was the one in which the great expounder of the Constitution denounced the abolitionists and defended the fugitive slave law.   It was this address that estranged his New England supporters and clouded the remainder of his public life.   Mr. Davis's recollection of it was simply that it was a great speech and made a profound impression on those who heard it.

Travel on the railway by public men gave young Davis an opportunity to meet some of those who came from the South and West.   They would journey over the Alleghanies in the stage to Cumberland, and there take the train for Washington; or they would travel from Washington to Cumberland, and take the stage returning home.   One of these famous passengers was General Sam Houston, who, after the liberation of Texas from Mexico, served as President of the new republic, and when it became a State was sent to Washington as one of its Senators.   He was a picturesque passenger, kindly in his intercourse, but not very talkative, according to the recollections of the young conductor.

Henry Clay was another famous passenger.   Davis came under the sway of Clay's magnetic nature as did a very large element of young America.   Clay was always amiable, and liked to talk with the conductor. When it was known that he was on a train, the people at the different stations would gather and ask for a speech. Clay usually was ready to gratify them, and the conductor saw to it that time was afforded for him to talk to the people. In recalling these addresses, Mr. Davis, who during his long life heard almost every great orator in the United States, some of whom were his colleagues in the Senate, was wont to declare that not one of them approached Clay in the mellowness of voice, the charm of manner, and the persuasiveness exhibited by him in these way-station talks.

During one of Clay's trips, Conductor Davis was witness of an incident that affected the Great Commoner beyond the power of speech. At Harper's Ferry, when the train was making its usual stop, it became known that Clay was on board, and the people came to the station and asked him to address them. He was about to begin when a man in the crowd, pushing himself forward, called out: "Mr. Clay, I want to tell you something about your boy Henry. He died in my arms."

The man had been a soldier in the Mexican war, in which Clay's son had been fatally wounded at the storming of Chapultepec.

The appearance of this comrade of his son, and the word he gave, was too much for Clay. He threw up his hands, reeled, cried out, "My God!" and as he sank into a seat beckoned the man to him. The crowd fell back in silent sympathy while Mr. Clay heard from a comrade the story of his son's death.

The magnetism of the Great Commoner cast its spell over the train conductor, who became one of his earnest political supporters. During a brief vacation one season, Davis went to Wheeling, and then took the packet down the Ohio River and visited Clay at Ashland. Returning, he became an active lieutenant of the Kentuckian; but this fact did not interfere with his railway activities.

Ten years' experience of this kind made Davis a practical railway man of the best type. He knew every mile of the line from Baltimore and Washington to Cumberland. He was popular in the communities through which the railroad ran, and that was in itself an asset for the company. He was liked by the train crews, out of whom, it was said at the time, he could get twice as much work as any other superintendent. He was an enthusiast on the resources of the country which the Baltimore and Ohio traversed, even more so than some of the higher officials, who did not possess his detailed knowledge of lands and timber and coal and all that goes to make railway traffic.

His worldly circumstances in this ten years had materially improved, but at no time was his salary large. As a freight brakeman his wages were thirty dollars a month. Later they were advanced to forty dollars, and then, when he became a conductor, to sixty dollars. He received as supervisor one hundred dollars per month. It is a trite truth that in the middle of the nineteenth century a dollar went much farther and represented much more than in later years; but, with full allowance for this higher value, the pay of one hundred dollars a month for the supervisor of the railway on its principal division could not be considered extravagant. It was in proportion, however, to the salaries of the higher officials, which were modest. Out of his pay Davis continued to contribute to the support of his mother and the family. He also saved something, for the principle of thrift was inherent with him, and was the foundation of his success in business.

Toward the close of this ten-year period of active railroading there was another event which exercised a deep influence on his life.   Frederick was an important point on the railway, and all the Baltimore and Ohio men from time to time made it their headquarters.   It was then, as it is now, the center of a very prosperous agricultural community.   One of the leading merchants of the town was Gideon Bantz, who was also a Judge of the Orphan's Court, and was familiarly known as Judge Bantz.   The Bantz family was one of the most substantial ones in all the region.   There was a daughter, Katharine.

The handsome young railroader, Davis, met her, courted her, and won her.   The romance was complete, but there were some parental objections, possibly on the score of family pride, since railroading was not then looked on as the path to social distinction.   An obstacle of this kind meant nothing to the energetic spirit of Railroader Davis.   He soon won the family to his suit, and in consequence in February, 1853, Henry Gassaway Davis and Katharine Anne Bantz were married at Frederick, and a life companionship began which lasted nearly fifty years.

Happily married, Davis began to plan more definitely for the future and to seek a wider field than was offered him as supervisor of railway operations.   He was then in his thirtieth year, at the apex of vigorous young manhood, and already displayed evidence of the qualities of industrial leadership which later matured.   It happened that his desire for a wider field corresponded with the plans of the Baltimore and Ohio Railway directors.

After frequent checks by the Virginia Legislature, some of them of a political nature and some of a sectional character, and after harrowing financial experiences, the main trunk of the railway had reached the Ohio River at Wheeling. In reaching the Ohio it had surmounted the crest of the Alleghanies, but there were still operating difficulties to be overcome in climbing to the summit. The climb was begun at Piedmont on the upper Potomac, where heavy, powerful locomotives were substituted for the light engines, and reached the crest at Tierra Alta. Piedmont, therefore, became a very important central station on the railway, since the motive power necessary to surmount the great summit dividing the eastern and western waters which took their source in the Alleghanies had to be operated from that point. The company had built what was described as a "large and handsome engine house of circular form, its walls of brick and the roof of iron, housing sixteen engines, at a cost of twelve thousand dollars."

It was Mr. Davis's wish to locate at Piedmont in order to take advantage of the opportunities which he saw would come from the development of the timber and coal resources of this region. It was the wish of the Baltimore and Ohio directors to have the right kind of man there. So they made Davis station agent. But his duties as station agent were in reality more those of a division superintendent, since the responsibility was placed on him of sending the trains up and across the Divide, designating the engineers and the train crews, and adjusting their labor. It is part of the record of economical and tactful railway management that the claim of the train crews that a trip up to the Divide should be considered a day's work was disallowed by Station Agent Davis, and the trip schedule fixed by him was accepted without a strike.

Piedmont, though in the heart of the bituminous coal region, at this time hardly had an existence as a community, since there were only eight or ten frame houses, and these of the most primitive kind. Station Agent Davis lived in a box-car for the first year, and then built a house, to which he brought his bride, who in the meantime had remained at Frederick. The estate of her father, Judge Bantz, who died in 1854, provided a substantial sum for Davis's investment.

Davis continued as station agent and superintendent of motive power for four years, but at the same time engaged in private enterprises in connection with his brother, Thomas B. Davis. Paying wages to his own kin did not seem brotherly, and so Henry G. made Thomas a partner. The latter also had been a brakeman on the railway, but had left its employment. The brothers started a general store, and engaged in what then was called merchandising, but they were a good deal more than country merchants. Their business continued to grow, so that in 1858 the station agent resigned, and gave all his time to the several enterprises in which they engaged. Later, William R., the youngest brother, who had been educated by Henry and Thomas, was brought to Piedmont and given an interest in the business, which took the partnership name of H. G. Davis & Company, and, with Henry as its head, continued under that name for many years.

H. G. Davis & Company bought the products of the farmers in the narrow valley of Piedmont, and sold them feed, groceries, dry-goods, and hardware in return; but their principal business was in supplying the railway company and in shipping coal. They delivered oil to the railway in barrels, and they supplied it with all kinds of lumber. They were among the first to open up the timber resources of the surrounding country and uncover its forest wealth. Their sawmills in the wilderness were the wonder of the day.   Their pioneer lumber camps were models for that period and for later periods.   This is the testimony of John Reilly, who was their foreman, and who survived all the brothers.   Their enterprise made them widely known.

Banking facilities, during the middle period of the nineteenth century and earlier, were not ample in regions that were still in the pioneer state of development.   Inchoate captains of industry, and ambitious men who undertook large enterprises, had to provide these facilities for the communities in which they operated.   It was therefore an inevitable sequence of their merchandise business, their coal and timber shipments, and their railway contracts that H. G. Davis & Company should establish a bank.   It was equally inevitable that H. G. Davis, as the most progressive man in the region and the head of its growing business, should be the president of the institution.

Thus was formed the Piedmont Savings Bank in the town of Piedmont in the County of Hampshire, in 1858, which was invested with all the rights, powers, and privileges conferred and made subject to all the rules, regulations, restrictions, and provisions made and imposed by Chapters 57 and 59 of the Code of Virginia, and the provisions of the Act Amending the Tenth Section of Chapter 57 of the Code of Virginia.   The bank was one of deposit and discount and not of issue, but later was changed into a State bank and then into a national one.

A printed copy of the charter and by-laws, with the list of officers, shows that, besides H. G. Davis, as the president, T. B. Davis and W. R. Davis were directors, so that it was preëminently a Davis institution.   From bank-book No. 2, in which was kept the account of Mrs. C. A. Davis, it appears that when the deposits were en-

tered the cashier receipted for them under the entry.
Business continued to prosper, while the head of the firm
and bank president, as an incident to his private affairs,
served as a member of the town council.

When the Civil War broke out, H. G. Davis & Company was the principal business concern in the upper
Potomac region. It also owned considerable coal and
timber lands, as yet undeveloped. One of the earliest
ventures of H. G. Davis, when station agent, had been to
lend fifteen hundred dollars on a mortgage on some of
the wild lands of Georges Creek. The mortgagee defaulted, and the impairment of his capital to the amount
of fifteen hundred dollars was a serious thing for H. G.
Davis. His associates shook their heads and condoled
with him on the loss; but he, according to the tradition
still prevalent, told them that he proposed to hold the
tract, and would realize at least one thousand dollars out
of it. Not very many years afterward it was sold for
sixty thousand dollars.

The upper Potomac country was the borderland between the Union forces and the Confederates. Hampshire County, as a local historian narrates, was never
free from soldiers from the day the Ordinance of Secession was passed by the Richmond Convention until peace
was restored. It was a perpetual battlefield. Usually
the Union forces were in possession, but the Confederates made daring raids and occupied the various points
temporarily. It was said that Romney, the county-seat
of Hampshire, was occupied alternately by Union forces
and Confederates fifty-six times in the four years of
fighting, a record surpassed only by Winchester, farther
down the valley. One half of the men in the county
were said to be in the Confederate army, but there was a
strong Union sentiment in the vicinity of Piedmont.

The Davises were Union men. Once a Confederate raiding force swooped down on the town with the declared purpose of carrying off its leading citizen. When the raiders first appeared, the family, like other families, took refuge in the cellar, but the head of it was off in the mountains. The Confederates were intensely disgusted at not finding him, but they did not molest the family beyond telling them that they hoped to find the leading citizen at home the next time they called.

The business of H. G. Davis & Company of course was interrupted by the activities of the Confederates. The bank was closed in order that its funds might not fall into their hands, and the general merchandising was more or less interfered with; but the more serious interruption was to the providing of coal and lumber, the supplies for the soldiers, and the speedy transportation of Union troops. The Baltimore and Ohio Railroad at this period was almost as vital to the cause of the Union as was the Union Pacific line in holding California. It was one of President Lincoln's constant anxieties. There was no danger that the Confederates could take and hold a considerable section of it permanently, but they could and did interfere with its usefulness to the Union forces by their destructive raids, and by their interference with supplies. Mosby's raiders in particular were active in this kind of warfare.

H. G. Davis & Company was equal to this situation. Its men constantly traversed the counties of Maryland, West Virginia, and Pennsylvania, buying the horses which they supplied to the Government. They also acted as timber cruisers and selected the most easily obtained timber. H. G. Davis & Company had large contracts with the Baltimore and Ohio Railroad, as well as with the Government, for supplying lumber in its different forms. The initiative and energy of the head of the firm was one of the marvels of that day. No one could turn standing trees into cross-ties and timber as swiftly as he. Lumber camps were established in the wilderness overnight, trams built, and sawmills set up. The firm also bought the product of other mills.

It was of greatest importance to the railway company to have ties, bridge timber, and other lumber always in reserve, and the quality of anticipation that Davis had shown as a water-boy at the Woodstock quarry was here brought out in its strongest light. He anticipated everything that could happen. The prospect that the company would want a certain quantity of ties was foreseen; but, besides that quantity there was always an equal quantity in reserve to provide against emergencies such as a raid by Mosby's men.

It was this circumstance that brought about Henry G. Davis's one interview with Lincoln. As the war progressed, he felt that he should do something more than he was doing for the cause of the Union, and he proposed to enlist. He was then forty years old. Governor Swann, who was charged with a share of the responsibility of maintaining the Baltimore and Ohio in operation, and who sometimes was sent for by Lincoln, heard of his intention, and called him to Baltimore. They went to Washington together. Governor Swann took him to the White House, and explained to the President the work he was doing, and how essential it was to the Baltimore and Ohio that he remain where he was.

In after years Mr. Davis sometimes spoke of the impression Lincoln made on him. He himself was a man of striking physique. He was an even six feet tall, strongly built, but without an ounce of superfluous flesh. "A big man," as the phrase goes, and he considered himself so. But when Lincoln, after listening to Governor Swann, came over and, placing both hands on his shoulders, looked down on him and called him "young man," he felt, as he said, that he wasn't so big a man after all. "Young man," said Lincoln, "so you want to carry a musket? Isn't it better to carry five thousand muskets? Swann says you are worth that many where you are now. I want you to stay there."

Davis went back to his post, and continued to supply the Baltimore and Ohio Railroad Company with ties and other equipment to meet emergencies. When the war ended, the firm, notwithstanding some heavy losses, had made substantial profits and had accumulated considerable capital, most of which was due to Henry G. Davis. This capital afforded the means of carrying out the larger plans that he long had had in mind, and which were based on his implicit faith in the resources of the upper Potomac region. Though the youngest brother opposed it and would not invest a dollar in the purchase of lands, H. G. Davis & Company bought several thousand acres of fine timberlands in the wild Cheat River country, at the summit of the Alleghanies, most of them in Garrett County, Maryland.

These lands were part of what had once been one of the largest private estates in the world, the six million acres that had comprised the property of Thomas, Sixth Lord Fairfax, the owner of the Northern Neck in Virginia. The boundaries of some of them ran from Fairfax Stone, in the corner of West Virginia and Maryland, which for more than a century had been a subject of contention between Maryland and Virginia. Several of the maps describing metes and boundaries of the tracts purchased bore the initials of George Washington as surveyor. This forest wilderness had an assured value as

Reproduction of daguerreotype of Kate Bantz Davis

timberland, although few men had the courage to make large investments in it. What wealth of coal might underlie it, no one could guess. Its development was to signalize the constructive capacity of Henry G. Davis and to form a leading chapter in his career as a railway builder following a period of public service.

CHAPTER III

EARLY PUBLIC LIFE

West Virginia a war-born State—Davis's belief in separation from the Old Dominion—Election to the Legislature as a Union-Conservative—Paucity of lawyers—Status of ex-Confederates—Reasons for test oaths and disfranchisement—Party passions—Committee assignments—Fiscal subjects and internal improvements—Delegate to Democratic National Convention—Election to State Senate—Repeal of test laws—Struggle over enfranchisement legislation—The debt question—Second election to State Senate—Democrats in power—Adventures of legislators in midwinter journey to Charleston—Work of the session—Election to United States Senate.

THE early public life of Henry G. Davis was contemporaneous with the early years of the commonwealth with which he was identified for more than half a century. When he entered politics West Virginia was still a State in the making. The framework of government had been set up and its functions performed during the closing years of the Civil War. But there had been little done, because in the midst of war there could be little done, to perfect the organization that was to endure for all time.

The new State had been a battle camp over parts of which contending armies fought, while its citizenship had been divided. Its people had separated from the Old Dominion on the great issue of the preservation of the Union, but some of them had been sympathetic to the cause of the Confederacy. Once the vital issue of the

34

Union was settled, it was inevitable that there should be a reaction from the passions evoked by the great struggle, and that many of those who had been instrumental in the formation of the new commonwealth should find themselves out of sympathy with their former associates who still favored extreme measures. This was the natural swinging of the pendulum from radicalism to conservatism.

The moderation that was characteristic of Mr. Davis was certain to place him in the ranks of the conservatives. A strong Union man throughout the war, he was equally strong in advocating conciliation after the war. The abuse possible in the application of the stringent laws passed to insure the control of the Government by those loyal to the Union, and the bitterness engendered through partizanship, were brought directly home to him when, at one election, through personal animosity, his own name was stricken from the voters' registration list. If the law could be so abused in his own case, he realized how widespread might be its abuse in the case of others.

While the trend of his political action undoubtedly was influenced by this incident, there was not the remotest suggestion of sympathy with those who were seeking to undo the work of the men who had formed the State of West Virginia, and were working to secure the reincorporation of the new commonwealth with old Virginia. He recognized that the northwestern and the eastern sections of the Old Dominion were separated geographically by the Blue Ridge and the Alleghanies. He fully understood the difference in sentiment and interest between the people west and the people east of the Alleghanies. With his faith in the industrial future of the western section, and the necessity of constructive measures for developing its great natural resources, he knew that the control which the old-school politicians of the tidewater region had exercised for three quarters of a century must end, and he was not the man to be influenced by sentimental pleas when that sentiment was made the cover for the continued aggrandizement of one section at the expense of another section.

This feeling was reflected in a speech made by Daniel Lamb at the Wheeling Convention in 1861, when the ordinance for the formation of the new State was under discussion. "We are," said Mr. Lamb, "in fact a different people. Our social habits are different. Our commercial relations are not with eastern Virginia. The productions of our soil and of our workshop do not go in that direction, nor do we purchase the articles we want from the cities of eastern Virginia. Every consideration which can be addressed to the wisdom of statesmen would demand a separation at the proper time and in the proper manner."

This was the conviction of Mr. Davis also, and it was made manifest in his opposition to all attempts to undo the new commonwealth. This is of some importance, because his political course in these early years lay with those who to some extent were sympathetic to the Old Dominion.

In the autumn of 1865 Mr. Davis was elected from Hampshire County to the Legislature as a member of the House of Delegates as a Union-Conservative. This was within six months after the close of the Civil War. The term "Union-Conservative" itself describes the political conditions which existed at that period.

The Fourth Legislature, as it was called, since annual sessions were held, met at Wheeling in January, 1866. This Legislature was a very remarkable body, remarkable in one respect for the small number of lawyers that it contained. It is doubtful whether any legislative assembly among the several States ever had so small a percentage of the legal profession. In the Senate, which was composed of nineteen members, there were three lawyers. In the House, among the fifty-two members, there was only one lawyer, Mr. Henry Clay McWhorter, afterward a Judge of the Court of Appeals. There were twenty farmers, twelve merchants, one of whom was Henry G. Davis; two ministers of the gospel; four physicians; one banker, one teacher, one clerk; and seven mechanics, who described themselves as millwrights, blacksmiths, wheelwrights, and ironmasters. The Committee on the Judiciary had the lawyer for its chairman, while the other members were a merchant, a farmer, a banker, and a clerk.

The membership of the Legislature was typical of the new State. The communities were isolated, for the era of railway communication was in its early stages. Farming was still the principal occupation of the people, since the industrial development, except along the Ohio River, had barely begun. The members were truly representative of the self-contained, virile, rugged people who elected them. Nor does it appear that the processes of law-making at this period suffered from the small number of members of the legal profession who took part in it.

Two fundamental subjects, somewhat antagonistic in their nature, confronted this Legislature. One was the political issues growing out of the Civil War; the other was the constructive measures of taxation, finance, administrative organization, industrial development, and internal improvement which were vital to the new commonwealth in solving the problem of continued existence. Mr. Davis, as a member of the House of Delegates, took a prominent part in the discussion of both subjects. Governor Boreman, in his message, said that permanent civil organization had been restored in all but five or six eastern counties. He recited the efforts of the ex-Confederates and their sympathizers in several of the counties to elect to office persons who were ineligible under the Constitution of 1863 and the laws enacted to make it effective.

These laws included test oaths for teachers, attorneys, jurors, voters, and all officials. There were also statutes under which ex-Confederates could be sued for damages done to the property of loyalists by the military commands under which they served, and a law to prevent the prosecution of civil suits against loyalists by persons who had been engaged in the Rebellion.

This statute, the Governor declared, was of doubtful expediency. He recommended amendments to the election laws under which the Governor would be authorized to appoint county registration boards, with power to designate the township registers, and to act as the court of last appeal in all election and voting contests. The purpose of this recommendation was to prevent the ex-Confederates and their sympathizers in sections where they had the numerical superiority, controlling the voting and thus electing to office candidates who, under the Constitution of 1863 and the subsequent laws, were ineligible.

There was much partizan discussion in both branches of the Legislature over this subject, in which the passions of the Civil War, still heated, flamed out. Mr. Davis took part in the discussion, and, as a Union-Conservative member, opposed the test oaths in all their forms, and voted against the further restrictions on suffrage which were proposed. It was, however, in the discussion of measures of a non-political character, and in the work of the committees, that his qualities of constructive leadership showed themselves. The principal committee on which he served was that on Taxation and Finance. It had not only to provide for the appropriations for the State government, but also to devise the measures of taxation, and to formulate much of the fiscal legislation essential to the functions of the new commonwealth.

Nathan Goff, Sr., of Clarksburg, was chairman of this committee. He was a man of great influence throughout the State and had the respect and confidence of all parties. He quickly recognized the value of Mr. Davis's business experience and sound judgment in dealing with all these subjects. They worked together in complete harmony, and a strong personal friendship sprang up between them. Subsequently Mr. Goff's nephew, Nathan Goff, Jr., was a member of the Legislature, and with him, too, Mr. Davis maintained a warm friendship. Years afterward, when President Hayes nominated Nathan Goff, Jr., for Secretary of the Navy, it was the privilege of Mr. Davis, as a Senator of the United States, to move his confirmation.

In addition to his work in providing for the fiscal organization, Mr. Davis took a leading part in bringing to a head various projects of internal improvements which were of great consequence to the State. He was a member of the Committee on Roads and Internal Navigation. The improvement of the turnpikes received much attention from this committee, but its labors also embraced the larger subjects of the James River and Kanawha Canal and the railway enterprises which were deemed worthy of encouragement as a means of developing the State. Among the transportation lines which, by the action of the Legislature, received a charter, was the Potomac and Piedmont Coal and Railroad Company, which, years later, was to become the basis of Mr. Davis's most important railway enterprise.

At this session Mr. Davis introduced and had passed the bill creating Mineral County out of Hampshire County. Thereafter his citizenship was in Mineral County instead of Hampshire.

The first year's experience as a State legislator had been very valuable to Mr. Davis. It had enabled him to form the close personal acquaintanceship of men from all sections. It had brought him in direct contact with many local political leaders who found themselves looking to him for advice. It was the first step in the political leadership of the State which, in after years, fell to him.

Mr. Davis did not seek reëlection to the House of Delegates. Business affairs occupied much of his time, and apparently he wanted a few months free from official responsibility. But that he had not lost his interest in politics was made apparent early in 1868, when he announced himself as a candidate for the State Senate. The result is given in a brief entry in his journal:

May 20, 1868. J. S. Vance and J. W. Key, candidates for House of Delegates. Vance nominated. H. G. Davis, myself, nominated unanimously for Senate. Colonel J. N. Camden, Wilson, Johnston, present. A large meeting.

Another indication of political influence, and also of the alinement of parties, was given about the same time, when Mr. Davis was chosen a delegate to the Democratic National Convention at New York City. It was no longer a question of Union-Conservatives and Radicals, but of Democrats and Republicans. He attended the convention at which Seymour and Blair were nominated, and for the first time met members of the Democratic party who were national leaders. With several of these he was to occupy important relations in later years.

The question of suffrage and the disfranchisement of ex-Confederates were the leading issues of the State campaign in 1868.[1] The radical wing of the Republican party, which was in control of the organization, advocated further legislation, claiming that this was necessary because of the disorders in the southern counties, where some of the ex-Confederates were charged with lawless acts. The great body of ex-Confederates had returned peacefully to their homes, and were doing their share toward the upbuilding of the State. To them it was a burning wrong that they should be denied the privileges of citizenship, since they had accepted in good faith the result of the war. A moderate element among the Republicans took this view, and it was to them that Mr. Davis, because of his conservatism, appealed for support.

In the campaign throughout the State those who advocated greater liberality toward ex-Confederates were described as "Let-Ups." This colloquial designation reflected very accurately the dominant political issue. The

[1] At the session of the Legislature in 1865, an amendment to the Constitution was proposed, which was afterward adopted, providing in effect that no person who had participated in the Rebellion, or given aid or comfort to the Confederacy, should be deemed a citizen of the State or allowed to vote at any election. Statutes were passed requiring attorneys-at-law, teachers, jurors, voters, and all officers to make oath that they had not since June 20, 1863, borne arms against the United States or the State of West Virginia, or voluntarily given aid and comfort to persons engaged in armed hostility thereto. The defendant in any suit could require the plaintiff to take such an oath. The statute also provided that no suit should be maintained against any person for acts done in the suppression of the Rebellion. The courts further held that suits might be maintained by loyal persons against those who had been in the Confederate army for injuries done by the said army. Under this statute there were some actions of trespass maintained, and judgments given against returned ex-Confederates.

question to be decided was whether or not the State in its political functions should "let up" on those who had been Confederates or who had shown themselves as sympathizers with the Confederacy.

Mr. Davis made an active campaign in his district. Some of the incidents are briefly described in the itinerary which his journal sets forth. This is one of several entries of a similar character:

September 14. I go to Berkeley Springs to attend a meeting. It was the first day of Court. Many people there. Governor Green, Clay Smith, and Judge Moore of Kentucky spoke with good effect.

The successful outcome of his canvass is tersely indicated in this manner:

October 30. Returns in; elected by 66 majority. Piedmont gives State ticket 63 majority; me 135.

Though the Democrats had made gains, they were still in the minority in the Legislature, which met at Wheeling in January, 1869. The number of lawyers had been increased slightly in the two years since Mr. Davis had served as a member of the House of Delegates. He now had four lawyer colleagues in the Senate.

Governor Boreman, in his message, reviewed the political and fiscal conditions of the Commonwealth. The State had been organized, he said, a little short of six years, created in the midst of civil strife during the terrible struggle for nationality and the principles underlying free institutions. This was the dominant note of the Republican majority in maintaining its position in regard to the suffrage. Governor Boreman resigned at this session, and was elected to the United States Senate.

He was succeeded by William E. Stevenson, who had served in the State Senate for several terms.

Governor Stevenson reflected the attitude of the more liberal members of his party, although he insisted on the necessity of continuing some of the restrictive measures. He recommended the repeal of the attorneys' and teachers' test oaths, while he questioned the wisdom of the further continuance of what was known as the suitor's oath in law cases. He also favored the amendment restoring citizenship to the disfranchised. The restrictive measures, he said, had not originated in a vindictive spirit. "They were adopted during a time of great public peril. They were prompted by that instinct of self-preservation which impels every community to shield itself from present or impending danger. . . . These disabilities were not, however, intended to be perpetual, but only to remain in force until all danger to the public peace was passed."

The majority, however, were still very determined in demanding the most thorough proofs of reconstruction on the part of those who sought to be restored to citizenship. A joint resolution was passed that the petition of any person would not be favorably considered except such petition should be accompanied by a written renunciation of former wrongs and an acknowledgment of errrors, discarding the false dogmas of exclusive States' rights sovereignty.

The legislative record of this period discloses several instances of the manner in which those who were seeking to exercise the full rights of citizenship were compelled to make their acknowledgment of loyalty. A single illustration, which appears in the bill authorizing Leonard S. Hall, of Weitzel County, to practise law in the courts

of the State, suffices.   The bill, which was passed by a
vote of 14 to 5 in the Senate, and which numbered Henry
G. Davis among those who voted in the affirmative, was
accompanied by the following letter:

> Wheeling, W. Va.,
> January 26, 1869.
>
> *To the Honorable the Legislature of West Virginia—*
>
> I respectfully ask you to permit me to practise law in this
> State without taking the attorney's test eath.   I cannot take said
> oath from the fact that I was in Richmond, Va., at the time of the
> breaking out of the war, and although I was never in armed hostil-
> ity against the United States, yet I adhered to the Confederate
> States, which I confess was wrong and the great mistake of my
> life.   I subscribe to the terms of your resolution of June 8, 1868,
> a copy of which is herewith filed, and I promise to faithfully obey
> your laws and conduct myself as a good citizen.
>
> Yours respectfully,
> L. S. HALL.

At this session Senator Davis presented numerous
petitions of citizens in his district asking for the repeal
of all the test oaths, and for modification of the registration act.   He was active in urging this legislation, and
equally active in opposing everything that looked to further restriction of the white suffrage.   He also strengthened himself politically with a large element in the State
by his opposition to the ratification of the amendment to
the Federal Constitution providing for negro suffrage.
Independently of the passing politics of the hour, he
viewed the conferring of the ballot on the negroes as a
grave mistake.   As a partizan manœuver he gave the
Republican majority some discomfort by moving to have
the ratification of the amendment referred to the people
of the State for acceptance or rejection.   His motion
was defeated, and the Legislature ratified the amend-

ment; but his action undoubtedly strengthened the Democratic party throughout the State.

While these political questions received much attention and gave Mr. Davis increasing prominence as a party leader, he found a much more congenial field in the measures of constructive legislation. He was a member of the Committee on Finance and Claims, Internal Improvements and Navigation, and Auditing Accounts. Serving on them, he was enabled to supplement and develop many of the measures that had received his support when a member of the House of Delegates.

Adjustment of the debt between Virginia and West Virginia was one of the subjects that claimed his attention, and from the beginning he took a definite position on this vexed question. His position in substance was that West Virginia should pay a just share of the debt, but that it must first be ascertained what a just share was. He favored the various propositions for commissioners to confer with commissioners from the State of Virginia, and was himself the author of one of the resolutions providing for the appointment of commissioners. In whatever he had to say on the subject during the discussions in the Legislature, he never accepted the assumption made by Virginia that West Virginia should pay one third of the debt.

The question was postponed because the suit of Virginia to cause the reincorporation of Jefferson and Berkeley counties with it was still pending in the Supreme Court of the United States. Later, when he was a member of the United States Senate, Mr. Davis reviewed the whole debt question from the standpoint of West Virginia in vindication of the stand he himself had taken and maintained.

At this session of the Legislature steps were taken for

appropriating proper funds for buildings to house the public institutions. The public school system was placed on a firm foundation, and numerous new schools were created. A significant step in higher education was taken when the Agricultural College at Morgantown was changed to the West Virginia University. This was the birth of the present great State University, which is so thoroughly representative of West Virginia's interest in higher education. Mr. Davis concurred in all these measures. His name also frequently appears in connection with the bills relating to internal improvements and provisions for developing the great natural wealth of the State.

Mr. Davis's second year in the State Senate was marked by the ending of the political controversy over the disfranchising of ex-Confederates. The liberal element in the Republican party had made its influence felt, and, moreover, the passions engendered by the Civil War had begun to die out. Governor Stevenson in his message, while insisting that a proper respect for the laws under which they lived and a satisfactory assurance of peaceful intentions in the future should be required from the ex-Confederates, nevertheless recommended the repeal of the test oaths and the adoption of an amendment restoring the privileges of those who were disfranchised. This recommendation was embodied in what was known as the Flick amendment. Bills were passed repealing the test oaths and also adopting the amendment.

When this Legislature adjourned, Mr. Davis was awarded much credit throughout the State for the legislation restoring the franchise to those who had been disqualified. Notwithstanding that his business affairs were pressing, he still gave a large part of his time to politics. He was renominated for the State Senate.

His opponent was W. H. H. Flick, the author of the enfranchising amendment.

Entries in his journal show the activities of that year and reflect the political tendencies. Some of them follow:

May 21. I was at New Creek to attend a Democratic and Conservative convention.

June 6. I start to Democratic-Conservative convention at Charleston.

June 10. Return from convention. Had a pleasant trip. Nominated J. J. Jacobs, of Hampshire County, for Governor. Col. Camden declined.

June 12. Republicans held their State conventions at Parkersburg yesterday. Nominated nearly all the prominent State officers.

July 21. Returned from Moorefield Senate convention. A large number of persons from several counties were there. Our candidate for Governor, J. J. Jacobs, spoke in the morning. I was unanimously elected the Democratic or Conservative candidate for State Senate. No other name put before convention.

September 6. Attended Congressional convention at Piedmont. Nominated O. D. Downey. The nomination was offered me. I declined in favor of Downey.

Joint debates between political candidates were common in those days, and Mr. Davis, although not professionally a speaker, followed the usual practise and debated the issues with his opponent. His journal has several references to conferences with Mr. Flick in which they decided on the dates and places for their meetings. There are also intimations of the mutual respect which the candidates felt for each other. Mr. Flick was, in fact, a formidable opponent. A broad-minded man, who subsequently received high honors from his party, he had strengthened himself by his support of liberal franchise legislation, and the Flick amendment was looked upon as a means of keeping the allegiance of Republican voters who had become dissatisfied with the restrictive legislation.

The outcome of the campaign and its political significance is briefly indicated in several entries in the journal:

October 27. Election day.
October 28. I go to Piedmont to get election returns. Mineral County goes Democratic. News looks favorable.
October 31. Our State (West Va.) has gone Democratic. We elected Governor and State officers and a majority to the Legislature, securing a United States Senator. My majority 238; two years ago it was 70 in the same district.

The significance of the victory secured, and so tersely described, was immediately recognized. It was the beginning of the political ascendancy of the Democratic party in West Virginia for twenty-five years. That the talent for organization shown by Mr. Davis and his shrewd political judgment had much to do with the result, was universally admitted. That an honorable ambition for further public service in higher councils had been nourished by him was also disclosed. The first evidence of it appears in these entries in the journal:

Novmber 1. I have just returned from a visit to Wheeling, Parkersburg, etc. Find my friends Camden, Jackson, Baker, etc., all right, and firm for me for United States Senate.
December 3. Went to Grafton to meet Lewis Baker. He is fine, and doing what he can in a discreet way. He thinks we must win.

Going to the Legislature, as it was familiarly spoken of, was not so easy at this period. The capital had been permanently changed from Wheeling to Charleston, and Charleston then had no railroad connection and could be reached only by stage or boat on the Kanawha and its

Finance Committee of West Virginia Legislature

tributaries. A few days before the Legislature was to convene in January, 1871, a large number of the members from the northern and eastern end of the State met at Parkersburg, only to find the weather very cold and the river navigation entirely closed by reason of the ice. Mr. Davis was one of the party. Another, a lad of thirteen, was Alston G. Dayton, later a member of Congress and a Federal Judge. He was with his father. Judge Dayton's recollection of the trip was vivid, after nearly fifty years.

The party, Judge Dayton recounted, secured hacks and horses. Soon after they started the weather moderated, heavy rains came on, and the roads thawed out so rapidly that they became almost impassable, while the streams were swollen so as to be dangerous to cross. One stream they got over in a flat-boat, carrying two or three at a time, and then swam the horses across. Late at night they reached Sissonville, on the Pocatalico River, which was full of running ice that made crossing it impossible.

Sissonville at that time was composed of a small mill, a country store, which the party found locked up, a small blacksmith shop, and an old-fashioned two-story house on the hillside. Senator Davis made straight for the house to arrange for shelter and succor for the party. He returned somewhat crestfallen, and gave a graphic description of his experience. After knocking for a long time at the front door, it was opened a few inches by a middle-aged woman, who told him that she was a "lone widder woman" with nobody in the house but her young daughter and small son, and she could not afford to allow such a pack of men to come in.

The elder Dayton then tried his persuasive powers. He went to the house and told the woman that the parties were members of the Legislature, and that they were all men of good character. It was related afterward with some humor that this only made her the more suspicious. Finally a solution was found. An express wagon loaded with a heavy iron safe and drawn by four horses, with a guard of four men, had been included in the party when it left Parkersburg. The expressmen had managed to get it across the streams and through the muddy roads. It was understood that the safe contained a large sum of money in transportation to pay off the men who were working on the Chesapeake and Ohio Railway. Mr. Dayton induced the woman to come to the window and look at the safe, and then argued that if she would let it be brought into the house overnight she could feel sure of the respectability of the legislators.

This argument prevailed. The safe was deposited in the front hall, the members of the party admitted, fires were lit and supper was provided—corn-bread, bacon, and buttermilk. The meal was partaken of in relays. Such bedding as the household possessed was spread on the floor, and the wearied legislators slept as best they could. In the morning they were given a chicken breakfast with soda biscuit. On asking the reckoning, they were told that there was no charge for sleeping on the floor, and that the usual price for meals was ten cents; but, in view of the extra work, the widow thought she ought to have thirty cents for supper and breakfast. Senator Davis pulled out from his pocket a silver dollar and gave it to her, and the members of the party formed in line and each one did likewise.

After further adventures the party finally reached Charleston, and settled down to the work of the session.

The fruits of State Senator Davis's political leadership, and the further evidence of his ambition for higher place, is indicated in a series of entries in his journal:

January 17, 1871. First day of session of Legislature. Each House organized by electing Lewis Baker of Wheeling, President of Senate, and E. E. Crocroft, of Wheeling, Speaker of the House.

January 18. Committees announced. I am chairman of Finance and Claims.

January 20. Senatorial contest is getting warm. I feel sure of success.

January 23. The senatorial question is the all-absorbing one. It is the talk of everyone. Many admit I must be elected.

January 26. Great excitement as to who shall be Senator. My friends say I will win, and I agree with them.

January 27. I was nominated for U. S. Senate in Democratic caucus last night on first ballot by a vote of 12 for Mr. Lamb, 12 for Col. Smith, and 27 for H. G. Davis.

January 28. All appear satisfied that I am to be next Democratic Senator.

January 31. At noon we vote for Senator. Senate, Brown 8, Davis 14; House, Brown 14, Davis 39. Total, Brown 22; Davis 53. So I have a majority in each House. Harman, Koontz, Gold and Stubbs, Republicans, voted for me.

This is a modest account of a very live struggle as to who should be the first Democratic Senator from West Virginia. Daniel Lamb and Colonel B. H. Smith, who contended with Mr. Davis for the honor, were both strong party leaders and each had a personal following, but their combined strength did not equal that of Mr. Davis in the party caucus. Mr. Brown, who received the Republican vote, had been prominent in his own party. The outgoing Republican Senator whom Mr. Davis succeeded was Waitman T. Wiley, of Morgantown, one of the staunch leaders in the formation of the new State.

Of deep human interest was the characteristic note in

which Senator Davis informed his wife of his election. This information was conveyed in the following letter.

Charleston,
January 31, 1871.

My dear Kate:

All O. K. I was to-day, by a vote of more than two to one, elected U. S. Senator for six years from 4th of March. I am well and in fine spirits. Write often. Hope all are well.

Yours,
HENRY.

During the remainder of the session Mr. Davis continued his work as State Senator, mainly on the Committee on Finance and Claims, of which he was now chairman by virtue of his party being in the majority. His principal labor was in helping to formulate a joint report of the House and Senate Committees on Taxation and Finance regarding the financial condition of the State.

Since a Republican State administration was under review, the inquiry had in it some partizanship, as was shown by a minority report dissenting from the statements of the majority; but there was much to which no partizan objection could be made. One of the recommendations was that the school fund, which was maintained by taxation, and the income from investments should always at the end of each fiscal year be set apart for its own purposes, and never should be estimated with the funds of the general treasury, which were subject to legislative appropriation.

This report contained, too, what might be called Mr. Davis's final word as a legislator of the State of West Virginia on the debt question: "It must be ascertained and met in that spirit of fairness which is the distinguishing characteristic of our people." Other details of legislation were faithfully attended to, and when the session expired Mr. Davis could look back on five years of faithful, constructive service to the new State in which both his head and his heart had been intimately concerned. His service to West Virginia was a fitting prelude to his service to the nation as a member of the United States Senate.

CHAPTER IV

SENATOR OF THE UNITED STATES—FIRST TERM

Notable members of the Forty-second Congress—The Democratic minority in the Senate—Partizan measures and sectional issues—Senator Davis's assignment to Claims and Appropriations committees—Speech in support of West Virginia war claims—Financial legislation in the Forty-third Congress—Panic of 1873 portrayed—Mobility of currency advocated—President Grant's veto of the Inflation Bill—Resumption of specie payments—Work as member of Committee on Transportation Routes—West Virginia waterways—Political revolution gives Democrats a majority in the House—Forty-fourth Congress—Senator Davis on Treasury accounts and government bookkeeping—National and State campaigns of 1876—Reëlection to the Senate—Support of Electoral Commission.

MR. DAVIS was in his forty-eighth year, the prime of a vigorous life, when he began his service as a Senator of the United States. He was that rare person, a business man devoting himself to public affairs. To the wider field which opened before him he brought the valuable legislative training that had come from his service in the Legislature of West Virginia. He also brought a ripe judgment and a comprehensive grasp of the fundamental questions that were paramount in the legislation of the nation at that day. To these qualifications he added the fruits of a matured political experience and a robust support of the principles of his own party, tempered with a keen insight into the principles of the party to which he was in opposition.

Mr. Davis took his seat in the Senate in the second year of President Grant's administration, at the opening of the Forty-second Congress, on March 4, 1871. It was a notable Congress in its membership in both branches. The war giants, who had been responsible for the measures which were enacted during the period when the preservation of the Union was the supreme issue, were still there, and were still shaping the legislation following the great struggle.

James G. Blaine was Speaker of the House of Representatives. James A. Garfield was one of the leaders of the Republican party in the House. Samuel J. Randall of Pennsylvania was one of the forceful men among the minority. Another was Samuel S. Cox, then representing a New York district, formerly of Ohio. His old railway chief, Thomas Swann, was a member of the House.

In the Senate were Roscoe Conkling of New York, Charles Sumner of Massachusetts, former Vice-President Hannibal Hamlin and Lot M. Morrill of Maine, George F. Edmunds and Justin F. Morrill of Vermont, Simon Cameron of Pennsylvania, Oliver P. Morton of Indiana, John Sherman of Ohio, Zachariah Chandler of Michigan, and Lyman Trumbull of Illinois, all of whom had taken a prominent part in shaping war legislation, and most of whom were radicals of the radicals on the Reconstruction measures. On the Democratic side the leaders were Allen G. Thurman of Ohio and Thomas F. Bayard of Delaware. They were reinforced by the entry, contemporaneously with Mr. Davis, of Francis P. Blair, Jr., of Missouri, and Matthew W. Ransom of North Carolina. Among the new Republican Senators were John A. Logan of Illinois, the greatest volunteer soldier of the war, William Pitt Kellogg of Louisiana, and Powell Clayton of Arkansas.   William Windom of Minnesota had come to the Senate from the House in the preceding Congress.

No general amnesty act had yet been passed, and those who had taken part in the Rebellion consequently were barred from membership, though some of the Southern States in which the Demcorats had gained control of the legislatures had selected men of this class.   The actual party alinement was fifty-eight Republicans and sixteen Democrats, although the political reaction which later was to result in the Liberal Republican movement already was manifesting itself, and several of the most prominent Senators were freeing themselves from the party allegiance which they had maintained during the war and immediately thereafter.

Among these were Carl Schurz and Lyman Trumbull. Yet the Republican majority was large enough to maintain the party solidarity necessary to carry through whatever measures bore a distinctively political character. The Democratic minority was a compact, aggressive body which had little difficulty in acting as a unit on most questions and which therefore never lacked the qualities of a determined opposition.

There are a few entries in Senator Davis's journal regarding his early experiences in the Senate.   From one of these it appears that a caucus was held at Senator Thurman's house in which the minority membership of the committees was agreed on.   From a later entry it is disclosed that the tradition that a new Senator must remain silent for two years sometimes was broken even in those days, the trespasser on one occasion being the fiery Missourian, General F. P. Blair.   Under date of April 3 is the simple entry, "Gen. Blair spoke all day."

Henry Gassaway Davis in 1868

At another date it is noted that Senator Sumner made his great speech on Santo Domingo.

The principal committee to which Senator Davis was assigned was that on Claims. It was an important one, since it had to do with the claims growing out of the war. Notwithstanding that he was a minority member, much of the work of this committee seems to have been assigned to him. The numerous bills reported by him, some favorably and some unfavorably, all showed patient investigation and impartial judgment. Naturally, many of these bills related to his own State, since it had been the borderland between the contending armies.

At this session Senator Davis presented the petition from the Legislature of West Virginia favoring the removal of the political disabilities imposed by the Fourteenth Amendment. On other sectional questions growing out of the war he acted consistently with his party, especially in opposing Senator Sherman's resolutions on Southern outrages.

The second session of the Forty-second Congress found him immersed in committee work, and also brought evidences of growing appreciation on the part of his colleagues. A year after he had become a Senator there is a terse entry in his journal: "I am learning the ropes about the Senate and feel somewhat at home." It was not long after this that his political leadership in his own State was shown by his election as a delegate to the Democratic National Convention at Baltimore. At that convention he agreed with other members of his party that the only course open to the Democrats was to ratify the nomination of Greeley and Brown which had been made by the Liberal Republican Convention at Cincinnati, but he does not appear to have looked on the nomination of this ticket as presaging party success.

Political questions, sectional issues, were paramount n Congress, and party feeling ran high. Senator Davis, while taking a pronounced stand with his party colleagues, managed to avoid the bitter personal controversies that were a feature of the debates. Both his personal feelings and his political principles made him a strong advocate of the General Amnesty Bill, under which ex-Confederates would be enabled to return to the halls of legislation. At the same time he was opposed to the Civil Rights Bill, which was supported by the majority party in both branches of Congress. The Amnesty Act was finally passed, and later the modified Civil Rights Bill.

In the Forty-third Congress political questions were still prominent, but they were not predominant. Financial legislation and various measures of internal improvements claimed much attention. To this Congress came several ex-Confederates whose disabilities had been removed through the passage of the Amnesty Act. Among them was L. Q. C. Lamar of Mississippi, who entered the House of Representatives. Other new members of the House who later filled a large space in the affairs of the country were Colonel W. R. Morrison, of horizontal tariff bill fame, and J. G. Cannon of Illinois, R. P. Bland of Missouri, the free silver advocate, and T. C. Platt of New York. The delegate from the Territory of New Mexico was Stephen B. Elkins, who soon was to become identified with Senator Davis in the intimate family relation of son-in-law, and who was to be associated with him in his business enterprises, although the two were always to remain opposed in national politics.

Among Senator Davis's new colleagues in the Senate were William B. Allison of Iowa, who followed in natural progression from the House, John James Ingalls of Kansas, John P. Jones of Nevada, and Richard J. Oglesby of Illinois. The new members of his own political faith included the dashing ex-Confederate cavalry leader, General John B. Gordon of Georgia. The Democratic strength was increased by several new Senators, and the influence of the minority, chiefly still in opposition, became a much more pronounced factor in national legislation.

At the special session of the Senate called by President Grant to confirm his Cabinet, Senator Davis was placed on the Appropriations Committee, and of this Committee he was destined to be a member during the remainder of his senatorial term. Senator Morrill of Maine was chairman. Two Republican members of the Committee with whom Senator Davis through all the remaining years of their lives occupied intimate personal relations were Allison and Windom.

The work of this committee was most congenial to Senator Davis. Through its complete control of the legislation affecting all public expenditures it was the most powerful committee in the Senate, a power of which it had not been shorn by the creation and development of other committees, the sequence of the growth of the Government itself.

During this Congress one of the great characters of the nation passed away. The event is thus described in the Senator's journal:

March 12, 1874. Mr. Sumner, Senator of Mass., was in his seat yesterday; to-day dead. Senate adjourns until Monday.

Senator Davis was still a member of the Committee on Claims, and was the author of a bill appropriating $500,000 to reimburse West Virginia for the war losses of her citizens. At the session in May, 1874, he made a speech in support of this bill in which he vividly pictured the events of the days of the war. After sketching the formation of the State, he said:

"The people whose cause I advocate suffered much for the sake of the Republic. They are the men of the border, those men who during the Rebellion were the living rampart of the States which adhered to the general Government. . . .

"West Virginia was one of the border States during the late war, and so had to bear the brunt of hard knocks and cruel blows from both the contending armies. She was the bulwark, the fortress, interposed between the loyal States of the North and the opponents of the Government. Her hills and valleys resounded with the march of hostile armies during the whole war, and on numberless occasions were the scene of hard-fought battles, and were drenched with the blood of the best and bravest of both armies.

"All the moral influence which she as a State could exercise was thrown in the cause of the Government. Being one of the principal theaters of action and the Gibraltar of safety for the Northern States, a large number of troops was kept in this State all the time. Thus it was necessary, as one of the consequences of war, to use her schoolhouses and other public buildings as quarters to shield the soldier from wintry blasts, or else as hospitals to protect and care for the wounded. . . .

"It was a misfortune both to the people of the South and the people of the North that this war broke out; but it did break out, and it raged like a flame upon the prairie, destroying everything within its reach. It swept over our State like a hurricane. It was our lot to have visited upon us all the events, all the horrors of war, all the effusion of blood, the desolation of families, the rapine, the acts of violence and the conflagrations incident to war. The two armies surged backward and forward through our State like the ebbing and flowing of the tide, first advancing and then retreating. Life, liberty, property, all went down before the storm. Ties of kindred —social, domestic, and religious ties—were snapped asunder. Our cultivated fields were laid waste, our homes destroyed, our industrial pursuits interrupted, nay, almost abandoned. Many of our people were driven away from their homes; their cattle, horses, and other stock were taken, their houses burned, and everything they had on earth destroyed. . . .

"This is but a faint picture of some of the horrors of war. Our neighbors who dwelt in affluence and safety, while we stood sentry over their treasures and loved ones, little knew the sufferings and privations we were called upon to undergo."

The financial legislation of this Congress was the sequence of the panic of 1873, the full effects of which were most acutely felt during the following Spring. There was much pressure from the West and South to increase the volume of currency as a means of alleviating the industrial and commercial distress. The agitation bore concrete form in the measure reported by Senator Sherman from the Finance Committee to increase the national bank circulation. This afterward came to be known as the Inflation Bill, although it was a compromise between those who favored increasing the currency and those who hoped ultimately to get back to specie basis.

Senator Davis, like most of his party colleagues, supported this measure; in doing this he made it clear that he did not think a greater volume of currency was necessary, but that what was needed was a more equal distribution in different sections of the country. He did not look upon the National Bank Act as sufficiently elastic, and, having been a country banker, he was not afraid even to advocate a return to the State banks by reducing the prohibitive ten per cent. tax. But during the debates on this subject he made it clear that the basis of the national circulation should be means for facilitating currency in all parts of the country as needed. It was nearly forty years later when the views he advocated found expression in the passage of the Federal Reserve Act.

When the bill was reported from the Committee, Senator Davis offered an amendment providing, in substance, for free banking. Under date of March 18, 1874, his journal recites that he made a speech on the finances which seemed to be well received. His views on the causes that lead to inflation are as pertinent to-day as they were in the year following the great panic. After reviewing in its historical aspect banking legislation, he continued:

"What is needed in our present currency is stability, a fixed value, and that measured by a standard recognized by the world. . . .

"Previous to the panic early in September last there was no one bold enough to say that there was not sufficient circulation for the trade and business of the country; in fact, it was generally stated that there was too much paper money. Its abundance led to wild speculations, and particularly to the building of costly railroads in distant and wild countries far in advance of the wants of the people. The experience of all countries, particularly that of our own, teaches us that an abundance of paper money causes panics. The prospects of a healthy fall trade were never more encouraging than at the beginning of September last. None complained that there was not currency enough for all the business wants of the country. Like a thunder-shower in harvest-time the panic came; all lost confidence; banks and people held all the currency they had and got all they could, holding tight to it to sell at a premium, or fearing a demand that would be made on them. This caused a want of confidence which it has taken and will take time to restore. When it is fully restored, and a transfer made of part of the excess of bank circulation held in the North to the States of the South and West, I fully believe that a majority of the people will agree that we have paper money enough."

Discussing the same subject and supporting his amendment to reduce the tax on the circulation of the State banks from ten per cent. to an amount equal to that paid by the national banks (one per cent.), he declared it would relieve the wants of the Southern and Western States by allowing them a local circulation. During the discussion of the various financial measures Senator Davis often spoke in aphorisms.

Arguing against inflation, and citing the experience of the Confederate States he said: "The more abundant you make anything, the less valuable." Again: "What gives gold its value is that it costs about what it is worth to produce it; make it as plentiful as brass or iron and it would no longer have its present value." And again: "You cannot legislate money into this or that place. . . . Money will find the trade and business centers."

The bill reported by Senator Sherman from the Finance Committee, as ultimately agreed upon by both branches of Congress, provided for an increase of the paper currency up to $400,000,000, with provisions for a reduction from that amount by retirement of the notes, to which interpretations were given to suit their own views by those who favored more paper money and those who favored reducing the paper circulation. Senator Davis supported the legislation, and when, on April 22, President Grant's unexpected veto was received, he voted to override the veto.

The act providing for the resumption of specie payments on January 1, 1879, was passed at the winter session of this Congress. Senator Davis, though not opposed in principle to the bill, had some objections to its form, and he was one of the fourteen Senators who voted against it. In a later Congress he declared that resumption had come and was apparently working well, and consequently he was opposed to taking a backward step. "Do not let us go back," he said; "let us keep forward."

It was during the Fifty-third Congress that Senator Davis found a congenial outlet for his constructive tendencies in connection with internal improvements. In his journal, under date of September 15, 1873, he says:

I am a member of the Senate Select Committee on Transportation. It consists of Hon. Wm. Windom, chairman; Conkling, New York; Sherman, Ohio; West, Louisiana; Mitchell, Oregon; Norwood, Georgia; Davis, West Virginia. We meet in New York City twice, and then go to the Lakes, Chicago, Wisconsin and Fox River, Richmond, Va., James and Kanawha canals. Next, Charleston, Cincinnati, St. Louis, and then home. December vacation of Congress we go to New Orleans by way of Atlanta and Mobile. Go down Mississippi River to proposed St. Phillip Canal. Stay at New Orleans four or five days, then home by way of Jackson, Mississippi, Louisville, and Cincinnati. Return home January 4th.

These hearings excited great interest throughout the country. Senator Davis soon developed into one of the most influential members of the Committee. His intimate knowledge of railroading and of the whole subject of transportation was quickly apparent in the pertinent inquiries he addressed to the various witnesses who appeared in advocacy of the projects which they thought essential to the development of their section of the country.

The report of this Committee was prepared by the chairman, Senator Windom. Its voluminous pages are still studied by students of the transportation problems of the present day. A sweeping conclusion as to the power to regulate commerce, embodied by the chairman in the report, was not in full harmony with the views of some of the members of the Committee, who were traditionalists. Senator Davis joined with his Democratic colleagues, Senators Norwood and Johnson, the latter having been added to the committee, in a brief statement that they did not agree that Congress could exercise power to regulate commerce among the several States to the extent asserted. Senator Conkling also, while saying that he concurred in the main, dissented from certain statements of law and of fact, and from the recommendations relative to the power of Congress and its exercise.

The academic dissent from some of the general conclusions did not prevent Senator Davis from giving most hearty support to the specific projects that received the indorsement of the Committee. In this matter he was not unmindful of the interests of West Virginia, and he was solicitous also for the interests of Baltimore and the Chesapeake Bay country. He believed that his own State had not received the consideration to which it was entitled in the River and Harbor legislation. He pressed on the Committee the value of the Great Kanawha River, and he secured the designation of the eminent Baltimore engineer, B. H. Latrobe, as the civilian member of the Committee appointed to report on the James River and Kanawha canals.

He also secured an appropriation to begin the improvement of the river, the first appropriation ever voted by Congress for a West Virginia waterway, and the first step toward making the Great Kanawha the important transportation route it has since become. It was during the discussion of the project for the Hennepin Canal, joining the waters of the Great Lakes and the Illinois River with the Mississippi, that he declared the Chesapeake and Delaware Canal to be on a par with the proposed Hennepin Canal. On other occasions he sought to secure recognition of Baltimore as one of the great Atlantic ports.

In one of the debates on internal improvements and foreign commerce Senator Davis drew from the brilliant and erratic Senator Nye of Nevada a plea that convulsed the Senate. Senator Nye was advocating a bill providing for a postal steamship subsidy between the Pacific Coast and Australia. Senator Davis moved the reference of the bill from the Post Office Committee to the Committee on Commerce. The chairman of the latter Committee, it was known, was not favorable to the measure.

Senator Nye, somewhat inattentive to the routine proceedings of the Senate, at first did not catch the import of the motion. When he did, he jumped up, exclaiming: "This bill of mine? I have not time to attend its funeral to-day. [Laughter.] I hope that will not be done. You see the undertaker here in his seat, and I do not propose to be led to the shambles with this bill *nolens volens.*"

The signs of a political revolution throughout the

nation were becoming clearer during the final session of the Forty-third Congress. As soon as adjournment was had, Senator Davis gave his whole attention to the campaign in his own State. The political developments are summarized in two entries in his journal:

October 13, 1874. Our State election. Democrats made nearly a clean sweep in this and other States. We elected about 4-5ths of Legislature which elects a U. S. Senator. Also a full (3) delegation to House of Representatives.

November 3. Twenty-three States voted to-day. Democrats make large gains, even carrying Massachusetts, electing Gov. Gaston and 4 or 5 members of House. N. Y. and Penna. go Democratic, which give Democrats House by 50 or 60 majority, and elects 10 or 12 Senators.

When the Forty-fourth Congress met in December, 1875, the House of Representatives, with its large Democratic majority, elected Michael C. Kerr, of Indiana, Speaker. The Democratic membership in the Senate was increased to 32, just twice what it had been when Mr. Davis entered the Senate. He now had a Democratic colleague from his own State in the person of Allan T. Caperton, who had succeeded Senator Boreman. From the neighboring State of Maryland came his lifelong personal and political friend, William Pinckney Whyte. Francis Kernan of New York, W. W. Eaton of Connecticut, and Joseph E. McDonald of Indiana, were among the other new Democratic Senators. A notable figure of the past emerging into political life again was former President Andrew Johnson of Tennessee.

In this Congress Senator Davis returned to a subject to which he gave much attention through a great part of his Senatorial career. This was government bookkeeping and the forms of statement of the public debt. In the Forty-third Congress he had introduced a resolution requesting the Secretary of the Treasury to inform the Senate whether annual reports of the balances due the United States had been submitted since 1865, and if not why not.

The purpose of this resolution may have been political, as was charged by the Republican leaders of the Senate, but Senator Davis insisted that the people were entitled to know "who the defaulters were." The resolution was amended and passed, and a reply later was received from the Secretary of the Treasury which had little value to the inquirer. Following this effort Senator Davis submitted a resolution for a committee to investigate the Treasury accounts. It was amended by directing the Finance Committee to make an investigation. Naturally, Senator Davis got little comfort from the report of the Committee, the majority of which was opposed to him politically.

In the treatment of this subject the Senate had a taste of Mr. Davis's tenacity and of his persistence in following up a matter in which he was interested. Ultimately he got a hearing, and the Senate, while not fully agreeing with his charges, apparently did agree with his main contention, which was that the debt statements and all the statements in regard to government finances should be clear enough to be understood. Senator Davis's own views were set forth in detail during the running debate in the Senate in January, 1876, when he returned to the subject on different days. He had several colloquies with Senator Boutwell of Massachusetts, who had served as Secretary of the Treasury, and under whose administration some of the changes that were questioned had been made. His contention was summed up in this statement:

"The largest railroad corporations, commercial and manufacturing establishments in the country whose accounts reach tens of millions when managed upon proper business principles, have no difficulty in making intelligible their books and being able to make a statement of the exact condition of their business at any time; and while I concede that the Government is on a larger scale, yet its management should be such that its financial affairs may be readily understood; and indeed the larger the operations the greater the necessity for rigid, prompt, and accurate accountability and careful and regular statements, which should always agree, and when once rendered should be, like the laws of the Medes and Persians, not subject to change."

Senator Davis's own view of the subject, as it presented itself to him at the time, is recorded in two brief entries in the journal:

January 13, 1876. I make a speech on alterations, etc., in Treasury Department. I show many millions not accounted for. Ex-Secretary Boutwell replies.

January 24. I reply to Ex-Secretary Boutwell and make some new charges. I sustain all I have said.

There is reason to believe that in later years Senator Davis changed his views somewhat on this subject. Secretaries of the Treasury who were of his own political party, on their part, altered the methods of government bookkeeping, and of public debt statements, and were criticized in turn by their political opponents. But in his principal contention, that the statements of the Treasury accounts and the public debt should be clear enough to be understood, he was on solid ground from which he never retreated.

The national campaign of 1876 occupied much of the

attention of Senator Davis. As usual, he was one of the delegates from West Virginia to the Democratic National Convention, and he came back from Cincinnati believing that the prospects were very good for the election of Tilden and Hendricks. He corresponded with Tilden concerning the campaign. But, while interested in the national ticket, he was not unmindful of his own political fortunes. After the adjournment of Congress in August, he gave his whole time to the State. The subsequent events are thus recorded in his journal:

August 31, 1876. I have looked over the State and many of my friends have written me. All agree that without a great change takes place I will be easily reëlected to the Senate. My term expires March 4, 1877.

January 12, 1877. West Virginia Legislature met the 10th at Wheeling. I go and stay three days. Mr. C. J. Faulkner and myself are the principal candidates for long term of the Senate. Herford and Brice for short to succeed Mr. Caperton, who died in July last.

January 20. I return to Wheeling. Election for Senator takes place 23d.

January 28. On the 27th, on fourth ballot, I was elected to Senate for six years from March 4, 1877, by a vote of 60 against 37 scattering, of which Mr. Faulkner got 18. Herford was also elected on same day, next ballot after me. . . .

There were 6 or 8 candidates for my place in the Senate. Most promising was Hon. C. J. Faulkner, Judge John Brannon, Hon. J. J. Davis, Judge L. D. Camden. Hon. J. N. Camden and his friends were for me; also Governor-elect Mathews. I think Hon. Lewis Baker, editor of *Register*, did more to elect me than any other man. J. N. Camden next. There was no caucus nomination. I was elected in joint session on fourth day and fourth ballot. There were 21 Republicans in Legislature. 20 voted for me, so I received 40 Democratic votes and 20 Republican.

The fact that the Republican members, themselves

being so greatly in the minority, preferred to honor Senator Davis with their support rather than to compliment one of their own number, was a source of great gratification to him. It showed the warm feeling which the opposing party always held for him, notwithstanding the inevitable incidents of partizanship.

In the exciting events at Washington following the disputed election between Tilden and Hayes, Senator Davis bore himself with his habitual moderation. He believed that Tilden had been elected President, and he voted for the Electoral Commission Bill in the expectation that the Commission would so find; but that body having decided that Hayes was elected, he acquiesced in the decision, and counseled acquiescence on the part of others.

His first term as a Senator of the United States was now ending. His six years' service had broadened his insight into national affairs, and had given him an experience by which he was certain to profit during further service. In his own party, in the caucus and in the cloak-room councils, his influence had become very pronounced. Senator Thurman, on whom the burden of minority leadership had lain somewhat heavily, always turned to him when questions of party policy were to be determined. Other leaders who were heard most often on the floor in the exposition of party policy also counseled with him.

Yet, while a strong party man, Senator Davis never failed to show the independence that was characteristic of a broad-minded public man. He had won the esteem of the dominant party, and its leaders, recognizing his enormous capacity for detail and his thorough study of every subject presented to him, frequently turned to him for advice on matters of legislation that were not of a political character. With many of them, also, he had formed warm ties of personal friendship. Thus he was entering on his second term with every prospect of usefulness and of increased influence.

Scene on West Virginia Central Railway

CHAPTER V

Parties as affected by President Hayes's Administration—
Remonetization of silver—Democratic majority in the Senate of
the Forty-sixth Congress—New colleagues—Senator Davis as
chairman of the Appropriations Committee—Advocacy of a Department of Agriculture—Modest provisions for the farmers—
Camden as a colleague—Treasury accounts again—An unqualified
protection Democrat—Defense of the tariff on coal—West Virginia and debts of honor—Business reasons for declining a third
term—Resolution of State Legislature—Résumé of public questions during twelve years' service—Growth of appropriations—
James G. Blaine's tribute to Senator Davis.

THE Senate of the Forty-fifth Congress was called
in the customary extra session by President
Hayes to confirm his Cabinet nominations and
other appointments. The inauguration is thus briefly
described in Senator Davis's journal:

March 5, 1877. The 4th being Sunday, Hon. R. B. Hayes was
inaugurated President, the Electoral Commission made by Congress having declared Hayes elected over Tilden by a majority of
one electoral vote, 185 to 184.

The Democratic membership of the Senate was further strengthened in this Congress. Among the new
Democratic Senators were James B. Beck of Kentucky,
William H. Barnum of Connecticut, Benjamin H. Hill
of Georgia, L. Q. C. Lamar of Mississippi, Augustus H.
Garland of Arkansas, J. R. McPherson of New Jersey,
and Daniel W. Voorhees of Indiana. Mr. Blaine, who
had served in the Forty-fourth Congress to fill the va-

cancy caused by the death of Senator Lot M. Morrill, now entered upon the full senatorial term. Samuel J. Kirkwood entered from Iowa. George F. Hoar of Massachusetts, after several years' service in the House, now came to the Senate. Henry M. Teller appeared from Colorado, the Centennial State. David Davis of Illinois, having resigned from the Supreme Bench to accept the Senatorship as an independent, thus breaking the deadlock, was one of the conspicuous members.

When the House of Representatives organized, it still contained a large Democratic majority, and Samuel J. Randall was elected Speaker. Among the new members of the House were Thomas B. Reed of Maine and William McKinley of Ohio.

At the beginning of Senator Davis's second term many of the political questions that had been the means of welding the Democratic minority closely together no longer existed. There was still political legislation, but the era of Reconstruction and of the party measures growing out of it was ended. The new era was marked by the policy of conciliation toward the South instituted by President Hayes. The split this policy caused in the Republican party, and the bitterness of the factions that respectively sustained and opposed it, exceeded the bitterness that had obtained in previous years when the two great parties were lined up against each other. These family quarrels of the Republicans had little effect on the legislative activities of Senator Davis. His personal relations with several of the rival leaders at times enabled him to act as a mediator between them. This was the strongest evidence that could be given of the degree to which his personality had impressed itself on his colleagues.

Senator Davis continued to serve on the Committee on

Appropriations. Though not a member of the Finance Committee, he gave much attention to the work of that Committee in the form in which it came before the Senate, sometimes joining with his colleagues of both parties to modify its recommendations, sometimes supporting them, and occasionally rejecting them outright.

The remonetization of silver was the leading financial question before the Forty-fifth Congress. The House passed the Bland Free Coinage Bill, the purpose of which was declared by its supporters to be to remedy "the crime of 1873" by which silver was demonetized. The Senate accepted the Allison Amendment, under which the coinage of not less than two million dollars and not more than four million dollars was provided per month. Senator Davis, before this bill came up, had been one of the forty-three Senators who voted for the resolution offered by Stanley Matthews of Ohio, to the effect that the bonds of the United States were payable in silver. On the proposed remonetization he favored the Allison amendment, and spoke in support of it several times.

The substance of his position was that he favored silver because it was one of our chief products, would make the money known to the Constitution more abundant, would relieve distress, and would lead back to prosperity. He held that its remonetization was important to the laboring, the agricultural, the manufacturing, and the debtor classes. When President Hayes vetoed the Bland-Allison bill, he stood by his original convictions and voted to pass it over the veto, which was done.

It was during this silver debate that Senator Davis set forth his views on the relations between labor and capital. In a sharp colloquy with Senator Sargent of California, he remarked, "The poor man appears to have found friends here." Continuing the debate, he said:

"In the discussion of this question I do not find it necessary to reflect upon capital and labor. I am a friend of both—and have a good word and a kind feeling for each. By laws man cannot control they are and ought to be friends; they should go hand in hand; they are necessary to each other; one cannot be well and the other sick. A nation cannot prosper for a long time when they are at war; they may be arrayed against each other temporarily, but bad results are as sure to follow and continue until their natural harmony is restored. One depends upon prosperity and health upon the other. They should support and uphold each other; they have equal and the same right to protection."

These were not mere academic expressions or the catch-words of a politician. They embodied the principle upon which Senator Davis as a capitalist, and for more than half a century a large employer, guided his relations with labor.

In the Forty-sixth Congress the Democrats held the majority in the Senate as well as in the House, and thus were enabled to control the organization. Among the new Democratic Senators were George H. Pendleton of Ohio, George G. Vest and Francis M. Cockrell of Missouri, and John T. Morgan of Alabama. Senator Davis, by virtue of his service as a minority member of the Appropriations Committee, now that his party was in the majority, became the chairman of that committee.

During the two years in which he served in this capacity he observed the same practice that he had followed when in the minority. He believed in public economy, but not in parsimony. Politically he was opposed to the party that was in control of the national administration, and the scrutiny of its expenditures was a fair subject for party capital; but no department of the Government, in asking appropriations, had reason to feel that its proper requests would be denied.

If the chairman of the Appropriations Committee declaimed somewhat against extravagance and exhorted to economy, he had done the same thing when he was a minority member, and where it seemed that the growth of the Government justified increased expenditures in some directions he advocated them and sought to provide for them. This was notably the case in regard to what would now be called encouraging agriculture. That greater support should be given by the general government to the development of agriculture had been one of his favorite themes. It was natural that the farmer boy of the Western Shore of Maryland who later had cleared the Alleghany wilderness, and whose farm at Deer Park filled so many entries in his journal, should take an interest in the farmers of the nation.

Senator Davis loved the farm and farm life. He had introduced various resolutions and bills to encourage farming. One of these resolutions was presented at the spring session in 1878. Its text showed how little encouragement the agriculture of the country up to that time had received from Congress. There was a bureau or Department of Agriculture, with a Commissioner at its head and a few employes. This resolution called for the printing of three hundred thousand copies of the Agricultural Report. Congress made some provision for distributing seeds; but in the course of the debate on the resolution Senator Davis, correcting Senator Saulsbury of Delaware, who had spoken of five hundred thousand dollars as the appropriation made for agricultural purposes, explained that the amount was only two hundred and fifty thousand dollars.

At the December session he introduced another resolution reciting that, since agriculture was the foundation of nearly all our wealth, and since it was mainly through the exportation of its products that we were paying off our large indebtedness, the Committee on Agriculture of the two Houses should investigate and report what could or ought to be done by the general Government the better to advance the agricultural interests. Previous to the introduction of this resolution he had corresponded with Governor Horatio Seymour of New York, who had, as he wrote to Senator Davis, talked a great deal and frequently at agricultural fairs. Ultimately the resolution was passed.

In order to get the whole subject before Congress in a definite form, Senator Davis made a set speech. Under date of January 14, 1879, he records in his journal: "I made in Senate an agricultural speech which is highly spoken of." In this speech he said:

"We are a nation of farmers, and because of the vast area of our soil and its great fertility we must remain so. Our agricultural products not only support our people but pay for what we buy abroad. They furnish our greatest source of revenue—and to them we are indebted for the balance of trade now being largely in our favor and that our bonds and other indebtedness held abroad are so rapidly coming home."

Continuing this line of thought, he analyzed the statistics and showed that three fourths of the country's exports were agricultural products.

In succeeding Congresses Senator Davis joined with Senator Windom in seeking to secure the establishment of a Department of Agriculture and Commerce. He introduced a bill for that purpose at several sessions. His final effort in behalf of agriculture was made in

January, 1883, just a few weeks before his retirement, in a speech supporting his bill for the establishment of a Department of Agriculture. In this speech he compared somewhat humorously the numerical proportion of lawyers and farmers. He said that in both branches of Congress there were two hundred and fifty-two lawyers and sixteen farmers, counting himself as a farmer. This was in striking contrast to the House of Delegates of West Virginia in which he began his public life. As has been shown in the foregoing pages, there were one lawyer and twenty farmers in that body.

At this session of the Senate Mr. Davis, as a member of the Appropriations Committee, was in charge of the Agricultural Appropriation Bill. It provided $60,000 for seed, and $414,000 for administrative and other expenses. Senator Davis lived to see the modest appropriation approximating half a million dollars, which marked the last stage of his Senatorial career, grow into an appropriation of $20,000,000 in 1915, to support what has become one of the greatest departments of the Government of the United States, and all within a generation. To his constructive mind, and to his sympathy with the farmer and his knowledge of the economic relation of agriculture to national development, is due much of the credit for the creation of the Department of Agriculture and the functions it performs in the Government.

West Virginia politics and national politics were not neglected on account of Senatorial duties. Senator Davis took an active part in the West Virginia State campaign in 1878. Under date of September 24 he records in his journal: "I make a speech at Grafton on the political situation of the country. It is printed in full in *Wheeling Register,* and in part in many of the papers of the State." Further entries relate to other speeches. The outcome is indicated in October in the statement that the Democrats have carried each of the Congressional districts, and a large majority in the Legislature. The majority of the Legislature was especially gratifying to Senator Davis. The reason for his gratification is indicated in a later entry in his journal:

Hon. J. N. Camden has been elected U. S. Senator for West Virginia, term commencing March 4 for six years. I was for him and will be glad to have him for a colleague.

Mr. Camden's career was in many respects similar to that of Senator Davis. He was a business man. Living at Parkersburg, he was one of the pioneers in the oil industry, and he did for the Ohio River counties what Senator Davis did for the mountain counties in developing their resources and providing systems of transportation. The two were associated with the campaigns following the Civil War, under which the Democratic party through organization and leadership was enabled to gain control of the State. Their political association and their personal friendship continued until the death of Senator Camden.

In 1880 Senator Davis headed the West Virginia delegation to the Democratic national convention at Cincinnati, which nominated Hancock and English. He did not, apparently, regard the ticket as a strong one.

During the sessions of the Forty-sixth Congress Senator Davis returned to the subject of the Treasury accounts. His party being in the majority, he was able to secure the appointment of a special committee of investigation. John Sherman, who had been chairman of the Finance Committee when Senator Davis began his agitation for information, was now Secretary of the Treasury. The bookkeeping of the Department under him was not criticized, but the report made by Senator Davis on behalf of the majority insisted that in previous years many erasures and changes had been made in the books, and that the systems of checks on officers handling large sums of money was faulty. A minority report was presented by Senators Ingalls and Dawes, in which the conclusions of the majority were combated. Some years later the Treasury Department revised the entire system of bookkeeping, and introduced further safeguards, while at the same time simplifying the methods of bookkeeping. From the beginning this simplification had been one of the principal contentions of Senator Davis.

Senator Davis was a protection Democrat without apology and without qualification. A Henry Clay Whig in his earlier political life, this was perhaps a natural inheritance; but, living in a State whose principal resources lay underground, and being himself an industrial captain seeking to develop those resources, protection was a natural course of political action for him. Yet he was not extreme in his views, and he did not oppose reduction in some of the schedules where the industries had been sufficiently fostered to stand this reduction.

In the Forty-second Congress, when the internal revenue taxes were removed from fish, fruits, and meats, and the duties on tea and coffee were abolished, he also supported the reduction of ten per cent. on cotton, wool, iron, steel, paper, rubber, and glass products. In the Forty-sixth Congress he supported a tariff amendment by Senator Bayard providing that the duty on wool should not exceed twenty-five per cent. *ad valorem,* and on woolen goods fifty per cent.

The reasons that guided his support of protection as a principle and as a policy were set forth when coal, the chief product of his own State, came under review. The

Tariff Commission appointed by President Arthur in the bill it recommended had proposed to reduce the duty on coal.   In the debates on this subject in January and February, 1883, Senator Davis reviewed the whole tariff question in its broad historial aspect—as well as in its local application.   The Tariff Commission Bill proposed to reduce the duty on bituminous coal from seventy-five cents to fifty cents per ton.   Senator Davis objected to this proposition, for one reason because other articles were reduced only ten per cent., while the proposed reduction on coal amounted to thirty-three per cent.

In the discussion he reviewed and justified his own stand as related to his personal interest.   Senator Morgan of Alabama had declared that the protection proposition was a man voting a tax into his own pocket out of the people of Alabama to enrich himself.

Senator Davis, speaking with feeling, in reply said:

"It is true that I am a coal-miner, and had been for many years before I knew the Senate, and I have continued ever since.   I, however, am one of a corporation in which there are perhaps one hundred people engaged. Every Senator here has voted on everything that has come up in the Senate when his people were interested regardless of his personal interest.   I might as well say that the Senator from Texas, or any other Senator, when he votes for the duty on cotton, or any other thing, votes to put money in his own pocket.   I do not choose to go into that; I do not think it just or proper. . . .

"I have uniformly voted for a fair protection, or what I believe to be a fair protection, for every interest that has come up for consideration.   I have been unfortunate in disagreeing with a large majority of my friends on this side of the chamber.   However, I am just as honest in my conviction that I am right as they are in theirs.

I heard it said—I suppose it was not intended for me—on some vote I gave here that I had better look out—'wait until coal comes up.' That is hardly a fair argument. I do not regard it as a fair way of meeting a question, because a Senator happens to be interested in an industry, to retaliate on his vote on something else by the idea, 'when we get a chance we will punish him.' I have no such feeling towards others. I act upon each question as it arises, according to my judgment of what is right in regard to it. . . .

"I suppose I am interested to the extent of one ten thousandth part of the coal mines in this country. My interest in the question, I suppose, would not be greater than that, and yet Senators speak as if that would have weight with me; as if my course on this question was an exception to my general rule of action, as if coal was the thing above all others, as if some little personal feeling actuated me. I find Senators on this side of the house who are especially interested in some particular thing, and they vote and act for protection to that, and they vote against protection to everything else. . . . That course of conduct seems to go all around the chamber. It is not confined to this side altogether; and yet, when a man who has been consistent, and voted for every fair proposition, asks for a reasonable rate on a great product of his State, some Senators are kind enough to say, or choose to say, that that man owns an interest in a mine. I do own an interest in a mine, and I wish it distinctly understood that I do."

In later years, as a private citizen, Mr. Davis protested before the committees of Congress against the free coal proposition contained in the Wilson bill, the author of which was from his own State and district. Much later, in newspaper interviews, he voiced his objections to the reduction of coal which was provided in the Canadian Reciprocity Agreement negotiated by President Taft.

The debt of West Virginia was a topic of discussion and criticism at various periods during Senator Davis's service in the Senate. He had numerous colloquies with Senators Sherman, Hawley, Hoar, and Edmunds on the subject at different times. The New England Senators in particular were inclined to be critical, and he resented their attitude. In the several debates Senator Davis explained his own action, when a member of the West Virginia Legislature, in seeking an adjustment of the question and particularly in providing for commissioners to go to Richmond to confer with Virginia officials. As to the action of members of the Senate in bringing up the subject, Senator Davis maintained that it was a local question and belonged to the two States respectively, and not to Congress.

He reviewed the whole controversy in a speech delivered early in May, 1881. In this speech, incidentally, he spoke of the resources of West Virginia, saying: "They are largely undeveloped as yet, the greater part of them lying dormant; but when the treasures of this mountain State are unearthed, as they must be in time, they will astonish the world."

Referring to the proportion of the debt which the undeveloped commonwealth that West Virginia was when it separated from the Old Dominion should pay, he asked: "Can you tax a mountain uninhabited at the same rate you would tax a valley well improved?"

In this address Senator Davis made his famous deliverance on debts of honor. "In my opinion," he said, "no individual, no firm, no corporation, no city, town, state or government can afford to ignore a just and honorable debt. A State cannot do so even with as much propriety as an individual. The law can compel payment by one; in the case of the other it is a debt more of honor, and I believe it is the duty of every citizen of the State to do his full share to have his State, no matter whether it owes much or little, do its part, its honest part, its just part, its equitable part, toward the settlement and payment of any debt it may owe, and so far as my voice goes it will always be in that direction. . . .

"I think I am as much of a debt-payer as anybody, and I believe it is the duty of every State and every individual to pay a just and honorable debt, let it be what it may. I think that a man who wants to look the world squarely in the face and do his full duty will at all times —whether he is able to pay may be another question— at least answer and say, 'I owe and will pay when I can.'"

Senator Davis had found public duties most agreeable. His two terms in the Senate had not caused him to tire of it, but the public service was made at some sacrifice to his growing business interests. These were not neglected, but necessarily they were secondary. Projects of industrial development which he had been maturing had now reached the stage where, if they were to be brought to their full fruition, they must have the first claim on him. Accordingly, he determined to retire from the Senate, although this did not mean his entire withdrawal from public life, for he expected to continue his interest in public affairs, and did continue them thereafter, but principally as a private citizen. His determination to retire is thus set forth in his journal:

November 20, 1882. I have for two or three years said I would not be a candidate for reëlection to the Senate, and to put all matters at rest I wrote and printed the following letter. I have no doubt of my election if I had been a candidate.

The letter, which was addressed to the *Wheeling Register,* follows:

Piedmont, W. Va., Nov. 18, 1882.

I have recently received a number of letters and personal inquiries from members of the Legislature elect, candidates for the United States Senate, and other friends, asking me if I would be a candidate for reëlection and expressing their preference for me if such was my intention. To all such inquiries my general answer has been that for the past two or three years I have often said in public and private that I would not be a candidate for reëlection. Business is more agreeable to me than politics, and I am now engaged in lumbering, mining, banking, and farming; in connection with some friends who are capitalists living both in and out of the State, am constructing railroad lines running north and south through an undeveloped region, rich in mineral, timber, and agricultural wealth, and intended when completed to connect with the Baltimore and Ohio and the Chesapeake and Ohio railroads. My ambition is to make a success of these enterprises, especially the building of the railroads. These and other private matters are reasons which forbid my being a candidate for reëlection.

In the many trusts heretofore confided to my keeping I have always endeavored to do my full duty, and I thank the people of the State, and especially my friends, for the political honors that have been conferred upon me.

The West Virginia Legislature unanimously adopted a resolution showing the appreciation in which Senator Davis was held by all parties. Its text, which is worthy of preservation, follows:

Whereas, Honorable Henry G. Davis will conclude on the 4th of March next his second term as a Senator of the United States from West Virginia, and, having declined to be a candidate for reëlection, will then voluntarily retire from the Senate, therefore be it

Resolved: That a legislative acknowledgment and public expression of thanks is justly due unto an honored and well tried public servant, and that, in accordance with what we believe to be the sentiment of the people of West Virginia, not restricted to the limits of one political party, we do hereby declare that by his devotion to the public service at all times, and especially to the interests of West Virginia, the Honorable Henry G. Davis has justly earned the gratitude of his constituents, and in the respect and good will of the people of the State he will find reward for a career of honesty, capability, and energetic endeavor in the public service.

The two terms of Senator Davis in the Senate included six years of President Grant's administration, all that of President Hayes, the brief period of President Garfield's, and a part of President Arthur's term. When he entered the Senate political and partizan issues, echoes of the sectional struggle, were the vital questions. When he retired, the Reconstruction measures were no longer an issue. The menace of a second civil war growing out of the disputed election of 1876 had been settled peaceably, and, though its echoes were still heard, these had little influence on the course of legislation. Specie payments had been resumed, and the silver question had been settled, as it was then thought, for good. Foreign relations, which were threatening in consequence of the dispute with England over the *Alabama* claims, had been rendered friendly through the Geneva Arbitration. Chinese immigration, as an economic problem, had first appeared on the horizon, and President Hayes had vetoed the bill passed to prohibit it. Congress had begun systematically to develop the rivers and harbors as part of the transportation system of the country, although the appropriations for that purpose were still modest.

The growth of the Government was shown in the provisions made for the annual appropriations. Dur-

ing Senator Davis's first year's service in the Senate,
when the population of the country was forty millions,
the revenues had amounted approximately to $365,000,-
000 yearly, of which a little more than $117,000,000 was
applied to interest on the public debt and a fraction over
$176,000,000 to the regular appropriations. The pen-
sion appropriation amounted to $28,500,000 annually,
and of this sum $240,000 was for pensioners of the War
of 1812. The appropriation for the Army was $27,-
700,000, and for the Navy fractionally less than $20,-
000,000. The Post Office appropriation amounted to
$26,000,000.

For the fiscal year 1883–84, the last one for which
Senator Davis helped to provide as a member of the Appropriations Committee, the annual appropriations were
$230,200,000. Of this amount, approximately $24,750,-
000 was for the Army and $16,000,000 for the Navy.
The appropriation for pensions had amounted to $100,-
000,000. The population was now 55,000,000, and the
internal and customs revenues were approximately $362,-
000,000 annually.

Of the party colleagues with whom he served in the
earlier years, there remained in the full vigor of life and
of active public service Senator Bayard, one of the leaders of the sixteen Democratic Senators when the Forty-
second Congress met in March, 1871. Among those
who had entered since that time, several of whom had
become his closest friends, were Blaine and Allison.
His cousin, Arthur Pue Gorman, and Benjamin Harrison had entered the Senate in the Forty-seventh Congress.

To one of these colleagues it was given to form the
estimate of Henry G. Davis as a public man. This was
James G. Blaine. The estimate was of Mr. Davis as he

entered the Senate, and also as he left it. In his "Twenty Years of Congress," in reviewing the members of the Forty-second Congress, Mr. Blaine wrote:

Henry G. Davis, a native of Maryland, entered as the first Democratic Senator for West Virginia. His personal popularity was a large factor in the contest against the Republicans in his State, and was instantly rewarded by his party as its most influential leader. Mr. Davis had honorably wrought his own way to high station, and had been all his life in active affairs as a farmer, a railroadman, a lumberman, an operator in coal, and a banker. He had been uniformly successful. He came to the Senate with the kind of practical knowledge which schooled him to care and usefulness as a legislator. He steadily grew in the esteem and confidence of both sides of the Senate, and when his party obtained the majority he was intrusted with the responsible duty of the chairmanship of the Committee on Appropriations. No more painstaking or trustworthy man ever held the place. While firmly adhering to his party, he was at all times courteous, and to the business of the Senate or in local intercourse never obtruded partizan views.

Senator Davis's own valedictory to his Senatorial career was characteristically simple. It appears in this entry in his journal:

March 4, 1883. My second term in U. S. Senate ended yesterday. I declined a reëlection. Hon. J. E. Kenna succeeded me. . . . I intend to devote most of my time to the interests of the West Va. Central Co. both building road, mining, and selling coal.

CHAPTER VI

THE RAILWAY BUILDER

East-and-west trunk lines through West Virginia—Undeveloped regions between the north and south systems—The Davis projects—His own story of prospecting trips—Early expeditions into the forest wilderness—Timber observations—Exploring unknown coal-fields—Surveys for West Virginia Central Railway—Planning the route—Notable statesmen and capitalists enlisted in the enterprise—Horseback trip to White Sulphur Springs—Opening of the line in 1881—Industrial communities created—Contemporary account of the railway and the region it developed—Controversy with the Baltimore and Ohio—Making the system independent.

RAILWAY projects are not conceived overnight; they grow in the minds of those who originate and carry them through. They are based on knowledge of the resources that are to be developed and on faith in the returns to be received from developing these resources. They are, in one sense, the product of environment, and they reflect that environment. There is, however, a substantial difference in the nature of the projects, and this difference is nowhere more apparent than in the mountainous regions that are to be opened up to trade and industry.

Trunk lines, and in particular east-and-west trunk lines, have been the normal course of railway development in the United States. In the case of West Virginia the geographical situation made this especially the natural course of transportation. The Baltimore and Ohio Railroad, which brought the Ohio and Mississippi valleys and the Great Lakes to tidewater, was the northern route, and when it reached Wheeling in 1853, the observation was made that the roughest region yet traversed by an internal improvement in America was that between Cumberland and the Ohio River.

The southern route, following principally the old James River and Kanawha turnpike, was evolved after the Civil War into the Chesapeake and Ohio system. Its difficulties, financial and otherwise, were not unlike those of the Baltimore and Ohio; but gradually they were surmounted, and there was a trunk line from tidewater at Norfolk and Newport News to the lower Ohio Valley and to the Mississippi Valley.

A vast region lay between these northern and southern trunk lines, easterly and westerly, which could be developed only by lines that would connect with them and that would also secure access for the coal and timber to the Great Lakes and the Mississippi and to tidewater. Railways that had financial difficulties in providing a main system are slow to strike boldly out and build feeders. They construct branch lines cautiously and conservatively. It is their preference to leave to the enterprise of individuals the building of new lines, whose traffic they will handle without the initial cost of construction added to their own financial burdens.

In this manner most of the internal development of West Virginia has been secured. "The largest chapter in the history of the State," wrote Professor James Morton Callahan in his " Semi-Centennial History of West Virginia," "is that relating to the great industrial awakening which had its origin largely in the increasing demand for timber, coal, oil, and gas, and was especially influenced by the inducements for the construction of railroads."

No man in the history of the State of West Virginia fills a fuller page in this large chapter than Henry G. Davis, and no man did more to supply the deficiency in transportation facilities resulting from the conservative policy of the trunk lines.   He realized more thoroughly than anyone else of his day the possibilities of the State, especially the region lying southwest of Piedmont, the upper Potomac and Elk Garden regions.   He also realized that the vast natural resources of the coal and timber counties might lie untouched by man forever unless transportation to the outside world should be provided.

His early purchases of coal and timber lands on the upper Potomac were adjacent to the Baltimore and Ohio Railroad, and an ordinary man would have been content to reap the gains from his foresight in purchasing those lands.   But Mr. Davis was not an ordinary man.   After having developed the Piedmont and New Creek region, and then having opened the wilderness on the crest of the Alleghanies, his vision swept a wider horizon, and the conception came to him of building the railway line along the banks of the Potomac to the source of the summit of the mountains, and continuing beyond into the valleys on the western slope of the Alleghanies.

It was this conception that found expression in the charter for the Piedmont and Potomac Railway, which ultimately developed into the West Virginia Central and Pittsburgh Railway.   In the northern counties of the State, and particularly the upper Cheat and Tygarts Valley country, was a wilderness of timber underlaid with coal.   Some estimate could be made of the worth of the timber, but no one could estimate the value of the coal that lay beneath the surface.   That was purely a venture.   The region was almost inaccessible and very sparsely populated in consequence of the lack of means of communication. The most that the local communities had sought in the way of opening their resources was to improve the turnpikes. A proposition to construct a double-track tramway fifty miles in length was looked on as extravagant.

Mr. Davis had familiarized himself with every square mile of this wild country. He had traversed it on foot and on horseback, always with the observing eye of an engineer and of a pioneer lumberman and mining prospector. A trained geologist could not have done better in locating coal deposits. Some of the entries in his journal afford vivid evidence of the manner in which he determined the feasibility of the railway project. They also give a deep insight into the habits of mind that formed the basis of his success, while they afford more than a passing glimpse of pioneer exploring and of indifference to its hardships. Here is the account of one of his prospecting trips:

Aug. 16, 1869. Bro. Thomas and myself start on a trip at Canaan. Stop first night at Greenland. Mr. M. D. Neul and Abraham Smith go with us. Go to Corners from there, to 1 creek; stay all night with Cap Lamberts. On 19th on east side of mountain to Gouldigen; he goes with us to vein of coal; it shows about four feet; think it is 6 feet. If we were to go again think the best way would be to go first to Greenland; there to Gouldigen. We went up the Creek to coal; found several veins, ours about 6 feet. It shows several small slates. Return to New Creek[1] by Greenland on 20th and come to Deer Park same day.

In his journal, under the heading "Look at Anderson and Clancy Pine," is a detailed account of a timber prospecting trip, which shows how thorough were the methods of Mr. Davis in his reconnaissances:

[1] New Creek was later named Keyser.

Oct. 28, 1872. Left Piedmont horseback. Met Jesse W. Clanny at Morrison's Mill. Went to take a look at Anderson, Clanny and Wilson timber on Savage and tributaries.

Went to Swager's Mill; found good timber about there. Mill is on horse pond. Run about four miles from junction with Savage; run very crooked. Pine timber on creek is about half a mile wide and three long; not much near Savage. Went from Swager's to Clanny's Mill; is on Big Blue Lick Run. A Mr. Jacobs has 75 or 80 acres of No. 1 pine near Swager's. Good farming country between Swager's and Clanny's, not much pine. Staid Clanny's all night. John C. lives with old man and attends to mill.

October 29. Leave Clanny's house and mill, walk down Big Blue Lick and up Little B. Lick. Not much timber except hemlock near Clanny's mill, in fact bottoms on Runs are hemlock; on side of hills, white pine. Clanny has 2,000 acres in all, has about 700 acres on Little Blue Lick tolerable good pine, considerable hemlock, say one half each, would not give much for any but 700 acres.

Mr. Anderson has, I would think, 1,000 or 1,200 acres of white pine and three times as much hemlock.

Clanny's Mill on Blue Lick about 2½ miles from junction of Savage and mile from Little Blue Lick. Clanny's Mill about 12 miles from Mount Crabtree or railroad junction. Blue Lick about 7½ miles from road. Water sawmills on Mr. Anderson's, 8½ miles. Horse pond run, 6½ miles. Not much timber from horse pond run to railroad. Tram could be easily made down Savage by crossing Savage about four times. Lochiel or Wilson's is above Clanny's on Savage, do not think much of it. Arrived house with Mr. Clanny about 5 o'clock.

A further inspection of the timber in the Savage district was made September 20, 1877:

Billy Davis, John Riely, Gen. Anderson, agent and myself go to Swager's Mill for the purpose of evamining pine timber.

There but little good timber near Savage; it is on headwaters of the small streams running into Savage. We carefully examined Horse Pond run, Poplar Run, on which is Swargen's Mill (from Savage to foot of Meadow Mountain). No timber worth naming for 3 or 4 miles from Savage. A tract of land belonging to a Mr. Ross called Brantz Mill seat crosses the run about 2½ miles from Swager's Mill and 4 miles from Savage, takes about 50 acres of good timber, then for a mile up there is but little timber, then there is a body of from one to two hundred acres good white pine. This is from near Mrs. Otto's to Swargen's land and say a mile on creek.

Above Swargen's on Horse Pond Run there is from 100 to 150 acres of good timber. This takes us to foot of Meadow Mountain and makes in all belonging to General Anderson say 300 to 350 acres of good pine on Horse Pond Run.

On Elk Lick Run, from what is known as Gov. Thomas' farm to Barton road within mile of Savage there is a body of say 250 acres of good pine timber, and between Barton road on one side and Broad Water on the other there is probably 400 acres of land, 250 well timbered; from Thomas' place by this run to Savage is estimated at 4 miles. Upon the whole, there is not as much timber on Savage and run as I supposed.

A coal-prospecting trip in the region where he was planning the railway line is thus described:

November 9, 1874. I returned from a trip to Tucker, Randolph and Barbour Counties. Went to look at coal deposits of which much has been said.

I find on Roaring Creek at or near Crawford Scott's and I. K. Scott's a vein of coal open in several places; the vein from top to bottom is about 11 feet, about 2½ feet top and bottom of coal, then a slate from 1 to 2 on this, and about 6 feet of piece or good coal in center. I do not think it the vein of this region or Pittsburgh; it looks more like the Meyersville or Connellsville and Uniontown vein.

A later excursion is told of in this manner:

December 1, 1875. Owen Reader and myself left Piedmont this morning to look at and examine new coal fields lately discovered or opened on Stony River and Difficult Creek. Staid all night at Mrs. Lee's. Found near northwestern road and on and near Difficult Creek two veins of coal, one full 4 feet on turnpike, one 7 or 7½ on Difficult one half mile below road. I take those two veins to be over 3½ and 6 feet, improved in quality and thickness; they are about right distance apart.

Below Rhiners on Stony River and about midway between Stony River Falls and N. W. Road an 8 foot vein, say 2 feet of coal, then slate 4 inches, then 4 feet of coal, then small slate coal; very good in appearance, comes out in long regular pieces, finger shape. This is unlike other coal here, but like Connellsville coal.

Several excursions in later years reflect the thorough manner in which the resources of the districts along the proposed line were studied. Here are two of them:

July 5, 1881. Mr. Elkins and myself leave Deer Park on horseback to examine country around and about Fairfax Stone; also on backwater of Cheat River. We find the timber very fine; some cherry and ash; mostly spruce and hemlock. Coal indications are very good, several veins open, one near Dobbin House of almost 8 feet pure coal. We stay at Dobbin House overnight, no one lives there. We had blankets with us, made pillows out of our saddles; gone three days. George Musser showed us where he and Brant opened 200 yds., east road going to Fairfax Stone on Levering land, five veins in same hill next to Potomac. One vein near top hill about 8 feet, thirty feet below, 4 foot vein fifty below that vein appears 7 feet and two small veins below. On same ridge and mile or more east Riordon opened vein about 8 feet above, five feet without stone. Near Dobbin House (old one) say one and one half miles north, or this side of new house, Riordon opened vein almost 8 feet thick; looks black, pure and good, little or no slate in it. This is the best vein I have seen, pitches east, and appears to underlay a large body of land mostly ours. Parsons is now making survey for our road near or in this region.

Public service in the Legislature of West Virginia and in the United States Senate had not entirely diverted Senator Davis from his development enterprises. It was during this period that his investments in coal and timber lands were expanded, the railway project for the line to the southwest of Piedmont conceived, matured, and its construction begun. In the meantime his financial standing had been strengthened and his position in the business world had extended beyond the local communities. His political activities had brought him into contact with men who were known nationally and the identification of whom with any enterprise was certain to secure for it public confidence.

In these circumstances, toward the end of his second term he was able to secure the necessary financial support, and the company was formed to build the West Virginia Central and Pittsburgh Railway. Augustus Schell, a sachem of the Tammany society and an important figure in financial as well as political affairs, in New York, had met Mr. Davis at several of the Democratic national conventions, and there had grown up a warm friendship between them. Schell agreed to place part of the bonds of the proposed railway. William H. Barnum, the Connecticut capitalist who had served for a brief period as a colleague of Mr. Davis, also interested himself.

Several of the Senators with whom he was on terms of closest intimacy became stockholders. Among these were James G. Blaine, Thomas F. Bayard, J. N. Camden, William Pinckney Whyte, and William Windom. Stephen B. Elkins had been associated with Mr. Davis from the time that he had transferred his residence from New Mexico to the East. Jerome B. Chaffee, who served in the Senate from Colorado, and who had been associated with Mr. Elkins in business enterprises in the Southwest, joined the syndicate. Senator Arthur Pue Gorman was heavily interested. There were also several Baltimore capitalists, among them John A. Hambleton, the head of a great banking house, William Keyser, prominent both in Maryland politics and in railway affairs, and Major Alexander Shaw. It is doubtful whether any railroad in the country at any time had so many men prominent in public life and in finances on the Board of Directors as had the West Virginia Central Railway. They were there because of their confidence in Henry G. Davis.

That the ideas of some of the statesmen identified with the enterprise as to the best methods of financiering were not always in accordance with the plans of the originator of the railway, appears in a letter from Mr. Blaine in which he said:

I had a long talk with Elkins yesterday. It is my belief that you have adopted the hardest mode of raising money for the railroad. I wish I could talk with you personally for an hour in regard to the matter.

Mr. Blaine apparently had the opportunity for an hour's talk; but, so far from convincing Mr. Davis, he was himself convinced that the plan adopted was not the hardest, for there is no further reference in the correspondence to his views.

The manner in which the route for the railway was worked out, with proper regard for the resources that were to furnish traffic, is disclosed in several journal entries. Their nature is indicated in the following one:

October 1, 1880. Mr. Elkins, Mr. Randolph, Tom [brother] and myself made a trip to Elk Garden, to examine our coal and other property, and the best way for our railroad and inclined plane to go and take out the big and other vein coal.

1. We examine three routes, one running on top of hill and down to river about one mile above Deep Run.

2. Next route is through Mrs. Dixon's to Weasmans, and make inclined plane through Weasman to Deep River near Cranberry Run.

3. From big vein coal at our opening No. 1 by way of Barber's Ridge to Deep Run; plane will come down to Deep Run about two and one half miles from Potomac.

The last-named is my choice of routes; it comes out on our land, has a No. 1 place to land, and enables us to open small veins. Distance on all the routes is about the same.

We were pleased with our trip, and think we have a great future to that coal and lumber region.

When the construction work was well under way, Mr. Davis invited some of his associates to make a horseback trip with him over part of the route, and beyond to White Sulphur Springs, which he expected to reach ultimately by extensions of the line. The journey was filled with fruitful incidents and was not lacking in some hardships for the travelers; it is all summed up succinctly in a page in the journal entries:

July 19, 1881. Senators Bayard, Camden, Secretary Windom, Maj. Shaw, Baker, Elkins and myself, etc. We had with us Conroy for guide and John as waiter. Took blankets and provisions to camp out. We left Deer Park and on the tenth day arrived at White Sulphur. Went first night from Deer Park to look at coal opening near Fairfax Stone. Staid all night at the engineer's hut on Dobbin Road. Sleep on small boards with saddles for pillows. Next day through Canaan Valley and Meade's Corners that night. Next day to 20th. Staid over night at Mullinix's on Dry Fork. We had trout for supper, breakfast, dinner.

22d. Staid over night at Mrs. Hill's; this is near divide between waters of Dry Fork and Laurel Falls of Cheat and Greenbrier. This is a fine bluegrass country, and at east end of Rich mountain, the highest point above tidewater, we christened Mount Bayard in honor of the noble Delaware Senator.

23d. . We stopped for the night at what is known as Traveler's Repose on Greenbrier River and Stanton and Parkersburg Pike. Country tolerably good.

24th. We stop over night at Major Isaac Moore's near Dunmore, Pocahontas County.

25th. Stay over night at Huntersville, County seat of Pocahontas County. This is a fair country. We passed through some
fair pine timber, and what appears to be good iron ore. The
country from Traveler's Repose to White Sulphur is a remark-
ably good country to make a railroad through.

26th. About night we arrive at White Sulphur Springs. All
well pleased with our trip.

There were not only the coal resources being developed. More easily available, as the foundation for
industry and traffic, were the timber resources. A large
part of Tucker County was absolutely a primeval wilderness. The flat top of the mountain at an elevation of
3,000 feet was covered by almost impenetrable forests.
It was literally true that until Mr. Davis began his prospecting and his engineering surveys a great part of this
tangled wilderness never had been penetrated by man,
not even by the aboriginal savages. There were no
trails. The interlacing rhododendrons and laurels beneath, and the interwoven vines and saplings above, rendered the wealth of spruce and hemlock valueless until
trails were hewed and blazed by the woodmen.

Blazing the trails was in itself a work of extraordinary
difficulty, but the very density of the forest gave a stimulus to conquering it. There were the spruce and the
hardwoods first to be opened by the ax, then to be sub-
jected to the sawmill, and later to furnish the material
for the great pulp and paper mills. In the heart of this
region on the plateau was laid out the town of Davis,
which at one time was selected as the terminal for the
railway. Later this plan was abandoned, and a branch
line was run from the main stem at the station of
Thomas, where were located the coke-ovens.

The first section of the railway, that to the Elk Garden coal-fields, was opened early in November, 1881.

It was a momentous event for the whole region, but it is described with customary brevity in the journal entries:

November 2, 1881. We formally open our new road (W. Va. C. & P.). We leave Cumberland at eight o'clock by way of Cumberland & Pennsylvania Road, come to Piedmont, then to our junction (one mile), then up over our road to Elk Garden. Day fine. We are mining coal; all passes off well. Senator Bayard, Governor Hamilton, Major Shaw, Hon. S. B. Elkins, Mr. Kerens, C. P. Bayard, J. A. Hambleton, etc., accompany us.

November 3. Hambleton, Kerens, Shriver and Randolph, the latter two representing Baltimore *American* and *Sun,* made a trip part in wagon, balance horseback, to headwaters Potomac and Black Water. We returned to Deer Park Saturday well pleased with our trip. Coal and timber is even beyond our expectation.

In 1884 the railway had been extended to the site of the town of Davis, which within a year had become the center of important mining and lumber industries. The main stem was thereafter pushed forward, with some short branches to the mines, until the terminal point which had been decided on in Tygart's Valley, in the heart of Randolph County, was reached, and the creation of a thriving little city was begun. The successive steps in the construction of the railway have been well described by Professor James Morton Callahan in his "Semi-Centennial History of West Virginia." Though they are principally of local interest, they have a direct bearing on railway development in West Virginia. Professor Callahan's account is as follows:

The construction of a railroad from Piedmont up the North Branch to tap the undeveloped resources of Randolph County was proposed long before it was accomplished. The Potomac and Piedmont Coal and Railway Company, incorporated by the Legislature in 1866, and begun in 1880, secured a new charter in 1881 in its new name, the West Virginia Central and Pittsburgh

Railway Company, which was organized with H. G. Davis as President. Passing over the divide beyond the headwaters of the Potomac, the new road continued south of the Great Back-bone Mountains to Davis in the heart of the hardwood forests by November, 1884. Early in 1889 the main line of the road, following the waters of the wild and picturesque Black Water Run, was completed down the Dry Fork through the mountain gap to Parsons on the main branch of the Cheat; and later in the year, after turning up Shaver's Fork for a short distance, it crossed Leading Creek and reached picturesque Elkins (pre-viously known as Leadsville), whch was established as a town with terminal facilities, and has had a steady growth, partly due to the proximity of the inexhaustive Roaring Creek coal-fields. From Elkins by gradual extensions one branch followed up the Valley River, sending off a smaller branch at Roaring Creek, five miles west of Elkins, and another returned eastward to Shaver's Fork, which it ascended, until finding a way through Shaver's Mountain crossed to Glady Fork, ascended it to the divide, and descended the west fork of the Greenbrier to Durbin, in Pocahontas. . . . By 1891 trains were running on extension to Beverly and to Belington, where connection was made with a Tygarts Valley branch of the Baltimore and Ohio from Grafton. By 1904 connections were made at Durbin.

The new road, after passing through Mineral and Grant coun-ties, penetrated the vast coal-fields of Tucker and Randolph. It carried into the silence of the pine-needle woods the hum of modern industry, and expressed its material usefulness in gigantic lumber plants and rich coal-mines and in newly made and grow-ing towns—living monuments to men such as Windom, Blaine, Gorman, Bayard, Wilson, Fairfax, Douglass, Hendricks, and Elkins. The opening of mineral and timber resources created towns such as Bayard, Thomas, Davis, Douglass, Hendricks, Bantz, and Parsons in Tucker; such as Montrose and Elkins in Randolph; and such as Belington in Barbour. Bayard received its earliest stimulus from the large Buffalo Lumber Company and the Middlesex Leather Company. Another factor in its growth was the North Branch Coal and Coke Company, whose principal office was located there. At Thomas were located the large Davis-Elkins Coal and Coke Works. Six miles eastward, on the branch from Thomas, the coal works and manufacturing industries, together with a tannery and lumber plant, soon supported a population of 1,500, forming the town of Davis, with quite a mercantile trade increased by that of the surrounding country. Elkins, located in a lovely valley bordering the northwestern bank of Tygarts Valley River, received its first stimulus to growth by the construction of engine and car shops by the railway company, and the erection of homes for many operatives of the road.

The completion of the railroad through the timber to Davis and beyond furnished an outlet for the timber in the eastern and central sections, admitting portable and stationary sawmills which have since continued to operate. Everywhere temporary railroads were forced into the heart of the woods, followed by sawmills, tanneries, pulp-mills, and lumber-camps to aid in the campaign of conquest and destruction of the previously unmolested forests.

The conception of the railway originally had been perhaps that of an adjunct to the Baltimore and Ohio, with which Mr. Davis had been so closely identified for more than a third of a century. His close personal relations with the officials of that road, and in particular with Mr. John W. Garrett, who was then the president of the company, assured coöperation and friendly traffic arrangements.

After President Garrett's death some changes in management resulted in a less friendly policy on the part of the controlling interests. They made Mr. Davis feel that, since the West Virginia Central was dependent on the Baltimore and Ohio for its outlet, he must accept whatever traffic terms they chose to make. Baltimore and Ohio officials of a previous generation would not have taken this arrogant attitude, for they knew the man with whom they would have to deal; but the newer element apparently did not know. They soon learned.

The West Virginia Central's connection with the Baltimore and Ohio was at Piedmont. At Cumberland, thirty miles beyond, connection could be had with the Pennsylvania system and with the Chesapeake and Ohio Canal. Almost before the Baltimore and Ohio knew it, a right of way had been secured along the Potomac and the extension of the West Virginia Central to Cumberland was begun. The building of the line was bitterly fought by the Baltimore and Ohio in the courts, and even physical obstructions to the working parties on the line were resorted to. This kind of obstruction did not stop men who had absorbed the spirit of the determined man for whom they were working. The courts also decided the litigation in his favor, and ultimately the West Virginia Central had a through line to Cumberland, thus relieving the Davis interests of further dependence on a single line of railway for their outlet to the market. Having secured the benefits of competition, Mr. Davis resumed friendly relations with the Baltimore and Ohio, but on a different basis from that which obtained when his company had been dependent on it.

Some extensions and branches that were built on his own account later were merged into the system. For a quarter of a century he was the president of the West Virginia Central system and contributed potently to the growth of the region which when he began its conquest was open to civilization only by scattered farms in the narrow valleys. This was the work of the Railway Builder.

Finance Committee of West Virginia Central Railway

CHAPTER VII

INTERNATIONAL AMERICAN CONFERENCES

Awakening of interest in the countries to the south—First Conference at Washington in 1889–90—Mr. Davis appointed a delegate by President Harrison—Andrew Carnegie a colleague—Secretary Blaine's address of welcome—Organization and work of the Conference—International banks and transportation—Bureau of American Republics—Mr. Davis appointed by President McKinley delegate to the Mexican Conference in 1901–02—His associates—High character of representatives from the other Republics—Golden Age of Mexico under Porfirio Diaz—Personnel of Mexican delegation—Tokens of respect for "The Senator"—Reasons for declining to be the presiding officer—Speech on the Monroe Doctrine—Important results achieved—Farewell tributes to Mr. Davis.

PRESIDENT JAMES MONROE promulgated the Monroe Doctrine in 1823, the year in which Henry G. Davis was born. Nearly half a century later Mr. Davis became actively identified with the nations that came within the sphere of the Doctrine, and continued to be identified with their interests and their aspirations for the remainder of his long life. It is not apparent just what directed his thoughts to the countries to the south. It may have been the championship that was given them at the dawn of their independence by his early political idol, Henry Clay. It may have been that his association in the Senate with statesmen whose eyes were turned southward first awakened his attention. Whatever the source of the inspiration, his horizon expanded from national to international affairs.

When Mr. Davis was in the Senate there were occasional resolutions and speeches on the need of closer relations with the sister nations of the New World. The Trade Commission appointed by President Arthur, which visited the South American countries and reported on the commercial prospects, had its inception during his second term in a resolution offered by his colleague, Senator Cockerill of Missouri. Later, as a delegate to the National Democratic Convention at Chicago in 1884, he had supported the resolution embodied in the platform favoring an American continental policy based upon more intimate commercial and political relations with the Republics to the south.

During the first administration of President Cleveland, Congress gave concrete expression to the aspirations for closer relations by making provision for an international American conference to be held in Washington. The official invitations to the several nations were issued by Mr. Davis's friend, Secretary Bayard. The measures for the assembling of the Conference fell to President Harrison's administration. Mr. Davis's journal, without preliminary suggestion of the subject, records that President Harrison and Secretary Blaine had appointed him one of the delegates for the United States.

The Conference assembled at Washington in October, 1889, and was one of the notable events of that period, exciting interest in Europe as well as in the countries of the New World that participated in it. The several Republics designated their resident Ministers in Washington as delegates, and supplemented them by other men of reputation extending beyond their own borders.

Señor Matias Romero, who had long been the Mexican Minister to the United States, and whose friendship with General Grant had given him much influence in the years when Mexico was struggling toward stability under Porfirio Diaz, represented that country. The Republic of Brazil, just emerged from monarchy after a mild revolution, was represented by Salvadore de Mendonça, an accomplished diplomat. From the Argentine Republic came Señor Roque Saenz Peña, who afterward became President. Other delegates also later filled important rôles in their respective countries.

President Harrison and Secretary Blaine had been at pains to select a delegation that would be representative of both the international element and the business classes in American life. The chairman was John B. Henderson of Missouri, who had served as United States Senator and who was an authority on international law. William Henry Trescott of South Carolina, the author of important works on the diplomatic history of the United States, was another representative of the international idea. The other delegates were Cornelius N. Bliss of New York; Clement Studebaker of Indiana; T. Jefferson Coolidge of Massachusetts; Andrew Carnegie of New York; Henry G. Davis of West Virginia; M. M. Estee of California; John F. Hanson of Georgia; and Charles R. Flint of New York.

At the opening of the Conference, Secretary Blaine made a speech of welcome which interpreted the aspirations of the delegates and in some measure indicated the results that were expected to follow. Among other things Secretary Blaine said:

The delegates I am addressing can do much to establish permanent relations of confidence, respect, and friendship between the nations which they represent. They can show the world an honorable, peaceful conference of eighteen independent American Powers, in which all shall meet together on terms of absolute equality; a conference in which there can be no attempt to coerce a single delegate against his own conception of his nation, a conference which will permit no secret understanding on any subject, but will frankly publish to the world all its conclusions; a conference which will tolerate no spirit of conquest, but will aim to cultivate an American sympathy as broad as both continents. And yet, we cannot be expected to forget that our common fate has made us inhabitants of the two continents which, at the close of four centuries, are still regarded beyond the seas as the New World. Like situations beget like sympathies and impose like duties. . . .

We believe that we should be drawn together more closely by the highways of the seas, and that at no distant day the railway system of the North and South will meet upon the Isthmus and connect by land routes the political and commercial capitals of all America.

After the organization of the Conference and the appointment of the committees, the delegates were taken on an excursion through New England and other parts of the country on what was said to be the finest special train that ever had been put in motion. Mr. Davis accompanied the visitors on this trip. After they returned to Washington, the delegates settled down to somewhat intermittent committee work. An occasional entry in his journal shows that Mr. Davis, with his methodical habits and his business training, found some difficulty in adapting himself to the leisurely methods of international assemblages. There are good-natured admonitions to his fellow delegates about the necessity of getting down to work.

The principal committees on which Mr. Davis served were those on the Pan-American Railway and on customs regulations, the latter proving very important because of the recommendations of a permanent nature which it made and which were adopted. Arbitration and other subjects of a somewhat academic character occupied much of the attention of the Conference; but at the same time there was an influence in the background guiding toward questions of a practical kind such as banking facilities, shipping, and railway communication.

Though he was not a member of the Committee on Banking, Mr. Davis was called into some of the meetings of that committee, and also helped shape the course of the Conference in modifying and adopting the recommendations made. The Conference went on record to the effect that commerce between the American countries might be greatly extended if proper means could be found for facilitating direct exchanges between the money markets of the several countries. The advisability of the Congress of the United States passing a law incorporating an international American bank with branches was discussed with special reference to the facilities that would be provided for making investments. This idea found fruition twenty-five years later, when, in consonance with the principle of the Federal Reserve Bank Act, Congress authorized the national banks of the United States to establish branches in foreign countries.

No more important action was taken by this Conference than the adoption of the recommendation of the Committee on Customs Regulations. It was this report that provided for the establishment of the International Bureau of the American Republics as a permanent agency for carrying forward the work begun by the Conference. The evidences of Mr. Davis's constructive ideas are apparent in this report. Out of it came the establishment of the Bureau of the American Republics, later to be broadened and expanded, with enhanced functions and an enlarged field of influence, into the Pan-American Union.

The chairman of the Committee on Railway Communication was Señor de Velarde of Bolivia; Mr. Davis was the second member. The report of this Committee and its significance, as well as Mr. Davis's part in formulating it, are discussed in the following chapter.

The first International American Conference concluded its labors in April, 1890. Its sessions, which had been opened by Secretary Blaine, were brought to a close by a brief address from him. Reviewing the work of the Conference, he said:

"It will be a great gain when we shall acquire that common confidence on which all international friendship must rest. It will be a greater gain when we shall be able to draw the people of all American nations into close acquaintance with each other, an end to be facilitated by more frequent and more rapid communication. It will be the greatest gain when the personal and commercial relations of the American States, north and south, shall be so developed and so regulated that each shall require the highest possible advantage from the enlightenment and enlarged intercourse of all."

The development of closer relations among the nations of the New World, while not exactly dormant, was quiescent during the next decade; but, following the war with Spain for the liberation of Cuba, the importance of a better understanding and of more intimate intercourse again impressed itself on leaders of public thought in the United States.

President McKinley, in his annual message of December, 1899, voiced this feeling, and diplomatic methods were employed to secure a sympathetic coöperation on the part of the other nations. Mexico took the initiative in calling the Second Conference, and, Congress having made provision for delegates from the United

States, President McKinley and Secretary Hay occupied themselves with the selection of the delegation. Although the appointments were purely honorary, since they carried no compensation, an ample number of persons were willing to serve.

The delegation as appointed consisted of Henry G. Davis, W. I. Buchanan of New York, Volney W. Foster of Illinois, Charles M. Pepper of the District of Columbia, and John Barrett of Oregon. Mr. Davis's comment on his own appointment was recorded in his journal under date of April 9, 1901:

I am just in receipt of notice, signed by President McKinley and Secretary Hay, that I am appointed delegate on part of U. S. to conference of American Republics to be held in the City of Mexico October 22, 1901; there are five delegates. It is an honorable appointment without pay.

Of the other delegates, Mr. Buchanan had made a high reputation as Minister to the Argentine Republic, and at the time was director of the Pan-American Exposition at Buffalo; Mr. Foster was a business man engaged in many large enterprises and was familiar with Mexico; Mr. Pepper as a journalist had laid the foundation for a knowledge of Latin-America in Cuba; Mr. Barrett was just back from the Orient where he had served as Minister to Siam.

Though the appointments were made in April, the Conference at Mexico was not to meet until October. When the delegates from the United States assembled in Washington to receive their instructions, the assassin's bullet had removed President McKinley, and President Roosevelt was the Executive under whose administration this step toward Pan-American unity was to be taken. He showed a very live interest in the prospective work of the Conference.

Mr. Davis was selected by his associates as chairman of the delegation. His fitness for the position was fully recognized, and there was, moreover, the desire to further his plans for giving impetus to the subject of railway communication among the different Republics.

A special train was provided by the Department of State when the delegates left for Mexico in October. Since several of the Ministers of the South American and Central American Republics in Washington had been appointed delegates by their governments, and since other delegates had first come to the United States, they were invited to be the guests of the United States delegation on the trip to Mexico. Williams C. Fox, of the Bureau of American Republics, John Cassell Williams, the Secretary, and Dr. W. P. Wilson of the Philadelphia Commercial Museum were the others who were identified with the delegation.

The meeting of the Conference in Mexico City was an historic event. Because of the acuteness of the question of arbitration and the recognition of the prospective influence of the Conference, all the countries had selected their delegates from among their ablest men. The Argentine delegation consisted of Garcia Merou, the Minister to Washington, who was distinguished alike in the public affairs of his country and in literature; Lorenzo Anadon, who had served in the Argentine Senate and had held various official positions of a fiscal character; and Antonio Bermejo, who had served as a deputy in the Congress, as Minister of Public Instruction, and Minister of Justice, and who subsequently became one of the Justices of the Supreme Court. Bolivia was represented by Fernando P. Guachalla, the Minister in Washington, who subsequently became President.

Brazil sent one of its most distinguished jurists in the

person of José Hygeni Duarte Pereira, who had filled many important positions and was a Judge of the Supreme Court. The Chilean delegation was composed of Blest Gana, who had made a reputation in early life by his historical novels and who for nearly forty years had held important diplomatic positions; Emilio Bello Codecido, who had been Secretary of State, and who was one of the leaders of the party that had affiliated with President Balmaceda in the Chilean civil war, and had married his daughter; Joaquin Walker Martinez, the Minister in Washington, who had served in various diplomatic capacities, and also in the Cabinet at Santiago, and Augusto Matte, one of the leading business men of the country, who had served in the Chilean Congress and Cabinet, and in various diplomatic positions, and who was especially noted as a financier.

The delegates from Colombia were Carlos Martinez Silva, the Minister in Washington, who had been a delegate to the First Conference, and General Rafael Reyes, a distinguished explorer, soldier, and statesman who subsequently became President.

The Peruvian delegation consisted of Isaac Alzamora, the Vice-President of the Republic, a facile orator who had served as Minister of Foreign Relations and as a Deputy in Congress, and who had filled the chairs of philosophy and political economy in the University of Lima; Alberto Elmore, a Justice of the Supreme Court, who had also served as Minister of Foreign Relations, and Manuel Alvarez Calderon, the Minister in Washington, who had won a high reputation for his diplomatic ability.

Ecuador was represented by Luis Felipe Carbo, Minister in Washington, who had also served his country in a diplomatic capacity in other countries. The representative from Paraguay was Cecilio Baez, a member of the Chamber of Deputies, who subsequently served as President. Uruguay was represented by Juan Cuestas, the Minister in Washington, who was the son of the President. The delegates from Venezuela who were present for part of the time were J. Gil Fortuol, a writer and historian, and Dr. M. M. Galvais, a well-known lawyer.

The Central American countries sent some of their most experienced men. Costa Rica was represented by Joaquin Bernardo Calvo, the Minister in Washington, who had served as secretary to the delegation from his country to the First Conference. Guatemala was represented by Antonio Lazo-Arriaga, the Minister in Washington, who had served as Speaker of the Guatemalan Congress; and Colonel Francisco Orla, who had served on the Government Boundary Commission and in the Army. Salvador sent Francisco A. Reyes, her Minister of Foreign Affairs, and Baltazar Estupinian, the Vice-President of the Congress and an authority on international law. Honduras was represented by José Leonard, a native of Poland who had been graduated from the University of Heidelberg, and who was filling a scholastic position, and Fausto Davila, a vigorous exponent of the progressive element in the politics of the country. The delegate from Nicaragua was Luis F. Corea, the Minister in Washington, who had filled various public positions.

The personnel of these delegations was the indication of the high character of the Conference and the importance that was attached to its proceedings. It was the Mexican delegation, however, that contributed the largest galaxy of talent. As the host of the Conference, Mexico sought to dignify its work by the character of the men selected to represent her. This was in truth the Golden Age of Mexico under Porfirio Diaz. The signs of the great work he had wrought were everywhere visible. The elements of destruction that some of them carried with them were not yet apparent.

Mexico then occupied a foremost position in the eyes of the world, and this was a fitting occasion on which to give proof of her position. President Diaz was surrounded by the group of able men who had grown in public life with him. Ignacio Mariscal, who had guided the foreign relations of the country from chaos through infinite embarrassments until by his skilful diplomacy the whole world recognized and respected her international status, was the Minister of Foreign Relations. José Yves Limantour, who had evolved financial stability out of anarchic finances until Mexican credit stood as high as that of the United States, was Secretary of Finance. Men whose work was concerned chiefly with domestic measures, but whose constructive ability was equally great, filled other Cabinet positions.

The Mexican delegation was of the same type as the nen who formed the Cabinet of President Diaz. Genaro Ragiosa, the chairman, was a distinguished lawyer. Alfredo Chavero was noted as an archæologist, lawyer, and orator, and was representative of the versatility of Latin public men. Pablo Macedo, a very able lawyer, was also a popular orator, and was the idol of what later came to be called the submerged classes. Joaquin Casasus, a lawyer and political economist and an authority on finance, was also a litterateur, and had achieved reputation as a classical scholar by his translation of Virgil into Spanish and as a student of English literature by his translation of Longfellow's "Evangeline." Emilio Pardo was a very distinguished lawyer who was then serving in the Mexican Congress. Rosendo Pineda was a leader in the debates in Congress.   José Lopez Portilla was a member of Congress and an authority on international law.   Manual Sanchez Marmol was a leading member of Congress and was famous as a wit.   Francisco de la Barra was one of the younger men from whom much was expected because of his attainments in international law and his relations with Young Mexico and the moderate clerical party.

It was in an international assembly of this character, representing all the Americas, that Mr. Davis received the tokens of esteem that made the occasion memorable for him and for his countrymen.   He was in his seventy-ninth year.   This in itself would have insured him the consideration of his fellow delegates, for among the Latin peoples the spirit of veneration for elders does not diminish as the fourscore mark is approached.   But coupled with this was a peculiar sentiment of affection which found utterance in the designation of "The Senator" with which he always was referred to.   There was, moreover, a deep respect for his judgment and a feeling of confidence in his sense of justice that would be especially desirable in meeting some of the issues that were likely to provoke outbreaks of feeling.

The Conference was opened in a notable address by Minister Mariscal on behalf of Mexico, which was felicitously responded to by Delegate Alzamora of Peru. Then came the question of selecting a presiding officer. General Rafael Reyes of Colombia, moved by his deep sentiment, had informally suggested the choice of Mr. Davis, and this sentiment had been felt among the other delegates.   They were privately advised that the delegation from the United States, reflecting the views of the Department of State at Washington, and also reflecting

Mr. Davis's personal wishes, desired that the honor should go elsewhere.

Notwithstanding that this information was conveyed to them, General Reyes presented a resolution nominating Mr. Davis as permanent president of the Conference and proposing that the selection be made by acclamation. This action would have been taken had not the United States delegation as a body, and Mr. Davis individually, intervened to prevent it. Delegate Pepper, speaking in Spanish, thanked the delegates for the desire they had manifested of honoring the distinguished Senator whose name formed a link between the First Conference and the one then in session, but he explained why the selection was not expedient.

Mr. Davis himself ended the suggestion by a speech in which he said:

"I am deeply sensible of the honor proposed, and I thank you heartily for it, but a consistent course, together with a sense of duty, compels me to say that I cannot accept it. We are here, not for office, not for preferment in any way, but to assist all of the Republics of America in whatever may lead to good, especially to peace, harmony, and good will to all. We wish to help to cultivate and bring about a better feeling than has heretofore existed, although even that feeling has been friendly.

"Our thought is that we should have additional communication, both water and rail; and I want to see— and I believe all here do—an international railroad from Argentina to the Rio Grande. I believe that harmony peace, and good will will come out of our work here, and that we will find a way to prevent any further war on this hemisphere; that peace will reign perhaps forever.

Eighty million people of the United States stand ready to assist, in any proper way they can, to bring about the best results for the good of the American public.

"We are, as you know, a happy, true, loyal, independent, and liberty-loving people, and we say to our friends on our south that we want no further territory; but we are firm, as firm as the Medes and Persians were, in what is known as the Monroe Doctrine, which means that your territory is to be protected, your political rights, your commercial rights, and your liberty forever guaranteed. I feel more than I can speak. I appreciate the compliment proffered me more than I can tell you; but, as I have said in the beginning, I think it my duty that I should decline."

The Conference respected the Senator's wishes, and Señor Raigosa was chosen permanent chairman. Mr. Davis's few pointed words on the Monroe Doctrine created a sensation in the Conference at the time, and they were commented on, when published in Europe and in South America, as an important utterance. They reflected the views that he always held.

In the work of the Conference, Mr. Davis was frequently appealed to as a mediator in controverted questions such as arbitration. At the First Conference the United States had favored compulsory arbitration. Events of the intervening years had changed its attitude somewhat. The skilful diplomacy of Mr. Buchanan aided the delegates to the Mexican Conference to travel over this delicate ground without serious complications; but the confidence felt in the impartiality of the chairman of the United States delegation had much to do with the avoidance of a break on the part of several delegations.

Mr. Davis served on several of the committees, and all of these, when the reports and recommendations came to be made, showed the impress of his constructive mind. The project of an international bank again had the benefit of his suggestions. In everything that the Conference did he was looking to the future, and this was one of the subjects that he thought big with possibilities. Yet it was in looking toward the broader future that his ideas found their fullest scope. At his suggestion a Committee on Committees was formed, of which he was named as chairman. This Committee submitted a report under which provision was made for continuous development of intercourse among the three Americas.

One of the committees provided for this purpose was that on future Pan-American Conferences, and during the final sessions Mr. Davis served on this Committee, and helped to formulate the resolutions under which the continuity of Pan-American Conferences was assured. The chairmanship of the Pan-American Railway Committee naturally fell to him, and the continuity of this great subject was assured when the Conference adopted the report providing for a permanent Pan-American Railway Committee.

The Conference made a forward step in several directions. It provided for the arbitration of pecuniary claims. It formally gave its adherence to The Hague, and it put in operation the machinery of various projects for commercial and industrial development. It also passed a resolution indorsing the Panama Canal.

As the sessions drew to an end many evidences were afforded of the esteem in which Mr. Davis was held. He was compelled to leave before the final session, and his departure afforded the occasion for a demonstration that was extremely gratifying to his associates. He delivered a brief farewell address in which he said:

"The Government and the people of the United States

have followed with interest the proceedings of this Conference. They appreciate the many courtesies extended to their delegates, and are pleased with the results accomplished.

"Personally, I owe a debt of gratitude to the officials and people of Mexico and to the delegates and all connected with the Conference for the many kind acts that made my sojourn in this country one of the most pleasant experiences of my life. I hope that the friendships made here will not terminate with the adjournment of this Conference, but that we will meet frequently, and that many of us will attend the next Pan-American Congress."

As Mr. Davis left the hall, every delegate rose to his feet, and following his departure the Conference adopted a resolution recognizing the important services he had rendered to the union of the American Republics. The President of the Conference, as a further honor, appointed a special committee to accompany Mr. Davis to the railway station. In the meantime, he had gone to the National Palace, where President Diaz had invited him for a farewell interview. The President expressed his high appreciation of Mr. Davis's services in the Conference. At the railway station, not only the members of the special committee, but virtually every member of the Conference and also many Mexican officials, assembled to say the final word of farewell. It was a demonstration that profoundly affected Mr. Davis, and it was, moreover, a fitting conclusion to his active identification with the representatives of all the Americas in their work of promoting unity and fraternity.

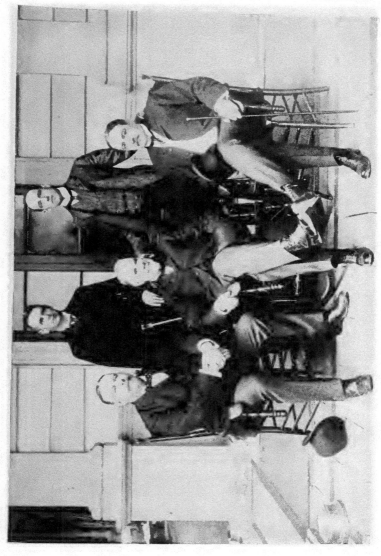

U. S. Delegation to Pan-American Conference at Mexico

CHAPTER VIII

THE PAN-AMERICAN RAILWAY

Intercontinental trunk line the concept of men of vision—Mr. Davis's faith shown at the First Conference—Activities on the survey commission—Value of engineering reconnaissances—Summary of the route—Support given the project by the Mexican Conference—Creation of permanent Pan-American Railway Committee—Its work—Special commissioner authorized by Congress —His report on status and prospects of the enterprise—Chairman Davis analyzes traffic and other objections—Relation to commerce and national development—Indorsement by subsequent Conferences—Steps to interest capitalists—Approval by International High Commission—Link between Harrison and Wilson administrations.

THERE are visionaries and there are men of vision, and usually the line between them is easily drawn. By many the project of an intercontinental trunk railway line has been looked on as the dream of the visionaries; yet even the skeptics must pause and give it more than passing thought when men of vision turn their attention to it.

There was nothing of the visionary in Henry G. Davis. A business man, a developer of natural resources, a builder of railways, with an intensely practical mind, he was essentially a man of vision. It was this quality that enabled him to see the natural wealth of his own State that was awaiting development. When his view expanded and swept over a whole hemisphere, the Pan-American Railway project appealed to his imagination with the same force.

The project itself was not any one man's conception. Statesmen and students of international relations alike had had it in their ken.   Hinton Rowan Helper of North Carolina had given the idea substance in his book on the "Three Americas Railway."   Juan José Castro, a Uruguayan engineer of eminence, had, with the aid of his Government, brought together the various factors in the project as they related to South America.   In the United States Senate, when Mr. Davis was a member of that body, his colleague and namesake, David Davis of Illinois, had introduced a resolution intended to secure recognition for the project.   It is probable that the interest of Henry G. Davis had been awakened before then, possibly through Richard A. Parsons, a distinguished Virginia engineer and railway builder who had sought to put the enterprise on a practical basis.

Whatever the original inspiration may have been it is certain that when he became a member of the First International American Conference the idea filled the mind of Mr. Davis, and he was eager to make use of the opportunity that it afforded to give the project tangible form.   In accordance with his wishes, he was appointed a member of the Committee on Railroad Communication, which was presided over by Señor Velarde of Bolivia. The report of that Committee bears his impress throughout.   In formulating it he had the coöperation of Andrew Carnegie.

The historical importance of this first step in an international enterprise with which the name of Mr. Davis will ever be associated justifies a special chapter on the subject.   The Committee in its report said that the first thing to be done was to ascertain the practicability and the approximate cost of the line by providing for an international commission to ascertain possible routes, estimate the cost of each, and compare their respective advantages.

The report further recommended that the railway, in so far as the common interests would permit, should connect the principal cities in the vicinity of its route, and that, if this would result in too great a change from the general direction of the main trunk, branch lines should be surveyed to connect with the main line; that the execution of a work of such magnitude deserved to be further encouraged by subsidies, grants of land, or guaranties of a minimum of interest; that the expenses incident to the preliminary and final surveys should be assumed by all the nations accepting in proportion to their population; that the railway should be declared forever neutral for the purpose of securing freedom of traffic; and that as soon as the Government of the United States should receive notice of the acceptance of these recommendations by the other governments it should invite them to name their representatives on the Commission provided for, so that it might meet in Washington as early as possible.

This provision was characteristic of Mr. Davis's forethought. He had little faith in resolutions and recommendations that did not point the way to carry them out. After a short debate, in which he took a leading part, explaining the main features of the report, it was unanimously adopted. The first step had been taken for building the Pan-American Railway.

The next step soon followed. It appears in the entry in the journal of Mr. Davis, to which is attached a newspaper clipping announcing the appointment of a commission to provide for an intercontinental railway survey. This reads:

October 4, 1890. The newspaper slip shows President Harrison and Secretary Blaine have made me one of three commissioners on the part of the United States on the Intercontinental Railway Commission. This looks to building road from U. S. to all the fifteen independent States of Central and South America. I look upon the work as great and important to the people of all the fifteen Republics. Trade is now against us. Europe can successfully compete with water, but not with rail.

I intend to give much attention and work to the above enterprise, and believe it practical; know it will be of great value to U. S. and its people. I hope and expect to live to see this road built from here to the most southern point of South America, and the balance of trade in our favor; now it is about $100,000,000 annually against us.

President Harrison, following the recommendation of the First Conference, had asked Congress for an appropriation to provide for the participation of the United States in the Intercontinental Railway Commission, and, the appropriation having been made, he designated Mr. A. J. Cassatt, President of the Pennsylvania Railway System and at the time by common consent the foremost railway executive in the United States, as the head of the Commission. With Mr. Cassatt were associated Henry G. Davis and Richard C. Kerens of Missouri. George M. Pullman had expected to serve, but at the last moment was compelled to decline through the urgency of private affairs.

Others of the countries interested had provided their quota of the appropriation and designated their representatives on the Commission.

The Commission held its first meeting at the Department of State on December 4, 1890. After a brief address the organization was effected. Mr. Davis was made chairman of the Committee on Finance, but he also, by special request, attended the meetings of the Executive Committee which had charge of the surveys and engineering reconnaissances.

The Survey was organized, with William F. Shunk of Pennsylvania as engineer-in-chief. Under his direction separate survey parties were put in the field for Central America, Colombia, and Ecuador. They were under the supervision of officers from the Engineer Corps of the United States Army. The survey corps made reconnaissances, prepared data, and submitted maps. The information thus gathered was of very great value. Much of it was entirely original and covered fields of investigation that had never before been touched.

The Intercontinental Railway Commission held sessions from December, 1890, until October, 1894, when its final report was submitted. This report was embodied in half a score of volumes and maps. Preliminary estimates were made for a line running from the northern boundary of Guatemala to the northernmost limit of the railway system of Argentina so as to form a through line connecting the railway systems of the United States and Mexico on the north with the Argentine system on the south, with branch lines connecting the railway systems of Chile, Brazil, Paraguay, and Uruguay with the main line.

In the summary of the surveys and reconnaissances as prepared by Captain E. Z. Steever, under date of January, 1896, it was stated that the distance from New York to Buenos Aires by the most available route, using existing railways as far as possible, was 10,228 miles, of which 4,772 miles, principally in the United States, Mexico, and the Argentine Republic, already were in operation, leaving 5,456 miles to be built. The practicability of the work, both as an engineering project and as a financial undertaking, was declared to be established.

While public interest was awakened by this report, and while the value of the information collated was appreciated, no steps were taken at the time toward furthering the project. But the subject was not allowed by Mr. Davis to be forgotten. He continued his efforts to arouse interest in it until the opportunity came to give it further prominence, and also to give it a definite direction which would insure that it would not ever again become dormant. This opportunity was afforded when he went to Mexico in the midwinter of 1901–2 as chairman of the United States Delegation to the Second Conference. As chairman of the Committee on the Pan-American Railway his enthusiasm soon infected the other delegates. They felt that what had long been considered, if not a dream, at least a vague and indefinable project, was now susceptible of becoming a reality.

The report of this Committee, which was principally formulated by Mr. Davis, covered much of the ground that had been made by the Committee on Railway Communications in the First Conference. Chairman Davis in submitting the report summarized the reasons for its adoption in twenty terse paragraphs, with special reference to the conditions as they existed at the beginning of the twentieth century.

The most significant feature of the report was the provision for the appointment of a permanent Pan-American Railway Committee with headquarters in Washington. The president of the Conference, in accordance with the resolution adopted, named the Committee. It consisted of Henry G. Davis, chairman; Andrew Carnegie; Señor Don Manuel de Azpiroz, Mexican Ambassador to the United States; Señor Don Manuel

Alvarez Calderon, Peruvian Minister to the United States; and Señor Don Antonio Lazo Arriaga, Guatemalan Minister to the United States.

The project having thus been given permanency, the energy of the chairman of the Committee did not permit its work to lapse. It was considered desirable to have a report on the whole enterprise as it then stood, and on the attitude of the various governments toward it, as well as to acquaint them with the friendly policy of the United States.

Several meetings of the Permanent Committee were held in the winter months of 1903, and it was determined to secure, if possible, the positive approval of Congress. A provision accordingly was inserted in one of the appropriation bills through the aid of Mr. Cannon, the chairman of the House Committee on Appropriations, and Mr. Allison, the chairman of the Senate Committee, by which this indorsement was secured. With the exception of the slight amount thus provided, the funds for the work were supplied by Mr. Davis and Mr. Carnegie. Mr. Charles M. Pepper was the choice of the Committee, and also of Secretary Hay, to visit the several countries. He was especially commissioned by President Roosevelt, under the authority of Congress, and thus became the representative not only of the Pan-American Railway Committee, but of the Government of the United States.

Commissioner Pepper spent a year in visiting the southern countries, during which his labors were facilitated by the several governments. He was able to explain to them the view taken of the project by the United States, to offer suggestions of a practical nature in regard to their own measures of coöperation, and to supply them with information in regard to what was being done in other countries. On his return he made a full report, which was transmitted to Congress by the President and was translated into Spanish.

This report reviewed the events that had stimulated the project since the First Conference, with special reference to the value of the work of the Intercontinental Survey, which, as a comprehensive study of railway development in Central and South America, had been of special benefit in various exploitation enterprises collateral to railway building, and also had formed the groundwork for further studies by geographical societies, scientific commissions, government engineers, and individuals. Analysis was made of the railway policies of the several governments, with detailed information concerning the progress of actual construction. It was shown that there had been an increase in mileage along the line of the main trunk, so that the total distance that remained to be closed up between New York and Buenos Aires had been shortened some five hundred miles since the summary made by Captain Steever of the Intercontinental Survey.

The publication of this report awakened fresh interest in the United States, and in Europe it also attracted attention to the existence of the permament Pan-American Railway Committee. Chairman Davis took advantage of the interest aroused, and in March, 1905, gave a dinner to the diplomatic representatives of the Latin-American countries and to others, at which the entire project was reviewed. Mr. Davis himself reiterated his faith in the ultimate realization of the idea. Senator Elkins added his word of confidence, saying that the project was no longer a dream, no longer a prophecy, since its consummation so long looked for now seemed practicable and possible. The diplomatic representatives of the Latin-American Republics in their addresses took occasion to express their appreciation of Mr. Davis, and they drank a toast to him as the man who with the utmost zeal worked for the accomplishment of the intercontinental railroad.

An incident of this dinner was a letter from Andrew Carnegie, who was unable to be present, in which he urged that the United States should give the hundred million dollars then spent on the Navy toward the Railway, conditioned upon the South American Republics pledging their credit for an equal sum. Afterward, in a letter to the *New York Tribune,* Mr. Carnegie elaborated this view, maintaining that the Railway would be a more effective means of maintaining the Monroe Doctrine than warships. He also urged the project on other grounds, both sentimental and practical, saying that it would enormously increase our trade, and that direct lines of steamers to South American ports would naturally follow.

In the discussion growing out of the activities of the Pan-American Railway Committee, Mr. Davis was frequently confronted with the geographical conditions that were alleged to make through traffic over an intercontinental trunk line impracticable as a business proposition. Some of his associates in large railway enterprises would good-humoredly suggest that diamonds as through freight from New York to Buenos Aires would be the only traffic that would pay. He was fully alive to the traffic objections to the project as well as to the engineering difficulties, but he understood better than most of his critics the collateral questions connected with the subject, and he also appreciated the indirect influence and the political or national objects that would be subserved by the several countries through the construction of the line.

In an article published in the *North American Review* for May, 1906, he reviewed the proposition on its business side, with incidental allusion to its historical and sentimental aspect. This article presents the best summary of his views that he ever made, and some parts of it are quoted below in their entirety:

It is proper to take into account the general subject and foundation of the proposed intercontinental trunk line and branches. The basis is a business one, whether looked at from the standpoint of the individual, of a single nation, or of the group of nations which constitute the American continent. Railroads are built to earn dividends. For the body of stockholders the dividends must depend on the net earnings to be obtained from the traffic that either already exists or is created. The capitalists who supply the funds may have additional reasons resulting from their ownership of mines, of timber areas, or of agricultural regions whose products can only be made marketable by providing means of communication. Sometimes, therefore, their investments do not depend solely on the actual net earnings. Yet the increased value of lands and the market obtained for their products of every kind are only another form of dividends.

For a nation, the dividends cannot be estimated in direct terms of interest on bonds, or of net earnings for capital stock. For it, the dividends are the development of the local resources, the wider market obtained for the products of the country, the increase of the population through immigration, and, in a word, the addition to the wealth of the nation. There is also the dividend which cannot be estimated in terms of dollars and cents because it comes from a better knowledge which the people of the different regions of the country obtain of one another, and from the cultivation of the national patriotic spirit. This is a clear case of the influence of frequent and cheap communication among diverse sections of the country.

It is because of the addition to the wealth of a nation by developing its resources, and the strengthening of the patriotic bonds which bind the different sections and their inhabitants more closely together, that all the progressive elements have aided railway construction. This will always be the policy of a new country with undeveloped resources, or of an old country which seeks to become a modern nation. It is this feeling which caused the United States to spend four hundred thousand dollars on surveys across the Rocky Mountains long before any feasible plans for a railroad to the Pacific were attracting the attention of capitalists, and later developed into a definite national policy when the Pacific Railways were aided by enormous land grants, subsidies, and bond guaranties. When the first transcontinental line was constructed many wise men doubted whether there ever would be traffic enough to pay the operating expenses. . . .

The international like the national dividends are wider markets and the enlarged trade which come from increasing the means of intercourse between different countries. A better understanding by one people of another people is certainly a desirable result, and this is secured by furnishing means of communication. The international dividend may be said to be one of dollars and cents in the way of more commerce, and of peace in the way of avoiding misunderstandings which come from lack of intercourse.

In the light of these facts the proposed Pan-American Railway may be said to offer returns to the individual, to the nations as separate Republics, and to them as a part of the family of nations of the western hemisphere. But the question at the root of railroad building always must relate to the commercial advantages, that is, to the traffic. It is not often that a rail line is built for traffic that already exists. Freight follows the rail line. The railway creates tonnage, and tonnage is commerce both local and international.

He then analyzed the commerce of Mexico, Central America, and South America with the United States, with the purpose of showing its relation to railway facilities. In discussing this phase of the subject he took up the matter of steamship service:

What will be noted in any detailed analysis of trade returns is that commerce grows in the ratio in which increased facilities are given not merely to steamship service but more especially to means of railway communication. The steamship service from its nature is of little benefit in developing the interior of the country.

The coast-line does not furnish a large traffic, and the points not reached by railroad create little tonnage. When this tonnage has to be brought to the market by pack mules or wagon carts the cost is often equal to the value of the product. The railway picks up freight every few miles, but the steamship service of South America on an average requires a land haul of one hundred and fifty miles each way, or three hundred miles in all. This is one reason, and a strong one, why intercontinental railway development through railway connection is desirable.

A common illustration familiar to all railway builders and traffic managers is that of the team with the load of wheat, which, by the time the point of shipment has been reached, has eaten up all the wheat. The same principle applies in mines. Iron ore, coal, copper, silver, may exist in great quantities in certain localities, but the mines never will be worked where the cost of transporting the ore is greater than the amount received for it. It is railway lines that make it profitable to develop the mines, and the traffic from this source is always to be considered in providing for railway systems. This probably is more especially necessary with regard to the localities to be reached by the Pan-American system than with those of any other part of the world.

The Pan-American routes as surveyed parallel the Pacific coast along the trend of the Andes, but they provide for branches or feeders which will shoot out toward the Atlantic as well as toward the Pacific. If their construction is much more difficult and costly than when the water line can be followed, there is in its business aspect the value of the traffic that comes from the tonnage of mineral regions. This tonnage is of the kind that quickly pays for itself.

The Third Pan-American Conference met at Rio de Janeiro in September, 1906, and was made historic by the presence of Secretary Elihu Root and the consequent impetus that was given to the relations of the United States with the countries to the south. For that Conference Chairman Davis prepared a full report reviewing not simply the activities of the permanent Pan-American Railway Committee, but giving also the progress in the way of actual construction. The Conference appointed a special committee on the subject, which accepted the report, made recommendations along the line of previous Conferences. commended the work of Chairman Davis and the committee, and recommended that it be continued. This resolution was adopted with many manifestations of appreciation.

Following the indorsement of this Conference, Chairman Davis continued his work both along educational and along practical lines. In February. 1909, he gave a dinner in Washington to the Pan-American Railway Committee, and his expectations are thus recorded in his journal:

February 9, 1909. On 7th inst. I gave a dinner to Pan-American Railway Committee. I am encouraged to think we may soon be able to move towards the building of the gap, at least the Panama Canal.

This dinner was followed by a visit to New York to talk over the subject with George F. Baker. the president of the First National Bank, with whom he had been for many years intimately associated in financial matters, H. P. Davison of J. P. Morgan and Company, and Frank A. Vanderlip. The entry in his journal records the encouragement he received:

February 10, 1909. Call on Messrs. Baker, Vanderlip and Davison in the interest of Pan-American Railway. Mr. Baker said he would join Mr. Davison and Mr. Vanderlip. Mr. Davison said he not only favored but they would join in building the road. Mr. Vanderlip was in favor and would join in building road. . . . I was well pleased. The three are the best men in New York, or elsewhere.

Unsettled financial conditions in the United States and uncertainty as to the willingness of Congress to grant a charter of the character desired prevented the coöperation of the capitalists mentioned in taking hold of the project at that time. Nevertheless, the energies of Chairman Davis continued to be directed toward giving the project concrete form as an international enterprise to be supported by the several governments which would be interested through their geographic and other situation. He had several interviews with President Taft and Secretary Knox, both of whom gave hearty support to his plans. Secretary Knox especially exerted himself in seeing that its importance be realized by the Fourth Pan-American Conference, which met at Buenos Aires in September, 1910, and the United States delegation received special instructions on the subject. To this Conference Chairman Davis, on behalf of the permanent Pan-American Railway Committee, presented a report showing the further progress that had been made since the previous Conference.

The Buenos Aires Conference confirmed the resolutions taken by its predecessor on the subject, acknowledged the important services that the permanent Pan-American Railway Committee had rendered, and continued its existence. It also further charged the Committee with the collection of fresh data and recommended the countries interested to coöperate with the Committee with a special view to preventing the project from being abandoned to the isolated action of each of the countries especially interested in it.

Following the action of the Buenos Aires Conference, the Committee, under the direction of Chairman Davis, continued its activity, in which it had the coöperation of the Department of State. Meetings were held during the subsequent year, at which the progress in actual construction was reported and measures were taken to secure further coöperation by the several governments.

It had been intended to present a report to the Fifth International American Conference, which was to meet at Santiago, Chile, in 1915; but the postponement of this Conference because of the unsettled conditions resulting from the hostilities in Europe rendered its preparation unnecessary. Means were found, however, for keeping the project alive. When the Pan-American Financial Conference met in Washington in the spring of 1915, reports were made by the respective delegations on railway conditions in their countries, and the majority of them gave prominence to the relation of the railway construction to the Pan-American project.

Out of the Financial Conference grew the International High Commission, a permanent body. Members of this Commission, with the Secretary of the Treasury at their head, visited South America in the spring of 1916. A special committee investigated the Pan-American Railway project and reported on measures to encourage it along the lines that the permanent Committee was following. Secretary McAdoo indorsed this report. The work that Chairman Davis had undertaken during President Harrison's administration was thus carried forward to President Wilson's administration, with the full recognition that it was the great idea not of a visionary but of a man of vision.

CHAPTER IX

POLITICAL ACTIVITIES AS A PRIVATE CITIZEN

Support of Senator Bayard in 1884—Cleveland's nomination at Chicago—Talk of Mr. Davis for Vice-President—He urges Hendricks—Campaign work—Visit to Albany—Explanation of his interest in Mr. Blaine—National conventions in 1888—Prophecy of Harrison's nomination—Mr. Davis declines to be a candidate for Governor—Visit to the President-elect at Indianapolis—Cabinet suggestions—Campaign of 1892—Disruption in the Democratic party—Support of Bryan and Free Silver in 1896—West Virginia politics—View of national election in 1900.

BUSINESS enterprises, exacting as they were, did not monopolize the attention of Mr. Davis after his retirement from the Senate. His interest in public affairs continued unabated. The duty of a citizen was never neglected by him. He liked politics. He participated in the primaries and in the local campaigns as well as those in which larger issues were involved. His political activities during the twenty years after he left the Senate give a panoramic view of the politics of the nation and of his own State of West Virginia.

He took part in conference and caucuses, attended conventions, declined suggestions and pleas that he himself become a candidate for several offices, wrote letters to the newspapers, and made speeches. Nor was his horizon confined to his own party. He was a keen observer of the tendencies and movements in the other organization, and the warm friendships he had formed with many leading Republicans gave a touch of personal interest. The political history of the country almost might be sketched from the activities and the observations of Mr. Davis during this period.

Senator Bayard was his choice for the Democratic nomination in 1884. This was partly the outgrowth of their association in the Senate, and partly due to the conservative character of both men in their views on public issues.

Mr. Davis, as usual, was placed at the head of the West Virginia delegation to the Democratic National Convention. After his election as a delegate to this Convention he began to interest himself actively in behalf of Mr. Bayard. The progress of the campaign for the nomination is indicated in his journal:

June 27, 1884. I returned from New York this morning. On Monday night about a dozen of Mr. Bayard's friends met at his house at dinner. By his request Senators Gorman, McPherson, and myself go to New York in Senator B's presidential interest. Convention meets 8th prox. at Chicago. I am a delegate. We find Bayard has a number of good reliable friends in New York, among them Aug. Belmont, W. R. Traverse, John Kelly.

It looked to us as if Gov. Cleveland had a majority of the New York delegation. Flower has considerable following. Tammany is opposed to Cleveland. Brooklyn or Kings County has not elected anyone. Upon the whole, Bayard's chance is only tolerable, owing largely to the fact that the country is disposed to go for whoever New York asks for.

At the Chicago Convention Mr. Davis exerted himself vigorously for his candidate, but his statement that Bayard's chance was only tolerable was borne out by the results. Delegates from other parts of the country did not accept the plea made by Tammany that Governor Cleveland, if nominated, could not carry New York

State. The unit rule was enforced and the Tammany delegates and other opponents of Cleveland in the New York delegation were voted solidly for his nomination.

On the first ballot Mr. Bayard received 170 votes. On the second, when Governor Cleveland was nominated, he had 81½ votes. Mr. Davis and one of his West Virginia colleagues, Mr. Beale, were among those who voted for Bayard on both ballots.

Following the nomination for President, the candidate for Vice-President was discussed in the usual aspect of availability as to geography and personality. Some of Mr. Cleveland's warmest supporters turned to West Virginia, while others looked to Indiana. Thomas A. Hendricks was the available candidate from Indiana, although some of Mr. Cleveland's friends were irritated with him. Others were not very kindly disposed toward Mr. Davis because of the persistence he had shown in supporting Mr. Bayard. It was known, however, that he would be very acceptable to Tammany and to the element in New York that had been opposed to Cleveland.

A conference was held which was attended by ex-Senator W. H. Barnum of Connecticut, ex-Senator Francis Kernan and Smith Weed of New York, John Kelly, the Tammany leader, W. L. Scott of Pennsylvania, Senator Gorman, George L. Converse of Ohio, and others. They sent for Mr. Davis, who advised the nomination of Mr. Hendricks. His recital of the circumstance is found in a very brief comment accompanying some newspaper clippings in his journal, to this effect:

From the newspaper extracts it will be seen that the nomination for Vice-President was between Mr. Hendricks and myself. No friend or myself made any move for my nomination; it came from Gov. Cleveland's friends unsought by me. I am told that W. L. Scott, of Pa., made an earnest effort in my behalf.

While Mr. Davis was deeply interested in the nomination of the candidate, he was also quite solicitous about the platform which should be adopted, and particularly what should be said in regard to the tariff. He was a member of the Committee on Resolutions, and served on the sub-committee which formulated the platform that the Convention adopted. He records its action quite briefly:

Sub-committee—General B. F. Butler, Massachusetts; Hon. A. S. Hewitt, New York; Hon. W. R. Morrison, Illinois; Henry Watterson, Kentucky; Governor Morton, Nebraska; General Burke, Louisiana; Hon. G. L. Converse, Ohio; H. G. Davis, West Virginia. We were about 48 hours in session, and at last agreed, less Gen. Butler.

Mr. Davis took his customary part in the campaign in his State, attending among other conventions the congressional convention in his district which nominated for the House of Representatives William L. Wilson, who was afterward to become famous as the author of a tariff bill with which Mr. Davis did not agree.

In October, in answer to a personal letter from Governor Cleveland, Mr. Davis went to Albany to confer about the prospects. His account of the meeting is given in a characteristic entry in his journal:

October 12. In response to letter of Gov. Cleveland, I went to New York and got Mr. Gorman to telegraph I was there. Gov. Cleveland asked me to come from cars to Executive Mansion, which I did; found the Governor waiting dinner for me. We dined together, no one else present. I was much pleased with the man and the way he received me. We talked over the situation and men generally for two or three hours. We concluded chances for Ohio were one in three, and West Virginia nine out of ten. Election in Ohio and West Virginia takes place October 14; presidential election November 4.

The outcome in those two States was indicated in the following journal entry:

October 18. The result of October election in Ohio and West Virginia is now known, Ohio being Republican and West Virginia Democrat; makes it a draw and very uncertain who will succeed in November election. Chances favor (slightly) Mr. Blaine.

The tension throughout the country over the closeness of the election is shown in these extracts from the journal:

November 5. Yesterday was general election day all over U. S. for Presdt. and Vice-Presdt. All passes fairly quiet. Contest very close. Not fully known to-day who is elected, but general impression is Cleveland and Hendricks. New York State is very close, and whichever way it goes will decide election.

November 12. Owing to New York State being very close between Blaine and Cleveland, there is now an official count going on. Cleveland has upon face 1,200 or 1,300 majority, and it is generally conceded he is elected.

In this campaign Mr. Davis's position was a peculiar one. Mr. Blaine was his warm personal friend and business associate. The chairman of the Republican National Committee was his son-in-law, Stephen B. Elkins. But as a leader and a believer in the principles of his party he felt impelled to support the candidate of his own political organization. Moreover, the chairman of the Democratic National Committee was Senator Arthur P. Gorman, his kinsman and business and political associate.

Immediately after the nomination of Mr. Blaine, and before the Democratic National Convention met, some question was raised in his own State in regard to his attitude. He answered the question in a brief letter to the *Wheeling Register,* in which he said that, while Mr. Blaine was his business associate and warm personal friend, he had no intention of supporting him. His own comment on the situation is given in his journal under the same entry, in which he recites Cleveland's election:

In the contest for President my political feeling and acts were and are with Cleveland; my personal feeling with Blaine. Mr. Elkins (son-in-law) and Senator Gorman (cousin) were at the head of the committees of Democrats and Republicans, so my relation to each is good and close.

When the President-elect was forming his Cabinet, some suggestions were made that Mr. Davis should be in it. He commented simply in his journal that the newspapers had considerable talk about himself for the Cabinet, but that nothing was known as to who would go into it, although all thought that Senator Bayard and W. C. Whitney would be offered places. Belief that Mr. Davis was in mind was strengthened in February, when he had an interview with Mr. Cleveland in New York City, but apparently that was not the purport of the interview. It is thus described:

February 7, 1885. Responding to telegraph from Senator Gorman, I went to New York last evening to call upon President-elect Cleveland. He had many callers. He treated me very nicely; talked to me half an hour.

This is the description of the inauguration of the first Democratic President since Buchanan:

March 4, 1885. I go down in the morning, go in Senate, witness inaugural address, etc., of Governor Cleveland as President of the U. S. Day is good. (*Very good.*) More people attend than ever attended an inaugural address before.

Mr. Davis's political relations with President Cleveland throughout his first administration were friendly, if less intimate than his personal relations. One brief entry in the journal indicates that he did not think that Mr. Cleveland and himself were so far apart on the tariff. It follows:

January 28, 1887. I was in Washington yesterday; had by appointment a long talk with President Cleveland. I suggested special message to Congress urging tariff legislation and reduction of revenue. He received the suggestion kindly, and I think he will act upon it.

Mr. Davis, as usual, headed the West Virginia delegation to the Democratic National Convention at St. Louis in June, 1888. There was no opposition to President Cleveland's renomination, and his old friend and senatorial associate, Allan G. Thurman, was nominated for Vice-President. This is his account of the proceedings:

June 3, 1888. I start to St. Louis in special car of Senator Gorman to attend Democratic Convention, which meets on 5th. I represent W. Va. on national executive committee. Gorman, Watterson, and Scott were the leading men of the Convention. I was with them most of the time. I declined reëlection on National Executive Committee. Cleveland and Thurman were each unanimously nominated. This is very unusual.

In this year the question as to who should be the Republican candidate was involved in much uncertainty. Mr. Davis, with his keen powers of observation, had reached the conclusion that the nominee would be General Benjamin Harrison of Indiana. Months before the Convention met, in correspondence with Mr. Bayard, who was then Ambassador to Great Britain, he expressed this belief. Mr. Bayard, three thousand miles away, saw no such probability, and so wrote Mr. Davis, asking him the grounds for his belief; and Mr. Davis responded reviewing the political conditions and the prospects. His prophecy was confirmed. His record of the event is thus given:

July 3, 1888. General Harrison has just been nominated by the Republicans for President. Elkins has had much to do with nominating him. In fact, I doubt his nomination but for Elkins. He is our personal friend.

There was a movement in the Democratic party to strengthen the ticket in West Virginia by nominating Mr. Davis for Governor. This movement, however, received no encouragement from him, and he finally set it at rest by a letter to the *Wheeling Register* under date of August 1st, as follows:

I have had many personal requests and a large number of letters asking me to allow my name to be used in connection with the gubernatorial nomination at the approaching State Democratic Convention to be held August 16.

To all such inquiries my general reply has been and is that my business affairs are in such condition that they demand all of my time and attention, and, without neglecting them and without great personal inconvenience and loss, I could not consent to become a candidate.

The people of West Virginia have been kind to me, and I owe them a debt of gratitude. They have always nominated and elected me whenever I have been a candidate. I would like to serve them in any way I consistently can, but cannot at the coming election be a candidate for Governor.

I deem it fair to my friends and party associates that I should make this public expression, so that they may be advised of my decision in the premises.

It is known that, among other things, I am engaged with others in building a north-and-south line of railroad through the State, which is regarded, in a measure, as a public advantage, as it will largely develop the resources of the State and add to its wealth and prosperity. It is feared by my associates and myself that my candidacy would interfere with the proper care and prosecution of this enterprise.

I hope and believe that the Convention will select and elect a worthy, sound, and progressive man, identified with West Virginia and its development, who will work for the advancement of the people and the progress of the State.

Notwithstanding the personal friendship to which Mr. Davis referred in his journal entry describing General Harrison's nomination, he entered aggressively into the campaign to defeat the Republican ticket. The gubernatorial question having been disposed of, he was free to give his energies toward the reëlection of President Cleveland, and this he did. He had misgivings, however, that the tariff issue would defeat the Democrats, and these were confirmed when the election returns were in. He thought that his own State would be close, but it went with the rest of the country and its electoral vote was recorded for the Republican candidates. Mr. Davis accepted the result philosophically, as he always did political reverses.

The friendship which General Harrison entertained for him was in no way affected by their political differences, and in December, by invitation, he made a visit to the President-elect at Indianapolis. The newspapers were filled with accounts of the visit and speculation as to what it meant. Mr. Davis's own explanation was given in his journal:

December 26, 1888. On 23d I left Baltimore for short visit to General Harrison and family. Arrived 11.30 P. M. Mr. McKee met me at the depot. Found General and Mrs. H. waiting up to receive me; they were very kind and good. I return on Monday evening. They asked and insisted upon my staying until Tuesday, which was Christmas. Newspapers have considerable to say about my visit. It was partly social, partly in interests of Mr. Elkins for War Department and Blaine for Secretary of State. The Harrison family and mine have been good and close friends for 8 or 10 years. I think Mrs. Harrison one of the best women I ever knew.

The inauguration of General Harrison, with comment on the weather, was almost as briefly described as the similar entry and comment on Mr. Cleveland's inauguration, four years earlier. It ran thus:

March 4, 1889. General B. Harrison, Republican, is to-day inaugurated as President U. S. He is a good and valued friend of mine and our family. It was expected he would make Mr. Elkins member of his Cabinet, but he did not. Messrs. Blaine and Windom are our friends. This is a very disagreeable day; it rained nearly all last night and this morning. Four o'clock— not raining, but cold and disagreeable.

Though President Harrison did not make Mr. Elkins a member of his Cabinet at the beginning of his administration, because of the complications, geographical and political, that usually beset Cabinet-making, he did this two years later. Mr. Elkins then became Secretary of War. Mr. Davis, while continuing his friendly personal relations with President Harrison, now found himself in stronger political opposition, since there was a national administration of the other party in power and to be held responsible. Yet he was not entirely in sympathy with the leading elements in his own party. He doubted the expediency of making Mr. Cleveland the candidate in 1892, although he recognized that the reaction over the extreme high-tariff legislation embodied in the McKinley bill would be favorable to the Democrats. He believed that Senator Gorman would be the strongest man for the nomination as representing the conservative element which entertained moderate views on the tariff. As usual, he was selected as one of the delegates from West Virginia to the Democratic National Convention. His journal, after noting the nomination of Harrison and Reid by the Republican National Convention, has this entry:

June 20, 1892. I am at Chicago attending Democratic Convention. I went out in interest of Senator Gorman. It was plain from time of our arrival that ex-President Cleveland had a majority of delegates. I returned the second day of convention, expecting Cleveland to be nominated on first ballot, which was done.

During the campaign Mr. Davis made a number of political addresses in support of his party candidates, State, Congressional, and national. In a speech at Piedmont the Saturday evening before election he said that the Force bill was the leading issue, and, while eulogizing General Harrison as a man, declared that his principles were wrong and he was to be blamed for that bill. The dangers of centralization, if the Republicans were continued in power, was another issue on which he urged the Democrats to support their candidates. On the tariff he declared that the Republicans were wrong in claiming that the Democrats were in favor of taking the duty off coal, and that the Republicans were responsible for the legislation reducing the rate on that product. He closed this address by introducing William L. Wilson and urging that he be supported for Congress.

The disrupting and antagonistic tendencies in the Democratic party during President Cleveland's second term were not pleasing to Mr. Davis with his conservatism and his constructive ideas. He was not in sympathy with either element in the party at that time, and in his own State he was out of touch with those who were in control of the party organization. The political condition known as the Bryan campaign was approaching.

Mr. Davis was not a delegate to either the Democratic National Convention in 1896 or that in 1900, but he kept his party allegiance and supported the national ticket in both campaigns. He made several political addresses in support of Bryan and Sewall in 1896, and wrote a letter to the *Wheeling Register* supporting the platform declaration for free silver. In this letter he declared that he did not fear the bad results that the Republicans claimed would follow Mr. Bryan's election. Regarding the tariff he said that, in his judgment, the interests of the people were best served by a moderate revenue tariff with incidental protection. He made a speech at Elkins in which he said he could not agree with all that had been said and done at Chicago, but he urged support of the ticket.

When Mr. Bryan came into West Virginia on his meteoric speaking trip, a meeting was held at Keyser at which Mr. Davis presided and made a speech indorsing the candidate and saying that his youth was no objection to him. He also said, speaking as a business man, that the business of the country would be in no danger from his election. Mr. Bryan in his speech, after complimenting Mr. Davis, referred especially to his age and experience and his standing in the business world.

"I am glad," said Mr. Bryan, "this man, ex-Senator Davis, living in the East, is not afraid to trust the executive office in the hands of a man who has always lived in the West. I am glad that this man of mature years is not afraid of those who have not reached that age in life. I am glad that one of the richest men in your State is not afraid to trust the government in the hands of the people. His position protects him from attacks which are made against me. He has been a Senator for twelve years; therefore our opponents cannot call him an ignoramus or a novice in legislation. His property interests protect him from being called an anarchist."

A passing view of the trend of the campaign is given in some extracts from the journal which follow:

Sept. 28, 1896. I have returned from trip to Baltimore, Philadelphia, New York, and Washington. This is presidential year. All the Eastern States, especially money centers, are for McKinley and gold standard. Western States appear to be all for Bryan and double standard, gold and silver. I am for double standard and Bryan; I have written a letter on the subject to the *Wheeling Register*. Candidate Bryan is to speak at Keyser on 30th. I am to introduce him, also preside.

October 1, 1896. Yesterday Bryan, Democratic candidate for President, came from Washington on B & O, spoke at Harper's Ferry, Martinsburg, Hancock, Cumberland, Keyser, and Grafton. I met Mr. Bryan at Cumberland. I was chairman, and introduced Mr. Bryan to the great crowd of people (at Keyser). Bryan spoke about 40 minutes. Estimated people present at 4,500. Rain and flood keep some away.

October 23, 1896. The political pot is boiling hot. Political meetings numerous. Mr. Elkins is giving all his time to electioneering and speaking for McKinley. I am for Bryan; have written a letter supporting Democratic ticket. Am giving financial aid. Many invitations, but have not made a speech. It looks like Republicans will succeed in New York; betting is about 3 to 1 on McKinley. West Virginia and Maryland are doubtful States, chances in favor of Republicans.

Nov. 2, 1896. To-morrow is election day. Democrats claim West Virginia and the election of Bryan. Republicans claim and feel sure of West Virginia and the election of McKinley. Betting in New York and Chicago is about three to one in favor of McKinley. Senator Elkins says West Virginia and the country for McKinley. I say, West Virginia and result doubtful. November 5. Presidential and State elections over. Republicans carry nearly all. McKinley about 300 electoral votes; 224 to elect. Majority on popular vote large. West Va. gives McKinley, also State ticket, about 12,000 majority; legislature about two thirds Republican.

In the mid-period of the Congressional and State elections Mr. Davis still continued to work for his party's success. In February, 1898, several newspapers began advocating his nomination for Governor, but he discouraged the movement. In August he presided over the Democratic Convention, which met at Elkins, and during the campaign he made several speeches. In the one he delivered at Piedmont he reviewed the general political outlook and gave some attention to the new question which had arisen as a consequence of the war with Spain to free Cuba. He said that the Republicans advocated the retention of all the conquered territory, and that this meant a colonial system, a new and dangerous principle in our government, a radical departure from our traditional policy altogether inconsistent with the Monroe Doctrine. He declared himself against the retention of the Philippines.

In this campaign Mr. Davis felt a close personal interest, because his brother, Colonel T. B. Davis, had been nominated to fill a vacancy in the House of Representatives. In his journal he recorded his gratification that his brother overcame a Republican majority of 290 and was elected by 186 votes.

The Legislature chosen at this election was of a mixed political character, reflecting the factional situation in both of the leading political parties in West Virginia. It was a question as to which party would succeed in choosing the United States Senator. Mr. Davis always had been able to secure Republican votes, and many of his friends thought that he would be the best man to present as the Democratic candidate. There were, however, ambitious Democrats who were close personal friends of Mr. Davis, and who had been his political lieutenants, that sought the nomination. There was also the fact that Mr. Elkins, his son-in-law, was a Republican United States Senator.

In his journal Mr. Davis records in November that he was asked by many to be a candidate, but had not said yes or no. A fortnight later he notes that, after a talk in which John T. McGraw and C. W. Dailey said they were for him, he told them he would not be a candidate. Under date of December 24, 1898, he writes in the journal:

The West Virginia senatorial canvass is hot. It is generally understood that I am not a candidate. Also, if I was I would receive Democratic vote.

Ultimately Nathan B. Scott, Republican, was elected Senator.

In the Presidential campaign of 1900 Mr. Davis again supported Bryan. He acted as chairman of the Democratic State Convention, which met at Parkersburg, and made a speech along the lines of opposition to imperialism and the Philippine policy of the Republicans. His personal interest in the election this year again related to the candidacy of his brother, Colonel T. B. Davis, who had been renominated, and who was elected. In his journal entry, under date of November 5, 1900, his views on the national outlook were recorded to the effect that it looked to him as if McKinley would be elected President. The outcome he summarized in this manner:

November 7, 1900. Elections, national and State, yesterday. Republicans carried nearly everything by large majority. I voted for Bryan, but it was a choice of evils. Hope this is the end of Bryanism.

But eight years later Mr. Davis was again to support Bryan for President.

CHAPTER X

SOCIAL LIFE AT DEER PARK AND WASHINGTON

Building a summer home in the Alleghany wilderness—Glimpses of the mountain farm—Mr. Davis's love of country life—Sowing oats and buckwheat—Shearing the sheep—Evolution of Deer Park into the summer capital—Distinguished visitors—Senatorial guests—Cardinal Gibbons—Ex-President Grant—President Cleveland's honeymoon—Fishing and other incidents—President Harrison and his family—Social side of official life in Washington—White House dinners—New Year's receptions—Entertainments for Senator Davis at the end of his term—Residence in Baltimore—First state dinner of President and Mrs. Cleveland.

THE intimate family, social, political, and business life of Mr. Davis for a quarter of a century alternated between Deer Park and Washington. The vast tracts of timberlands in Garrett County, Maryland, which he and his brother purchased at the close of the Civil War, were traversed by the Baltimore and Ohio Railroad, but it was unbroken wilderness that was thus crossed. In the heart of these forest lands he determined to build a summer home on the crest of the Alleghanies. The home was actually an extensive farm for which the greater part of the lands had to be cleared. The wild deer had roamed through the region and when a railway station was established it was fittingly named Deer Park. The beautiful animals for many years slaked their thirst in the stream that ran through the Davis grounds.

Colonel Thomas B. Davis

It is at Deer Park that the best evidences are afforded of Mr. Davis's love for the open and of his fondness for farm life. It is here, too, that he appears as a practical farmer as well as a pioneer lumberman and railway builder. He opened the homestead in the spring of 1867, and continued to live there during the summer months until 1892, when he removed to Elkins.

The entries in his journal during the earlier part of this period offer many pleasing pictures of the practical farmer in the midst of congenial surroundings, frequently noting the weather conditions and prospects, as every farmer must do, plowing, sowing, and harvesting different crops, opening new lands, experimenting with new varieties of grains, looking after the various farm animals, and not forgetting the farm garden.

Incidental to these farming operations are the development of the lumber business, installing new sawmills, laying tramways, and marketing the product. There are also numerous prospecting trips into adjoining forest regions, with shrewd comment on their nature, and often details of purchases and sales. The picture of farm life is a minute one, with few of the details left out. Excerpts from some of the journal entries give the outlines:

April 26, 1867. Moved to Deer Park.

April 29. Sowed a few oats on hill in front of house.

May 4. Weather so wet we cannot sow oats.

May 8. Ground white with snow. We have sowed about twenty bushels of oats.

Our mill, Greenwood, was commenced last week in March. About April 15, sawed some little lumber. May 1st just beginning to work right.

May 13. There have been 3 or 4 close days. We are sowing oats in the glade in front of house. Brother Thomas is here.

May 17. Received cow and calf from Mr. Thompson. We

finished sowing oats to-day. The carpenters are about done on our house.

May 20. We have planted nearly all our garden.

May 30. We counted our sheep, and marked them. All marked "H D." Wethers have an additional H on shoulder. Young lambs have D on shoulder. We have 134 total sheep. Our mark is crop of left ear and undercut on right. We will turn our sheep out to-morrow.

June 17. Bought of E. Bell 206.80 acres of land on hill joining Lawson tract at $20, all timber-land.

June 21. Sowed buckwheat in the meadow on Black Run.

June 25. Sowed buckwheat on hill.

August 31. Considerable frost last night; fear our buckwheat has been killed.

September 1. Frost killed buckwheat here, but not on high ground.

October 25. Examined trees bought and planted last spring; found dead two apple trees, eight dwarf pears, two plums, one cherry, one quince. This is as near as I can tell; may not be quite correct.

November 2. We send cattle and colts to New Creek to winter.

November 18. Mrs. Davis closed our house for the season. We are still plowing.

December 2. Weather cold; snow in the glades, and we have to stop plowing.

The first season on the new homestead was thus closed, but during the winter various purchases of implements were recorded with a view to the following season, and early in the next spring the family returned to the farm. Its cultivation continued to receive the personal attention of Mr. Davis, notwithstanding his absorption in larger business enterprises. Some of the incidents of the season are thus set forth:

April 18, 1868. Weather good. We sow oats, also commence plowing on glade hill.

April 25. Weather has been cold but good since 20th. We,

this morning, commenced sowing oats. Sowed black oats in front of Mr. Tillson's, and opposite, on other side of Zock. We also sow blue grass and timothy on some ground.

April 27. Weather good; we are still sowing oats. T. B. Davis sent 20 cattle, 12 mules, making 32.

May 12. Still sowing oats and plowing. Weather cool, and looks like rain. We planted or sowed China wheat to-day; it is something new.

May 15. Cloudy and raining. John Rhine brought up two mares and colts; 24 calves.

May 23. Have been plowing and sowing oats for two days. I was stopped this evening by rain. One day more will let us finish.

May 26. Fine day; we are sowing oats.

May 27. Close, warm rain; hard in the evening. Sheared and counted sheep to-day—47 ewes, 4 wethers, 2 rams, 13 ewe lambs.

June 16. No rain since last of May, three weeks.

June 18. Sowed some buckwheat in the wet places in glade. New sawmill about ready to saw.

August 2. We commence cutting oats.

August 13. Some frost last night; bit slightly buckwheat in the glade.

November 20. Quite a snow-storm.

December 2. About two inches of snow on the ground; we stop plowing. We leave Deer Park for the winter.

Subsequent seasons widened the farm work, but always it had the direct oversight of Mr. Davis. In the midst of political conferences, service in the State Legislature and the United States Senate, railway building, purchases of coal and timber lands involving millions of dollars, he continued to give his attention to the farm. His journal records that on May 5, 1870, the weather was good, that they finished sowing oats, and that "the last sowed was Poland oats, near the barn." Early in August, 1875, he notes that the army worm had made its appearance in oats and corn, doing great damage. A week later he records that they commenced cutting oats, though quite green, to prevent the army worm from eating them up. The loss to the farmer is thus indicated:

We will make but little more than our seed, owing to army worm.

How greatly the Deer Park farm had expanded and become something more than a farm is indicated in an entry under date of May 12, 1878:

On yesterday Professor Baird sent to Deer Park a fine lot of young salmon trout. We put 11,000 salmon in ice pond near house, 2,000 trout in pond near barn, 1,000 in little pond, 1,000 trout in Pond Big Run.

Other consignments of salmon and trout from the Smithsonian Institution are also noted at later dates.

Some of the incidents of farming in the later years are thus described:

September 1, 1879. This is a fine morning. We are done stacking oats. Are now cutting second grass crop, which is good; first crop was bad or short.

September 1, 1881. This has been a dry summer, but our oats, buckwheat, and hay crops are good. We are raising about 6,000 bushels, weighing 34 lbs. to the bushel, 300 bushels of buckwheat, 300 tons of hay.

July 12, 1882. We are cutting grass; it is only tolerable good. Grass near house is very good, but north or west hills are bad or short.

Mingled with the notes on the crops and other incidents of farming, after the first few seasons, there are increasingly frequent entries regarding social affairs, in which the names of distinguished men of the nation are given as visitors. These entries mark the transformation of the Alleghany summit from a wilderness into one of the great mountain resorts of the county. This transformation really was largely the evolution of the Davis farm and timber tracts, for it was Mr. Davis who saw its advantages and who planned and carried forward its development. At his instance, John W. Garrett, who was then president of the Baltimore and Ohio Railroad, examined the region and was so impressed with its attractiveness that he built a summer home for himself there, while his son, T. Harrison Garrett, built another. He went further than this, and in conjunction with Mr. Davis erected a large summer hotel and numerous cottages to provide for the summer guests who began coming to Deer Park.

All through these years the kindly and unostentatious hospitality of Mr. Davis and his family had been extended to their friends both in public and in private life. In a short time Deer Park had become the summer capital of the nation. Railway officials found it convenient to spend the heated months there. To Baltimore and Washington especially it was a haven of rest, easily accessible and therefore sought.

It was there that the messenger from the Vatican, Count Mucciola, brought the notification from Pope Leo XIII which raised His Grace, Archbishop Gibbons, to His Eminence, James, Cardinal Gibbons, the second American Cardinal. Thither came the leaders of both parties in Congress, escaping the heat of Washington for brief periods, most of them as guests of Senator Davis and his family. Rarely did a week-end pass without the Senator bringing a number of his colleagues. There, too, came Presidents of the United States for rest and recreation and former Presidents as well.

Some of the incidents of these visits of distinguished men are given as recorded in the journal:

July 10, 1875. Judge and Mrs. Thurman of Ohio arrive
They expect to spend two weeks with us.

July 11. General Bristow, Secretary of the Treasury, Judge
Pierpont, Attorney-General, and Governor Dennison of Ohio
took tea with us to meet Judge and Mrs. Thurman.

June 6, 1881. Mr. W. W. Corcoran [the philanthropist] and
Carter Robbins are here on first visit of a few days. We are
glad to have our friend Corcoran with us.

June 25. Hon. Wm. Windom and wife made us a visit from
Saturday to Monday. They are close friends of ours.

June 27. Hon. A. P. Gorman, Senator of Maryland and my
first cousin, made us a visit.

September 3, 1883. Senator T. F. Bayard and two daughters have been on a visit to us for nearly a week. They left
yesterday for home. During their stay here several entertainments were given them. One at Mr. T. Harrison Garrett's was
a nice affair.

Ex-Senator McDonald (of Indiana) and wife have been at
the hotel for some time. Bayard and McDonald met and talked
several times at our house. Rode and drove together. Both
are prominent candidates for Democratic nomination for President next year.

September 8. Mr. Bayard wrote me a very friendly and kind
letter, telling what a pleasant visit he had with us.

August 11, 1884. Senator Pendleton of Ohio left us yesterday. He paid us a visit of a few days. We like him very much.

September 15. Ex-Senator Barnum (of Connecticut) made
us a short visit Sunday last.

Senator John Sherman was another visitor, usually
one of the guests on a week-end trip from Washington,
while General U. S. Grant and Mrs. Grant came as the
guests of Mr. and Mrs. Elkins in the midsummer of
1883 and remained for several days.

A Presidential honeymoon was one of the incidents
resulting from Deer Park's attractiveness and the reputation for hospitality that its leading resident had given
it. The story of the honeymoon, which at the time

filled columns of the newspapers, is given with idyllic
brevity by Senator Davis in his journal entries:

May 22, 1886. President Cleveland sent for me through
Colonel Lamont, his private secretary; told me he is to be married early in June, and asked me to arrange so he can go to Deer
Park with bride and spend a week. The marriage and place
they go is known to but very few; newspapers have not yet got
hold of it.

June 2. I came to Baltimore last evening. Stopped at Washington and saw Secretary Lamont and President Cleveland.
Presdt. marries Miss Folsom this evening, and goes to Deer Park
to-night to spend a week or two.

June 8. President Cleveland and bride, Miss Folsom that was,
came here last Thursday morning, the 3d. They occupied one of
the B & O Railroad cottages. Weather has been fine. Mrs.
Davis and I call. President and Mrs. Cleveland return our visit.
About three o'clock Mrs. Davis and I go over to President's cottage and take President and Mrs. Cleveland a drive to Oakland.
At night we call to see the President and Mrs. Cleveland.

Saturday, June 5. President and Mrs. C. went to Bantz at
Deep Creek to fish; we caught a fair lot of trout. Sunday Pres-
ident and Mrs. C., Colonel Lamont, and Mrs. L., Mrs. Davis and
I went to Oakland to church. Sunday evening President and
Mrs. C., Colonel Lamont, and Mrs. L. dine with us at seven
o'clock. Monday President and Colonel Lamont took my moun-
tain wagon and horses and went to Leeland's place on Deep
Creek; got about 50 trout.

There were other fishing trips, and the family legend
is that young John Davis, who was often one of the
party, usually saw part of his catch transferred to the
President's basket without Mr. Cleveland's knowledge.

In the newspaper accounts of the honeymoon, it was
told how President Cleveland and his wife in the early
morning were seen wending their way up to the sawdust
walk leading to the Davis cottage, throwing aside all
ceremony and instead of waiting for the first call paying

a visit themselves, thus relieving the ex-Senator of any embarrassment that he might have felt in the matter of calling on the newly married couple. There was also an undercurrent of political talk at the time, growing out of the resignation of Daniel Manning as Secretary of the Treasury, and the possibility that President Cleveland might ask ex-Senator Davis to take the vacant place. The end of the visit was told in the journal entry of June 8 in this manner:

President and Mrs. C., Colonel Lamont, Mrs. Davis, Kate and I drive to Boiling Spring. At one o'clock President and party left on special train for Washington. President said he had a very pleasant visit and might return during the summer.

The forerunner of another Presidential guest at Deer Park is found in several notes of visits by Senator Benjamin Harrison. The friendship between the Davis and the Harrison families was an intimate one and was the more cherished because of the difference in politics of the heads of the two families. In August, 1887, Mr. Davis recorded in his journal:

General and Mrs. Harrison of Indiana are staying with us. Have been here a week or more, and will remain a week longer. Mrs. Davis and I gave them a dinner.

There were subsequent visits, and after General Harrison became President he found relief from official cares in going to Deer Park, although at the time he humorously explained that, while the office-seekers did not intrude on him there, nevertheless an unusually large number of people seemed to happen in at Deer Park in order to pay their respects. The incidents of President Harrison's visit the first summer following his inauguration are recorded in this pleasing manner:

July 3, 1889. Mrs. McKee, daughter of Presdt. Harrison, has been with us several days, arranging and fixing up cottage for President and Mrs. Harrison. Mrs. Harrison and party came to Deer Park to-day and went direct to their cottage. We give Mrs. H. an Alderney cow and Mrs. McKee an Alderney calf.

July 12. President Harrison came from Washington to-day and joined Mrs. Harrison and Mrs. McKee. Secretary and Mrs. Windom and daughter also came, and are our guests.

July 26. Attorney-General Miller came on 24th to make us a visit of several days.

July 29. Attorney-General Miller left for Washington to-day. He made himself very agreeable.

President and Mrs. Harrison have been quite friendly, coming to our house often, and we are going to their cottage, sometimes to meals.

August 31. At seven-thirty we expect the President and Mrs. Harrison to dinner with us. Have invited fourteen or sixteen persons.

Among the guests at this dinner were various public men and their wives and several railway officials of national reputation.

At this period Cardinal Gibbons was in the habit of seeking rest at Deer Park, and was an occasional guest of the Davis family. He met President Harrison at an informal dinner given by Mr. Davis. The delicate question of etiquette was solved by seating the Cardinal on the left of the host with the President on the right.

The Davis hospitality at Deer Park during these years was a reflex of the hospitality extended at Washington. Some passing glimpses of official functions at the national capital are given in the journal entries. Among these functions during the first part of the Senatorial career was a state dinner by President Grant at the White House which Senator Davis had not expected to attend, Mrs. Davis being ill at the time, and the invitation to dine with the President being nevertheless a command, the Senator found it necessary to make a personal call on President Grant and explain the circumstances. A state dinner at the White House during the term of President Hayes, in February, 1879, is described in this way:

Mrs. Davis and I dined with President and Mrs. Hayes at seven; it was a state dinner. We, at about ten o'clock, got through and went to British Minister's, Sir Edward Thornton, to a reception.

At that period the social side of official life was somewhat restricted, owing to the lack of facilities for entertainment. Representatives and Senators in Congress, Cabinet officers, and other officials lived mostly in boarding-houses or hotels. A few Senators and Representatives rented their homes, but for a member of Congress to own a house in Washington was to risk his political future, because the folks at home would not understand.

During a large part of his senatorial term Senator Davis and his family lived at the Arlington Hotel. Many of the leading public men also made their homes there, while distinguished strangers, such as the Emperor Dom Pedro and the Grand Duke Alexis, were entertained at the Arlington during their visit. The family thus was in the very center of official life.

At that time the New Year's reception at the White House was the function of a public character which inaugurated the social season, and the making of New Year's calls was as much a part of Congressional life as attending the sessions of the House and Senate. A New Year's day toward the close of the senatorial career is thus described:

January 1, 1881. This has been an unusually cold, stormy winter, with much snow; it is said to be the coldest winter for years.

Mrs. Davis, Hallie, and others received callers at Arlington parlor; more than 100 callers came. I make about twenty calls, among them Secretary Schurz, Sherman, and Ramsey. Also General Sherman, Senators Pendleton, Kernan, Windom, Allison, Bayard, Edmunds, and Beck.

Senator Davis, besides the entertainments given by himself and Mrs. Davis, was a frequent giver of dinners for gentlemen. One of these at Wormley's, which was then famous for its colored owner and for its good cheer, included Mr. Blaine, a large number of his colleagues in the Senate, and some prominent railroad officials.

Toward the close of his second term, when it was definitely determined that he was retiring from public life, a series of dinners were given in honor of the Senator and Mrs. Davis by his colleagues. One was by Senator Gorman, one by Senator Bayard, and another by Mr. Blaine. A few lines in the journal tell the story of the Blaine dinner, though it was a very notable one:

February 24, 1883. Ex-Secretary Blaine at his new house gave Mrs. Davis and me a dinner; commence at seven and one half; return home eleven o'clock. Left dinner table about ten. Guests, Senator and Mrs. Allison, Senator and Mrs. Windom, Senator and Mrs. Gorman, Justice and Mrs. Miller, Senator Bayard, Senator Camden, and General Sherman.

After his retirement from the Senate, Mr. Davis, on account of his business interests, for a time made his winter home in Baltimore. He entertained there with his customary hospitality and his former colleagues were frequent guests at his table. The friendship with Mr.

Blaine was cemented by several visits.   One of these is
thus described:

March 13, 1884.   Mr. and Mrs. J. G. Blaine came over from
Washington to dine with us.   There were present Mrs. Benjamin
Harrison, Mr. and Mrs. J. A. Gary, Mr. and Mrs. J. A. Hambleton, Mr. and Mrs. Samuel Spencer, Mr. and Mrs. Elkins, General Felix Agnus, and our daughter Kate; fifteen in all.

After a few years Washington again became the winter home and the social life at the national capital was
resumed.   It was during this period of residence in
Washington that the sequel of President Cleveland's
honeymoon occurred in the form of the first state dinner.   The story of this social event is given in full in a
newspaper excerpt pasted in the journal, with this comment under date of January 21, 1887:   "Mrs. Davis
and I attended dinner given by President and Mrs.
Cleveland.   It was a grand affair.   See preceding
page."

The newspaper account runs:

At seven-thirty o'clock to-night the guests assembled for the
first White House state dinner this winter, which was also the first
at which its young mistress has presided.   It was given for the
Cabinet, and was noteworthy as the first appearance of Mrs.
Lamar, bride of the Secretary of the Interior. . . . The bride of
the White House wore for the first time one of the most elab-
orate dresses of her trousseau, a pale blue silk starred with silver
daisies and veiled in clouds of tulle.

The order of escort to the table was as follows: The Presi-
dent and Mrs. Manning, the Secretary of the Navy and Mrs.
Lamar, Lieutenant-General Sheridan and Mrs. Fitzhugh Lee,
Ex-Senator H. G. Davis and Mrs. August Belmont, Commodore
Harmony and Mrs. Goodyear of Buffalo, Governor Lee of Vir-
ginia and Mrs. Andrew of Massachusetts, the President of the
Senate and Mrs. Sheridan, the Secretary of the Treasury and
Mrs. Endicott, the former being Mrs. Cleveland's left-hand neigh-

bor, while at her right sat her escort, the Secretary of State. Beyond these, still at Mrs. Cleveland's right, were the Postmaster-General and Mrs. John Sherman, the Speaker of the House and Mrs. Harmony, Assistant Secretary Fairchild and Mrs. Davis of West Virginia, Senator Beck and Mrs. Sicard of Buffalo, Mr. John A. Andrew and Mrs. Fairchild, the Secretary of the Interior and Mrs. Carlisle, the Secretary of War and Mrs. Vilas, who was the President's left-hand mate.

Further chapters in the social life in Washington in which Mr. Davis participated might be written, but it is well to end the chronicle with the golden memories of those gracious days of President Cleveland and his bride in the White House.

CHAPTER XI

VICE-PRESIDENTIAL NOMINATION AND AFTER

State of the Democratic party in 1904—Revival of conservative forces—Mr. Davis a delegate to the St. Louis Convention—Cleveland elements in control—Mr. Bryan's fight in the Platform Committee for silver—Compromise by omission—Judge Parker's nomination for President—Mr. Davis's story of his own nomination for Vice-President—Welcome by his neighbors at Elkins—Turn given the campaign by Judge Parker's gold telegram—Objections to Mr. Davis on the score of age—Notification at White Sulphur Springs—Speech by John Sharp Williams—Response—Campaigning at eighty-one—Philosophic acceptance of result—Activities during the four years that followed—Urged by his party in West Virginia for various offices—Reasons for declining—Delegate to the Baltimore Convention in 1912—Support of Wilson and Marshall

AFTER two national campaigns in which it had met defeat, the state of the Democratic party in the nation in 1904 was not encouraging. The inevitable reaction had occurred. Free silver, under Mr. Bryan, had not won in 1896. The same general attitude, together with opposition to imperialism, had not brought victory in 1900. The radical forces in the party having been in control and having failed, the conservative forces were now becoming influential.

It was apparent that Mr. Bryan was about to be displaced from his leadership. This was to be done under the element in the party which was known as the Cleveland Democracy, although it included many prominent party leaders who never had been Cleveland Democrats. All these forces were united in their determination to free the organization from the silver issue. They believed that this question had been settled for good and therefore should be eliminated if the party was to have any chance of success. The desire to get back into power was also a strong motive for burying the dead issue by many who originally had believed in it.

In West Virginia, as in other sections of the country, the conservative forces in the Democratic party began to assert themselves, and thus in a natural way the leadership of Mr. Davis was again sought. Having supported free silver and Mr. Bryan in both campaigns, he was not unacceptable to the following of Mr. Bryan in the State, although he was opposed to what were called the Bryan tendencies. The prevailing sentiment found expression in the first instance in suggestions that he accept the nomination for Governor. Various entries in his journal refer to this sentiment. In one case he remarks that he is being urged to be a candidate, but says to all that he is not a candidate and not hunting for a job. Again he says he is being urged to accept the nomination for Governor, but has not agreed to do so.

The Democratic State Convention met at Charleston in April, 1904, to select the candidates for Governor and other State officers, and to choose delegates to the National Convention at St. Louis. Mr. Davis was a potent figure at this convention. In his speech he said:

"An important part of our duty is to select conservative, representative Democrats as delegates to the National Convention at St. Louis. Let us name good men without reference to past differences of opinion. In the coming election we are likely to have a strong, popular, and conservative candidate in the person of Gorman or Parker."

Mr. Davis had been exerting his influence to secure delegates favorable to Senator Gorman, and this was made apparent when the delegates-at-large and the district delegates were chosen, twelve of the delegation being for Gorman and two for William R. Hearst. Mr. Davis was placed at the head of the delegation. The other delegates-at-large were former Senator Johnson N. Camden, former Governor William A. MacCorkle and the Hon. Owen S. McKinney.

When the National Convention met at St. Louis early in July, the nominee virtually had been selected in the person of Judge Alton B. Parker of the New York Court of Appeals. A careful literary campaign had been conducted for months with the purpose of making him known to the public at large. Antagonistic leaders supported him. Former President Cleveland had indorsed him in newspaper interviews and former Governor David B. Hill was in personal charge of his campaign. The vital struggle in the Convention, therefore, was not to be over the candidate, but over the platform.

It was known that the supporters of Judge Parker were likely to have their way; yet many of the delegates were not quite ready to ignore their past record on silver, or to accept the complete domination of the conservative element in the party, since this element drew its main support from the East and therefore raised the sectional question.

William J. Bryan appeared as a delegate from Nebraska. The conditions were strikingly different from those that obtained at Chicago in 1896 when he had ridden the whirlwind and dominated the Convention. They were also strikingly different from those that were to obtain eight years later, when he was again to ride the whirlwind, dominate another National Convention, overthrow the candidate who had an actual majority of the delegates, and make possible the nomination of a candidate who had entered the Convention with little prospect of success.

His political ascendancy was at its lowest ebb. In the early stages of the Convention the name of Mr. Cleveland was wildly cheered, while Mr. Bryan's was received with coldness. However, he made an aggressive and undaunted fight, giving out interviews denouncing Judge Parker as the plutocratic candidate, and declaring that there should be no repudiation of the stand the party had taken in previous campaigns on silver.

With the nomination of Judge Parker assured, the first battle over the platform was in the Committee on Resolutions. Mr. Davis was the West Virginia member of that committee, as he had been in many previous conventions. There was a sharp struggle over the tariff plank between the conservative and the radical tariff members. Mr. Bryan won on this plank. Some of the gold Democrats were in full agreement with his tariff views, but there were intimations that others who did not agree with him consented to it as a strategic move to oppose him on the silver question. Mr. Davis acquiesced in the phrasing of the tariff plank, although it was not entirely acceptable to him.

The great struggle was on silver. The Eastern delegates insisted upon a recantation of the former pronouncements for silver and a declaration upholding the gold standard. Mr. Bryan, according to the newspaper reports at the time, stood like a rock against such a declaration, and the committee was given to understand that if it was adopted he would bolt. A compromise plank was phrased, which recited in substance that the discoveries of gold during the last few years and the great increase in its production had contributed to the maintenance of a standard of value no longer open to question, removing that issue from the field of political contention.

Mr. Bryan made an aggressive, determined fight against the adoption of this plank by the convention. When it became evident that no declaration framed on this line could be adopted, a sub-committee of three was appointed to devise an acceptable compromise. This sub-committee consisted of David B. Hill, John Sharp Williams, and Mr. Bryan himself. The newspaper reports of the sub-committee's meeting were to the effect that Mr. Bryan interposed his unyielding opposition to every proposal that included the faintest favorable mention of gold; and at last Mr. Williams, worn to the limit of endurance, exclaimed:

"Gentlemen, we never can get together; let us omit the mention of money. Let us go back to the Convention and report a plantform freed completely of this troublesome question."

"That is satisfactory to me," said Mr. Bryan.

"Will you support the ticket and platform?" asked Mr. Hill.

"I certainly will," replied the Nebraskan.

The Convention ratified this compromise platform, took a recess, and reassembled in the evening to listen to the nominating speeches. The voting began after midnight. Mr. Bryan made one of his electrifying speeches in opposing Judge Parker, and supporting Senator F. M. Cockrell of Missouri. "I return to you the standard you gave me to bear," he thundered. "I may have failed in wisdom, and I may have lost the fight, but I defy any man to say that I have been false to my trust or untrue to the faith of Democracy."

Judge Parker was nominated on the first ballot, and the Convention took a recess. The Parker leaders were in doubt regarding the most available candidate for Vice-President. Some of them inclined to former Governor Judson Harmon of Ohio, who had served in Cleveland's Cabinet and who represented the same conservative tendencies that Judge Parker was assumed to represent. But John R. McLean, the owner of a powerful newspaper and himself a political factor of consequence in Ohio, was strongly opposed to Judge Harmon. Governor Hill and others of the men representing the dominant element consulted. Finally some one suggested Henry G. Davis of West Virginia.

Having been for free silver, and having supported Bryan, it was felt that his nomination might sweeten the ticket for Mr. Bryan. At the same time his large financial interest and his conservatism would make him acceptable to the Eastern element of the party. Moreover, West Virginia was a doubtful State, and if it could be carried for the Democratic national ticket his personal popularity would be the means of carrying it. Search was begun for Mr. Davis and word was brought that he had left on his special car the evening before. Nevertheless it was decided to nominate him, and this was done when the Convention met after recess. A telegram notifying him of the action of the Convention reached him at Greenville, Ohio.

Mr. Davis's own recital of the events that brought him into the vortex of national politics again is given with his customary terseness in the journal entries that follow:

July 3, 1904. I go to St. Louis as a delegate-at-large from West Virginia.

July 6. Democratic National Convention meets. W. Va.

delegation stands 12 for Senator Gorman, 2 for Hearst. Gorman refuses to let his name be presented to Convention. Considerable sentiment among delegates for him.

I am selected by W. Va. delegation on Committee on Resolutions. Senator Daniels, Virginia, is chairman sub-committee of ten. Among the members are Senator Hill of N. Y., Mr. Bryan, and myself. After two days' work and an all-night session, we get a unanimous report which is adopted by Convention.

When platform was adopted I thought my work was done. I went to my car and started for home. On my way I was telegraphed I was being voted for Vice-President. This was a great surprise to me. I was nominated on the first ballot, and made unanimous.

July 10. Sunday. Came from St. Louis Democratic Convention. Was met at Belington by a band which came to Elkins. Was met at depot by a thousand or more people and escorted home.

This very modest statement gives a faint idea of the reception of the candidate. Politics were forgotten and he was received as a fellow citizen. C. Wood Dailey made a brief speech introducing him to the friends and neighbors who knew him so well. In replying to it he spoke with deep feeling, saying:

"My strongest feeling at this moment is my gratification at this remarkable expression by the people of my own town of their kindly feeling and good will toward me personally. In this gathering I see many who do not hold my political faith, and among them our distinguished fellow townsman, Senator Elkins. All this testifies there are some ties between them that for the time at least make them forget party politics and lead to the expression of personal feeling and regard.

"It is the expression of your personal feeling for me for which I wish to thank you; and now, as it is Sunday, and this besides is only for the expressions of feeling of kindly interest, let me retire, and in doing so I will introduce my friend Senator Elkins, who, differ with me as he may in politics, feels an interest in our town and rejoices in every honor that comes to it."

Senator Elkins, in speaking briefly, said:

"This quick gathering and cordial welcome is without party significance. It is the enthusiastic outburst and expression of the respect, confidence, admiration, and affection which neighbors and friends entertain for Senator Davis, who has done so much to promote the growth of this town and the prosperity of our great State.

"His nomination for the office of Vice-President brings not only honor and distinction to him, but to us as well, and as neighbors and friends we share in it with him. I am sure I speak for every member of this great assemblage when I say, as neighbors and friends we are each and all glad that the great honor which the distinguished Senator so richly deserves came to him without his seeking it, or even without his knowledge, and as neighbors and friends we rejoice with him."

The signs of public interest throughout the country and of interest in his personality appear in this entry in the journal:

July 12. Many letters and telegrams of congratulation on nomination for Vice-Presdt. Many callers and newspaper reporters at Elkins. Publishing everything that occurs or has happened.

Meanwhile a new turn had been given the campaign probabilities in the closing hours of the Convention. When the news was received in the East that the Convention in its platform had omitted all mention of gold or silver, there was much dissatisfaction. Judge Parker acted of his own accord to correct the omission by sending the following message to William F. Sheahan, one of the New York leaders:

I regard the gold standard as firmly and irrevocably established, and shall act accordingly if the action of the Convention to-day shall be ratified by the people. As the platform is silent on the subject, my view should be made known to the convention, and if it proves to be unsatisfactory to the majority I request you to decline the nomination for me at once, so that another may be nominated before adjournment.

ALTON B. PARKER.

This telegram was presented to the Convention after the nomination of Mr. Davis for Vice-President at a night session. It stirred afresh the opposition of the Bryan supporters, and Mr. Bryan made an impassioned speech of denunciation. The Convention, after an angry debate, authorized the sending of the following telegram to Judge Parker:

The platform adopted by this Convention is silent on the question of the monetary standard because it is not regarded by us as a possible issue in this campaign, and only campaign issues were mentioned in the platform. Therefore there is nothing in the views expressed by you in the telegram just received which would preclude anyone entertaining them from accepting a nomination on the said platform.

Having directed this resolution to be sent to the candidate for President, the Convention adjourned with Parker and Davis as the ticket.

For a time there was a question regarding Mr. Bryan's intentions, which he finally answered by supporting the ticket in his own way and with his own interpretation of the issues of the campaign.

The nomination of Mr. Davis seemed likely to raise a collateral issue. This was whether any political party was justified in nominating a man of his age for the Vice-Presidency, since there was always the possibility that the Vice-President might become President. Mr. Davis was then past fourscore. His eighty-first birthday would be celebrated ten days after the election in November. Should he be elected, he would be well in his eighty-second year when he assumed office, and he would be expected to retain his physical and mental vigor until he was in his eighty-sixth year.

The Republican newspapers took the matter good-humoredly, explaining that his age was of no consequence, since there was no possibility of the Democratic ticket being elected. A more serious view was taken by some of the Republican leaders. Elihu Root in a political speech, while making kindly reference to Mr. Davis, criticized the action of his party in nominating a candidate of his age, and drew a somewhat gruesome picture of its possible consequences.

Mr. Davis was unperturbed by the discussion of his age. He was so accustomed to looking forward and his mental make-up was such that he gave no more attention to the chances of mortality for himself than he would have given to any man nominated at half his age. After a short period of rest he entered vigorously upon his campaign. In the middle of July he went to New York to attend a meeting of leading Democrats which Governor Hill had called. From there he proceeded to Esopus to see Judge Parker. His own account of the interview appears in his journal:

July 21. I go up to Esopus, Judge Parker's home on the Hudson. Spend several hours with the Judge; like him very well. Canvass starts off brightly.

In accordance with the wishes of Mr. Davis, the formal notification of his nomination was made at White Sulphur Springs. His account follows:

Aug. 10. At White Sulphur Springs Hon. John S. Williams of Mississippi, leader of House of Representatives, notified me officially of nomination for Vice-President. I replied. A great crowd at Springs and at notification.

Mr. Williams in the course of his speech, after discussing the public issues, turned to the personality of the candidate for Vice-President and, addressing Mr. Davis, said:

"The people see in you one of the best products of the best period of American institutions, a period whose salient characteristics were local self-government, individuality, equal opportunity, and freedom—freedom to work, freedom to buy and sell, freedom to compete in industrial life, resulting in self-dependence; freedom to develop as one's own master and not merely as the well trained and well managed industrial servant of another. They see in you what Oliver Wendell Holmes said is a rare thing, a self-made man who is yet not proud of his maker. . . .

"In real conclusion, Mr. Davis, it is a sincere pleasure indeed to know and to be able to help place in high position a man of your character and sense and modesty; a man who, as the result of a life of continence, temperance, self-containment and usefulness and honest industry, presents a picture in virile though advanced age of *mens sana in corpore sano* which is a delight to the eye, a satisfaction to the soul, and was thought by wise ancients to be the *summum bonum* of individual earthly existence."

In his speech of acceptance Mr. Davis touched on

one point with a deep degree of sentiment. He said:

"I find it a great pleasure, standing here upon the borderland of the two Virginias, to receive and accept any commission you bear, and to send greetings through you to the Democracy of the entire country. Is it not significant of a closer and truer brotherhood among us that, for the first time since the Civil War, a nominee on the national ticket has been taken from that section of our common country that lies south of Mason and Dixon's line— a happy recognition of the obliteration of all sectional differences which led to and followed that unhappy struggle?"

Continuing, he attacked the Republicans in the national administration for extravagance, held them responsible for unfavorable business conditions, recalled that they had favored the double standard, and spoke particularly of his own attitude on the rights of labor. He paid this tribute to Judge Parker:

"He is a man of courage, yet prudent; of high ideals, yet without pretense; of the most wholesome respect for the Constitution and the majesty of the laws under it, and a sacred regard for their limitations; of the clearest sense of justice which would rebel against compounding a wrong to an individual or a nation; positive in conviction, yet of few words; strong in mental and moral attributes, and yet withal modest and reserved; possessed of a sturdy constitution and magnificent manhood, and yet temperate in his actions and dignified in his demeanor."

Referring to his party, he said that, while there had been differences in the preceding campaigns, yet at St. Louis they were all harmonized and a common ground was found upon which all could stand and do battle for Democratic principles. Concerning the platform he said:

"I heartily indorse the platform upon which I have been nominated, and, with the Convention and its nominee for President, regard the present monetary standard of value as irrevocably established."

A further exposition of his views was promised in his letter of acceptance, to be made public in September. In it Mr. Davis criticized the increasing cost of government under Republican administration. A paragraph was given to imperialism in which he noted its tendency to drift to absolutism and centralized power. The policy, he insisted, was always dangerous to liberty. Concerning the tariff he declared in favor of a wise, conservative, and gradual change that would equalize burdens of taxation and make honest competition possible; but expressed the opinion that in making such change due regard should be had for capital and labor involved in industrial enterprise. He reiterated his conviction that local self-government could be maintained only by strict observance of the Federal Constitution. He discussed in some detail civil service and the race issue, and he renewed his tribute to Judge Parker. Concerning arbitration he observed: "The spirit of arbitration is kindred to the love of law and order."

It is part of the political history of that campaign that it was not without friction, and that the managers had some trouble in holding the various party leaders together. In September Mr. Davis went to New York to meet the members of the Democratic National Committee and Judge Parker. In October a ratification meeting was held at Baltimore, over which Senator Gorman presided. Mr. Davis made a speech, also Governor Hill, Senator Daniels, and his warm friend, former Governor William Pinckney Whyte. After that, the greater part of his time was given to meetings in West Virginia. He traveled on a special train and spoke constantly. His journal records making "eighty or ninety" speeches, which in itself showed what a vigorous campaigner he was at eighty-one.

An incident of great interest in the campaign was the visit of William J. Bryan. Late in October Mr. Bryan entered the State at Parkersburg, and from there went to Huntington and Charleston. Mr. Davis met him at Parkersburg. Mr. Bryan in his speeches supported the ticket in his own way and interpreted the platform after his own manner, but he showed his appreciation of the loyal support Mr. Davis had given him when he was the candidate.

As the campaign drew to an end very little doubt remained concerning the outcome. Mr. Davis had excellent opportunities of learning the Republican view from his son-in-law, Senator Elkins, who was active in the Republican national campaign. The recollection of the family is that during the canvass the Democratic candidate for Vice-President and the Republican Senator, when they met at their homes in Elkins, discussed the weather, the crops, the continuous development of West Virginia, the railway enterprises in which they were interested, and kindred topics. There is even a legend that Senator Elkins, at several of the passing interviews, was carried away by the beauty of the mountain scenery surrounding them, and complimented Mr. Davis on his foresight and energy in turning this part of the wilderness into the dream city that it had become.

Mr. Davis was very anxious to carry his own State, and in ordinary circumstances the large personal following he had among Republicans, and the deep esteem felt for him by men of all parties, might have influenced the voting. Had he been the candidate for Governor there is little question that this esteem would have found expression; but his Republican friends looked upon the national campaign as one of issues and not of men, and were not inclined to vote the national ticket of the opposition party in order to show their esteem for the candidate for Vice-President.

There is no reason to assume that during the last few weeks of the campaign Mr. Davis deceived himself into believing that the Democratic national ticket would be successful. His philosophic view of the campaign is summed up in his journal in this manner:

November 8, 1904. Election day. It is generally believed Roosevelt will be elected. I make a good vote in Elkins and Randolph County.

At about ten o'clock we hear enough to know we lose and Republicans win. Victory for Roosevelt is great.

The objection made during the campaign by his opponents and the thought which lodged in the minds of many of his political supporters, that if elected he might not live throughout his term, or might become incapacitated for performing the duties of Vice-President, or President should the chief executive die, is interesting to recall in the light of the activities of Mr. Davis from March, 1905, to March, 1909. His business affairs having been neglected during the campaign, he applied himself assiduously to them, and particularly to the favorite project of his later years, the Coal and Coke Railway.

His journal records, during 1905, various conferences with railway officials of connecting lines to make traffic arrangements, a horseback trip over part of the route, and the actual opening of the road for traffic. In the three years following there are similar entries regarding the progress of the road, inspections of timber and coal properties, and various details of financing the line, as well as particulars regarding other business enterprises.

Interest in his own business during this period did not preclude broader interests. The annual meeting of the West Virginia State Board of Trade rarely found him absent. When the State Bankers' Association met he was almost invariably present; and at its annual meeting in 1907, at Elkins, he entertained his successful competitor for the Vice-Presidency, Charles W. Fairbanks, who delivered an address. During this period he gave his regular annual dinners to railway presidents, and supplemented them by dinners to the permanent Pan-American Railway Committee.

Philanthropies and benefactions received the attention he had for many years given them. The Young Men's Christian Association and the Child's Shelter of Charleston, both of which were very dear to his heart, are frequently mentioned in his journal in connection with his visits and contributions to them. There are similar entries concerning the Davis and Elkins College at Elkins, with various details, and in particular the building of a house for the president of the college. Home-coming week at Baltimore, in 1907, was one of the passing incidents of the period, as were his benefactions to the Odd Fellows Lodge with which he had been affiliated.

Political affairs, notwithstanding his absorption in business and philanthropies, still filled a large space in his activities. In 1906, and again in 1908, his party talked of him as the candidate for Governor, but this talk he discouraged. In February, 1907, he made an incidental visit to the Senate, when Vice-President Fairbanks, noting his presence, and also the presence of two other octogenarians, Senator Pettus of Alabama and former Senator William Pinckney Whyte of Maryland, gracefully sent each a white rose. Mr. Whyte and Mr. Davis had been colleagues in the Senate thirty years earlier. Edward Everett Hale, the chaplain, was also an octogenarian, and was a great believer in the peace-making influence of the Pan-American Railway, of which Mr. Davis was the sponsor.

As the Presidential year approached, Mr. Davis showed his usual interest in the candidates of both parties, and indicated his personal preference by a newspaper interview favoring Judge George Gray of Delaware as the Democratic candidate. In his journal entry on Washington's Birthday, 1908, he noted that it looked as if Bryan, Democrat, and Taft, Republican, would be the nominees for President. He did not seek election as a delegate to the Democratic National Convention, but in the campaign he supported Mr. Bryan actively and heartily.

When inauguration day, 1909, came, the day that would have ended his term as Vice-President had he been elected, he was in the full possession of his powers and was giving very close attention to his railway and to his philanthropies. In 1910 he helped his party in its State campaign, and there was a move for his election as Senator, after it became assured that the Democrats had a majority in the Legislature. The *Washington Star*, in an editorial article in November, commented on this possibility, with special reference to Mr. Davis's position on the tariff:

It would be an event of the highest national interest if at eighty-seven, and after a long rest from office, Henry Gassaway Davis should reappear in the Senate. Despatches from West Virginia mention his name. Other names are mentioned, those of men of merit and ability, but that of Mr. Davis is the most prominent of all, and in the country generally will command much attention.

This well preserved veteran has had a remarkable career. Beginning life in humble circumstances, he addressed himself first to business and then to politics, and achieved notable success in both fields. He made both money and reputation, and when he reached the Senate took rank there with the men known as workers. He was heard more frequently in committee than in open Senate, though not a silent man when the debates played around subjects that quickened his thought.

Other newspapers also discussed the possibility of Mr. Davis becoming a candidate, and the entries in his journal indicate conferences with some of his party friends on the subject. The talk was not displeasing to him, but there is no reason to suppose that he gave it serious consideration.

At the Jackson Day banquet of his party in Washington, on January 8, 1912, Mr. Davis was one of the most notable figures. A thousand prominent members of the party from all parts of the country were present, including several candidates for the nomination for President, and a former candidate in the person of Judge Alton B. Parker. When Mr. Davis came in he was cheered for several minutes, and escorted to the toastmaster's table, where he made a brief acknowledgment. The following day he told one of his friends that the address that had mostly deeply impressed him was that of Governor Woodrow Wilson of New Jersey.

Mr. Davis's interest in national politics this year was keen, and was exerted, as usual, toward conservatism. He attended the Democratic State Convention at Parkersburg in June, and was elected a delegate-at-large to the National Convention. The State Convention instructed for Speaker Champ Clark; but Mr. Davis told the Convention that his choice for President was Governor Harmon of Ohio.

Developments in the Republican party are described briefly in these journal entries:

June 19, 1912.　Republicans are having a lively time in Chicago National Convention.　Taft and Roosevelt are candidates, and are very hostile and bitter.

June 20.　Taft had majority of convention of about seventy, and was nominated.　Roosevelt bolts, and becomes a candidate.

Mr. Davis went to Baltimore in the latter part of June. It was the ninth National Convention of his party that he had attended.　Forty-four years earlier he had made his first appearance as a delegate in the Convention that met at New York and nominated Seymour and Blair. Owing to the great heat, he did not remain at Baltimore until the end of the sessions.　While not in full sympathy with some of the tendencies that were manifested, he gave his hearty support to Wilson and Marshall, and during the campaign coöperated with the Democratic National Committee.　Though unable to make speeches, he prepared newspaper interviews in which he reiterated some of his favorite views about the prosperity of the country under Democratic rule and the extravagance of Republican administrations.　In these interviews he quoted freely from Governor Wilson's speech of acceptance, and approved the candidate's pronouncement in favor of an early and gradual revision of the tariff downward.

Railway train in the mountain region—Point Lookout

CHAPTER XII

APPROACHING fourscore, Mr. Davis had found there was still work for him to do. The scope of his activities as he reached the allotted biblical age are indicated in an entry in his journal in April, 1901, apparently made casually, like so many other entries. This is it:

My health is good, and I am quite a busy man. Am President West Va. Central & Pittsburgh Railway; Piedmont & Cumberland Railway; Coal & Iron Railway; Davis Coal & Coke Company; Empire Coal & Coke Company; Washington Coal & Coke Company; Mill Creek Coal & Coke Company; Marshall Coal & Coke Company; Valley Coal & Coke Company; Queen's Coal & Coke Company; Davis National Bank, Piedmont; Trust Company of West Va.; United States Delegate Conference American Republics, which meets Mexico City October 22, 1901; West Va. Tax Commision, appointed by Governor to revise tax laws.

Circumstances contributed to give a fresh start to these business activities, and at fourscore and beyond to make him an even busier man than he had recited in his journal.   Twenty years of his management and development of the West Virginia Central Railway had made it a very valuable property, with greater possibilities in the future as part of one of the larger railway systems of the country.   The representatives of a number of important lines had seen these possibilities, and had begun negotiations for its purchase.   One of these lines was the Wabash, then under the control of the Goulds.   They wanted a railroad into Pittsburgh from the region tapped by the West Virginia Central and they had purchased the Western Maryland with this object in view.   This road then reached Hagerstown, and an extension to Cumberland was projected.

At Cumberland the West Virginia Central would make a natural prolongation.   The negotiations for its purchase were begun in the autumn of 1901, before Mr. Davis left for Mexico as one of the delegates to the Pan-American Conference.   They were continued with Senator Elkins and others of those who were largely interested, while Mr. Davis in Mexico City, by letter and telegraph, kept a guiding hand on the whole transaction. The outcome was that the West Virginia Central was sold by its owners on a basis of complete transfer.   It was characteristic of Mr. Davis that, having been the head of the system and responsible for its management, he did not care to be further identified with it after he had parted with his interest beyond exerting a friendly personal influence toward the new management.

The sale of the West Virginia Central Railway was consummated early in January, 1902, after Mr. Davis had returned from Mexico.   In consequence he found himself in the possession of several million dollars cash capital.   At fourscore he might have invested it in Government bonds or similar securities; but this would have meant idle capital, and the idea of idle capital was as repugnant to him as that of himself becoming an idle individual. Moreover, his ambitions for West Virginia in the way of developing the country had not yet been satisfied. There was a large region in the very heart of the State, contiguous to the section he had already developed, whose vast resources of coal and timber were imprisoned resources because no means of transportation for them existed.

This region stretched off toward Charleston, the capital, on the Kanawha River. A railway line reaching the Kanawha there would open up these resources through the Baltimore and Ohio and the Western Maryland systems on the north, and through the Chesapeake and Ohio and the Kanawha and Michigan Railway on the south. It would be a real artery for West Virginia. Tidewater would be accessible, and also the Ohio Valley and the Great Lakes.

The railroad would involve engineering difficulties greater than those encountered in the building of the West Virginia Central, because much tunneling would be required. This may have been one of the reasons why it appealed to Mr. Davis, since his whole career had been to undertake projects when impelled by obstacles. Railway building on the prairies would not have appealed to him.

He had studied the region with his usual thoroughness. Away back in 1874, when the West Virginia Central was a concept rather than a project, his journal had recited the details of a trip to Tucker, Randolph, and Barbour counties to look at coal deposits "of which much has been said." Regarding one section of this region he further recorded:

I find on Roaring Creek at or near Crawford Scott's and I. K. Scott's a vein of coal open in several places; the vein from top to bottom is about 11 feet, about 2½ feet top and bottom of coal, then a slate from one to two on this and about 6 feet of piece or good coal in center. I do not think it the vein of this region or Pittsburgh; it looks more like the Myer's Mill or Connellsville & Uniontown veins.

Upon the whole, I do not think as well of the Randolph or Roaring Creek coal deposit as I had been led to suppose. The Clarksburg vein I think is more over toward Buckhannon and Weston, say in Upshur County.

Later inspection seems to have given him a more favorable idea of the coal prospects in this district, and when his determination to continue developing the region had been reached, he began making extensive purchases. Quite simply in his journal in February, 1902, he records:

I have bought from E. J. Berwind, New York, his Roaring Creek coal property and railway (twenty-two miles, $875,000).

In the meantime he had formulated his plan, so that there was little delay in the organization of the Coal and Coke Railway Company. It was entirely Mr. Davis's individual enterprise, and remained so until the line had been actually completed, when some of his former associates joined with him. His first move was to gain possession of a link that already had been built. Pittsburgh capitalists and mine-owners had constructed a railway known as the Charleston, Clendennin and Sutton from the Kanawha at Charleston to Sutton, a distance of sixty-four miles. It had the disadvantage, in railway terms, of ending nowhere, and its extension had not proved inviting enough to secure the coöperation of capitalists.

Mr. Davis acted in his usual direct manner. He

fixed an upset price, and sent to Pittsburgh a confidential representative, who quickly closed the transaction with the owners. Then the construction of the intervening links of this line was begun. Henry G. Davis, railway builder, eighty years old, was at work again. He gave his personal attention, as usual, to every detail of the building of the railway, overseeing the letting of the contracts and also the way in which they were carried out. His own story of the construction is told with his usual simplicity, or rather is gathered from the occasional entries in his journal. In February, 1902, he recorded the purchase of coal lands in Randolph, Upshur, Braxton, and Gilmer counties. Two months later, noting further purchases, he said: "We have bought in all about one hundred thousand acres."

In June he states: "I am pushing along Coal and Coke Railway. No one has an interest except myself." Later in the same month he records:

On the 11th Bower, Robb, Moore, and I left Elkins by way of Roaring Creek Junction; rode over line of Coal and Coke Railway now being constructed by myself, intended to go through our coal-fields to French Creek coal-field, west of Buchan River, five or six miles above the town of Buckhannon. We staid overnight at Ford's Half Way House; next day by way of Gray Run to Sago, a station on railway. We returned by way of Middle Fork of Valley River and Sand Run.

In October of the same year he records: "We are pushing along Coal and Coke road; between 500 and 600 men at work grading and in first tunnel."

There were numerous other trips over the route in the following months. Quite casually is recorded in some detail a horseback trip in May, 1903. Mr. Davis was then well along in his eightieth year. Other members of the party, very much younger, after they got back spoke of it as a hard trip, but there was no indication of hardship in the account given by the eighty-year-old leader.   It runs as follows:

May 27, 1903. On Morning of 18th inst., John [son], Lee, Bowers, Robb, and myself left Elkins for Charleston, W. Va., over contemplated route Coal and Coke Railway from Elkins to Charleston.

Went by rail to tunnel No. 1 at Kings, from there by way Grassy Run to Sago; staid overnight.

From tunnel No. 1 and Sago on horses by way of French Creek and Ball Run to Burnsville, stop overnight, then by Little Hand 4 miles to Copen Run, up that Run to Peshens Run, stop for dinner at Mr. Peshens, then over 24 tunnel to waters of Otter Creek and Elk River. Staid at Mr. Bogg's at Frametown overnight. Next morning we started on horseback about 6.30. From Frametown to Big Otter, end at present of our Charleston & Sutton Road, then to Charleston by rail (64 miles). Staid Charleston Thursday evening to Saturday morning and started back home.

Sutton Sunday for dinner, then over Nole's Creek Route to Burnsville, engineer Chatman accompanied us going and coming. Between Frenchton and Elk River distance about 56 miles. We reach Elkins noon on Tuesday 26th.

I was in 3 coal openings each about 7 feet, 1 with two postings amounting to say 10 in., one opening on Gray Run, one on Copen Run, one Elk River (O'Brien's). Was fairly well pleased with route. Think average cost of road between Elkins and Charleston (175 miles) will be about $25,000 per mile. Mouth Copen Run also Jacob . . . bell good ground for siding stations.

There were numerous other trips, sometimes on construction trains, sometimes on horseback, and sometimes over difficult sections on foot. The eighty-year-old pedestrian was as hardy as the eighty-year-old horseman, and his younger companions always marveled that he did not seem to share their fatigue. The grading and the tunneling were the subject of frequent observations on his part, but there were also notes regarding sidings, the best points for station yards and towns, and provisions for operation and traffic. Further land purchases also were recorded. There were likewise interviews with officials of connecting lines.

A visit to Elkins by George J. Gould and Mr. Joseph Ramsey, the president of the Wabash, is recorded, in which the relations of the new road are discussed. The interview was thus told:

I talked to Messrs. Gould and Ramsey about our new road under construction from Charleston here. They talked fair and liberal. Upon the whole the interview was agreeable to each of us.

In November of the same year the rapid progress that the road was making is stated in a brief entry:

Last week General Manager Bower and I took cars to Tunnel No. 2 as far as Coal and Coke was completed; then horseback to Sago, Tunnel Mill beyond the Buckhannon River, returned same day. Found construction going on fairly well. Hope to get road completed to Buckhannon River by January, 1904.

One of the final stages in the construction of the line is indicated in the journal entry of June 15, 1905:

Returned last night from a horseback trip over Coal and Coke Railway as far as Gassaway. We expect to get road through by November. We are urging the contractor to push the grading. The town of Gassaway is improving fast. We are putting in foundation for engine house, and will soon start shops.

The main line was completed in December, 1905, and the first train was run through from Elkins to Charleston in January, 1906. A local newspaper gave this brief account of the consummation of the Railway Builder's latest project:

Saturday last in the small hamlet of Walkersville, Lewis County, the last spike was driven fastening the rails of the northern and southern ends of one of the most stupendous enterprises in the way of railroad construction ever undertaken in this State. Three years ago Senator Davis laid the plans for the building of a line of railway between the cities of Elkins and Charleston to develop and carry to market the coal from the vast holdings in the counties of Randolph, Upshur, Lewis, Braxton, and Gilmer. This enterprise does not stop with the aim that may be construed, but brings into close business relation counties of the interior and opens an avenue of commerce that will do more for the undeveloped portions of the State than any line heretofore constructed.

Under the generalship of W. H. Bower, general manager, work has been in progress almost night and day without interruption on the 175 miles. While it is true by the purchase of the Charleston, Glendennin & Sutton Railway, 63 miles of road is used, it was necessary to reconstruct it by relaying of heavier rails and filling of trestles, all of which work was done without interruption to the large traffic. On the 100 miles of new road it was necessary to pierce the mountain twelve times, making a total distance of four miles underground. Thirty steel bridges were built, crossing the many streams. Cuts and fills along the mountains reach a height of 100 feet. The roadbed is being covered with crushed limestone sixteen inches deep. This gives but a rough idea with what thoroughness the construction has undergone.

The Coal and Coke Railway in reaching the Kanawha crossed five rivers—Tygart's Valley, Middle Fork, Buckhannon, Little Kanawha, and Elk. This, taken with the tunnels, afforded some idea of the engineering difficulties. But these streams also offered the prospect of developing great timber tracts as well as coal-mines. The line also traversed some oil lands, so that there was the normal basis for industrial development.

Communities sprang up along the line just as they had come to life along the line of the West Virginia Central.

About midway of the route, where the road crossed Elk River, the new town of Gassaway was established. Here the company's shops were located and it became the principal divisional headquarters of the railway. Other towns sprang up through the development of the natural resources, particularly timber and coal, in the surrounding regions.

Mr. Davis was in his eighty-fourth year when the railway was opened for traffic through from Elkins to Charleston. Before that, in order to reach the State capital from the northern counties, a roundabout journey had been necessary, requiring two or three days over different railway systems. Thenceforth it was possible to make the through trip in a single day. He had covered every section of the road with the engineering parties. He had watched the construction of every mile of it. But, far more than this, he had traversed the surrounding regions on foot or on horseback, so that he knew what their resources were.

The Railway Builder who went to work again at fourscore might have considered his labors ended at eighty-four; but he continued to give the enterprise his close personal attention, directing the details of its management, making inspection trips, stopping at all stations, as an entry in his journal recorded. In 1907 some of the responsibilities of financial management were lifted from him by Senator Elkins and his brother, Thomas B. Davis, but he continued his general supervision of the line. In May, 1908, he jotted down in his journal: "I have been for two or three months looking closely to the management of Coal and Coke Railway, and have reduced expenses $5,000 per month, $60,000 per year."

There was a period of several years in which the coal and coke trade of the whole region was dull, and he notes these periods quite methodically, reciting also sometimes that the gross earnings were small, although usually entries of this kind are supplemented with the statement that the net earnings are improving. During this period he made several trips to Baltimore and Philadelphia to confer with the managers of other railways regarding new lines or extensions that would interweave the different systems and increase the traffic of all of them. He was very insistent on the other lines giving his road fair treatment in the matter of the traffic that it turned over to them.

In the meantime his horseback excursions were continued. In June, 1910, he notes in his journal a horseback ride to West Elkins, when the river was unusually high and backwater "say three feet," which apparently did not interfere with his continuing his exercise. Difficulties with employees over wages sometimes arose, but they usually were settled by conciliation. On one or two occasions he took the trainmen into his confidence, and told them how he had put his money into the railway and how he had carried it through dull times, when the earnings were lean, because he was unwilling to reduce their wages. The discovery of oil at one point is noted in April, 1912, by the brief statement, "Quite an oil-field recently come at Blue Creek on our road."

Responsibility for the active management of the railway was relinquished by Mr. Davis late in 1912. He records it briefly:

On November 23, at a meeting of directors held at our Washington office, we elected Hon. R. C. Kerens first vice-president Coal and Coke Railway. Our railway and coal company doing fairly well. Coal and coke each in good demand at increased price. Car supply short. I was eighty-nine November 16; health good for age.

In the following year there were several entries in his journal showing that the railroad was doing "fairly well" and that coal and coke were in good demand at advanced prices. In 1914 the state of the coal and coke business and of the railway traffic was indicated usually as good, although in some months the trade was dull and the road was doing "only tolerably." The following year the entries were similar with dull business, followed later by improving business; and a month before his death, that is, in February, 1916, an entry was made reciting that the railway and coal mines were doing fairly well. Thus he never lost his interest in the enterprise that he had created.

The larger activities involved in building the Coal and Coke Railway included minor ones incidental to it. There were local development enterprises to be organized, coal and timber properties to be refinanced. Much travel was involved in this work. There were numerous trips to New York, Baltimore, and Philadelphia, as well as over the route of the railway line. Mr. Davis's travel was as incessant at this period as it had been a quarter of a century earlier when he was building the West Virginia Central Railway.

Besides the railway and collateral enterprises there were other investments of a personal character to be looked after and fiduciary obligations to be discharged. There were the responsibilities of the banker to be fulfilled by giving that close personal attention which insured that conservatism in handling the money of other people was observed. In all these activities the railway builder and the man of business showed that the qualities that had been preëminent in middle age were not lacking at fourscore and beyond.

CHAPTER XIII

WEST VIRGINIA

Commemorating the half century of a war-born State—Recognition of Henry G. Davis's part in upbuilding the commonwealth —His early exposition of its resources—President of Board of Trade—Tributes to him as a pioneer in development—Head of Bankers' Association—Service on Tax Commission—Memories of epochal events—Speech on anniversary of first Battle of Philippi—Semi-Centennial celebration at Wheeling—Mr. Davis's modest account of his own work—Golden Jubilee Honors for the Grand Old Man—His review of the moral and material progress of West Virginia—Promises of the future—Poetic interpretation of achievement and aspiration.

THE Semi-Centennial of West Virginia's Statehood was celebrated at Wheeling in June, 1913. It commemorated fifty years' growth of a State born in the stress of civil war and cradled in blood and battle. Few of those who had molded the young commonwealth, carried it through the earlier period of civic development and social and institutional progress, awakened its sleeping resources and guided their transformation into a brilliant chapter of material prosperity, survived. Among the few was Henry G. Davis.

In whatever related to the evolution of the State, civic, social, and industrial, he had borne a strong man's part. After the lapse of half a century he was still a vigorous exponent of all that was best in the commonwealth, and was addressing himself to its welfare with undiminished activity. It was, therefore, both fitting and natural that when the Semi-Centennial Commission was appointed by Governor Glasscock, Mr. Davis should be selected as chairman. He was the incarnation of West Virginia, of her early hopes and aspirations and of their realization.

His appointment met with universal approval. It also served to recall the part he had had in building the commonwealth. Much of this is given in the chapters relating to his railway and other enterprises and to his public life. Some of these events may again be briefly reviewed, with a word about the activities that extended beyond the semi-centennial celebration even to the day of his death. As early as 1868 he had served, by appointment of Governor Stevenson, as a delegate to the National Commercial Convention that met at Louisville.

During his two terms in the United States Senate his labors in behalf of West Virginia were unceasing. He secured the first appropriation for river and harbor improvements by means of the James River and Kanawha Canal, and he obtained recognition of the justness of these improvements which resulted in subsequent measures.

The resources of the State, both agricultural and mineral, were the study of his lifetime and formed one of his favorite themes. He never neglected the opportunity to make them known. In his best known address on agriculture in the United States Senate, as far back as 1879, he had wandered from the general subject to give special information about the resources of West Virginia, her soil, her timber, coal, and petroleum. It was especially the mineral resources that he described, and speaking on this subject he said:

"They are largely undeveloped as yet, the greater part of them lying dormant; but when the treasures of this mountain State are unearthed, as they must be in time, they will astonish the world.   In minerals such as coal, iron, and salt, West Virginia stands unrivaled with the one exception of Pennsylvania.   In the production of oil, which has become one of our largest industries and one of our most productive sources of national revenue, West Virginia and Pennsylvania are entitled to all the credit.   The coal-fields of West Virginia are beyond question the most remarkable in the world.   The timber of our State is probably as good in quality and large in amount as that of any State in the Union."

Talks of this kind helped to awaken the people of the State to the natural wealth of which they were the heirs; it also drew the attention of capitalists and encouraged the development of the resources by the construction of railway lines and the opening of the coal-mines.   It was through the efforts of Senator Davis that the first appropriation for a geological survey of West Virginia was obtained, and this survey more than justified all that he had said about the mineral wealth.

When West Virginia began to take systematic measures to attract immigration and capital, Mr. Davis was foremost in the movement.   He was not afraid of being called a boomer.   In February, 1888, he was a member of the convention that met at Wheeling to adopt measures for advancing the interests of the State.   A few weeks earlier he had written a letter outlining the steps that should be taken to insure developing the still latent resources.   When the convention met he made a speech on the same subject, and, as chairman of the Committee on Immigration and Development, he submitted a report, which was adopted, providing for the organization of the West Virginia Immigration and Development Association.

Years afterward the efforts to give organized expression to the business interests of the State resulted in the formation of the State Board of Trade. He was one of the active men in its formation in 1905, and thereafter he rarely failed to be present at the annual meeting. In 1906 he was elected president of the Board. He was then eighty-three years old. In February, 1907, at a meeting of the Board at Wheeling, Mr. Davis received many proofs of the esteem in which he was held as a commonwealth builder. Commenting on his presence, the *Wheeling Intelligencer* said:

Wheeling is always glad to extend a cordial welcome to Hon. Henry G. Davis, and in this particular Wheeling is not different from any other West Virginia town.

Henry G. Davis was a pioneer in the development of West Virginia. Over fifty years ago he began to show his faith in the future of West Virginia, and year after year he has given the strength of an acute mind and vigorous body to the upbuilding of the State. He has won wealth, fame, and honor. His gray hairs have been richly crowned with the laurels of honorable achievement; but, though his years have passed the limits of active life allotted to most men, he is still planning, still thinking, and still doing those things which in a broad sense make for the betterment of mankind.

The *Wheeling Register* in its tribute said:

Hale and hearty, vigorous in mind and limb, despite his more than fourscore years, Henry G. Davis was himself even more interesting than the admirable address which he delivered at the annual banquet of the Board of Trade. The speech he delivered showed a grasp of current affairs not less noteworthy than his familiarity with the early history of this city and State.

When the State Board met at Huntington, in October, 1909, Mr. Davis delivered one of the principal addresses, and in it he reviewed at length the resources of the commonwealth and the measures taken for its development, with especial reference to the importance of railways as the means of such development. Speaking of the evolution into industrial communities, he said:

When the State began its career there were but few towns of any size, nearly the entire population being engaged in agricultural pursuits. There are now about one hundred and fifty incorporated villages, towns, and cities, with a score or more containing over five thousand people. The new ones are to be found along the railroads and principally where the mining industries have flourished. Not until there is utilized within its borders the valuable essentials it contains for manufacturing life will there grow up marts of trade and centers of activity such as have made the neighboring State of Pennsylvania great and powerful. We have spent nearly fifty years in demonstrating to the world that we possess nearly all the requisites of commercial greatness. Now let us begin the next half century with a determination to use the material we have to build our own house instead of our neighbor's across the way.

As a lifelong banker, Mr. Davis took great interest in every movement that brought the bankers of the State together. He rarely failed to attend the annual meeting of the State Bankers' Association, and usually made one of his short, pointed speeches filled with statistics, but statistics that were pertinent and illuminating. He served as president of the State Bankers' Association one year. The annual convention in the summer of 1913 was held at Elkins, and was attended by prominent financiers from beyond the State. One of these was United States Treasurer Burke, and another former Governor Edwin Warfield of Baltimore. Mr. Davis was then in his ninetieth year, but in his address he showed his interest in finance as clear as at any time during his active business life.

A typewritten outline of his address to the bankers is

Davis Child's Shelter at Charleston

prefaced with this comment in his own handwriting: "My remarks brief; a talk, not a speech." The talk ran through an historic review of banks, from the Venice Bank in 1171 to the organization of the first United States Bank, and then to the banks in the United States, their resources, their capital, and their circulation. From this general review it was a natural transition to the growth of West Virginia banks and their functions in developing the State.

Identification with the economic and the public life of West Virginia and the large part he bore in the industrial development naturally caused Mr. Davis to take a live interest in the fiscal affairs of the State. Because of his knowledge of these subjects and of his sound judgment in whatever related to them, he was looked to when the Legislature, in 1901, passed an act creating a Commission of five members to consider the subject of taxation, as one of the best fitted of all the citizens of the State to serve on the Commission. Governor A. B. White recognized this, and in a letter to Mr. Davis said:

I respectfully write to know whether you would consent to serve the State in this capacity and give the Commission the benefit of your valuable experience and thought on these matters. It would be very highly appreciated if you would, and I am sincerely desirous that you serve on this Commission. . . . The purpose is to consider the whole subject of taxation with reference to securing some reform legislation on these matters. I trust you can see your way clear to give the State the benefit of your services for which your long business experience has so eminently fitted you.

Mr. Davis accepted the appointment thus proffered him, and he also appreciated the compliment conveyed, since the State administration was Republican. The Commission as ultimately organized consisted of former Governor W. P. Hubbard of Wheeling, Henry G. Davis

of Elkins, L. J. Williams of Lewisburg, John H. Holt
of Huntington, and John K. Thompson of Raymond
City. Mr. Holt had been the Democratic opponent of
Governor White in the State campaign.

The Commission, after carefully considering the de-
fects in the system of taxation, determined to devise a
plan by which the expenses of the State government
would be paid by taxes upon corporations, charters,
licenses, capitation, etc., leaving the taxes collected from
real and personal property to pay the county and munici-
pal expenses. To Mr. Davis was assigned the subject
of the State revenues and the manner in which they
should be collected and disbursed. While serving on this
body he also attended, as one of the delegates of West
Virginia, the National Conference on Taxation, which
met at Buffalo. He gave much of his time to the work
of the Commission, and helped to formulate the preliminary report, which was submitted in December, 1901.
The final report was submitted in October, 1902, and
was signed by Mr. Davis along with the other members.
Many of its suggestions and recommendations bore the
stamp of his personality.

Many chapters might be written of Mr. Davis's part
in the fiscal history of the State, but they would be
merely the cumulative recital of a deep knowledge of
the economic resources and of the relation of taxation
to their development and to the application to the administrative affairs of the State.

The subject of West Virginia recurs to the Semi-Centennial celebration and the part of Mr. Davis in it.

Before the actual semi-centennial celebration there
had been a half-century observance of the first battle
that was fought within the borders of the new commonwealth. This anniversary was celebrated at Philippi

in June, 1911.   Speaking on that occasion, Mr. Davis recalled the thrilling days of half a century past, and the
principles for which men then fought.   He also reviewed
the creation of the new State.   On this point he said:

"Many good people thought the act of creating West
Virginia out of a part of Virginia was harsh and illegal.
Previous to the war there was a feeling of discontent
among the people of what is now West Virginia.   They
felt that they were not being treated fairly in legislation,
and were compelled to pay heavy taxes on account of
internal and other improvements in what is now Virginia, while but a small part of the money so raised was
expended in the part which is now West Virginia.   As
it was also opposed to secession, bordering largely on the
free States of Pennsylvania and Ohio, it was ready for
the separation which came.   There seems to be something not altogether inappropriate or illogical in the fact
that the first battle of the Rebellion occurred in the only
State that was created by that conflict.

"Virginia is the only State that lost part of its territory in the Civil War.   In the days of the Revolution
it did more for our independence and liberty than any
other State in the Union.   It gave the country Washington, Jefferson, Madison, Henry, Marshall, and other
great men.   The State of West Virginia honors the old
State, and will always look upon her with the pride and
affection of a devoted daughter.

"A half century has elapsed since these beautiful hills
and valleys were occupied by hostile forces.   Long since
have the sounds of cannon ceased and the wounds of
conflict healed.   Soon, in the progress of time, as the
participants in these scenes pass away, the dark days of
1861 will become hallowed in memory, and their story
softened by romance and legend.   It is sufficient for

those of us who can remember them to know that the mellowing effects of time have already obliterated all animosity and that on all sides peace and good will prevail."

Mr. Davis's part in preparing for the Semi-Centennial celebration, and his active participation in it, are related in his journal with a brevity that gives no hint of the degree to which it embodied honors to him as the first citizen of the State—the Grand Old Man, as the orators and the newspapers insisted on calling him. These are the entries in the journal:

November 4, 1911. The West Virginia Semi-Centennial Commission appointed by Governor Glasscock met at Waldo Hotel, Clarksburg. Eleven of the fourteen commissioners attended. Governor Glasscock presided. Wheeling and Charleston ask for the celebration to be at their town; Wheeling selected by a vote of eight to two.

I presented a program of the intended celebration which, with a few amendments, was adopted. I was unanimously elected permanent chairman of the Commission, Secretary of State Reed vice-chairman, with the full understanding Reed was to do nearly all the work that naturally devolved on chairman.

May 29, 1913. Returned last evening from Wheeling, attending Semi-Centennial Commission meeting. I am chairman, which is giving me considerable work.

June 20. Went to Wheeling 18th to attend Semi-Centennial. Great crowd expected 20th, Statewide Day. Parade, State, national troops, cadets from State University, arch on streets, great display of flags. I presided at the great meeting and made half hour speech.

This account is the essence of modesty. The historian of the future would have to seek other sources to obtain a correct idea of what the celebration meant as a tribute to Henry G. Davis. They are found in the newspapers, in the official publications, and in the contemporary story of the Semi-Centennial as given in permanent form in the volumes published at the time. A program of the ceremonies was published in which the title page was an appreciation of Mr. Davis, as seen below:

THE GOLDEN JUBILEE OF WEST VIRGINIA
1863–1913
To the Hon. Henry G. Davis of Elkins
West Virginia's "Grand Old Man"
A prime factor in the development and progress of the State and the up-lift of its people, these pages are respectfully and appreciatively inscribed.

The newspapers in their special issues were full of appreciative tributes. In one of them by Roy B. Naylor, Secretary of the West Virginia Board of Trade, was this eulogy:

He came to what was then western Virginia as a young man with no capital save a clean heart, a clear brain, and a strong right arm. . . . To-day, in his ninetieth year, his face set towards the future with the enthusiasm of a man of thirty, well has he earned the title that fits him best, West Virginia's Grand Old Man, and justly is he regarded as one of the remarkable men of our times. In him we have the ideal citizen, vitally interested in all the activities of his State, a creator of wealth, a doer of good deeds, a Christian gentleman. With all the success that has come to him in every walk of life, he remains, as always, kindly, courteous, and unspoiled, with the mind of a master builder and the heart of a little child.

Another tribute, in verse, by Ignatius Brennan gave prominence to this thought:

He looms as a connecting-link of time—
   A link that starts when our domain was young,
Then stretches 'cross the cycle, so sublime,
   And joins all with a clime of every tongue.

Before the locomotive raced the rail;
Before the harnessed-lightning pierced the vale;
Before a thousand things of wondrous make—
He lived, and gave his being for their sake.

In the several addresses made during the celebration there were summaries of the moral, the material, and the civic progress of West Virginia in its fifty years of Statehood. The chief address on Statewide Day, June 20, was made by Mr. Davis himself, and in this speech he described both the moral and the material progress of the commonwealth. Among other things Mr. Davis said:

"The men whose faith and strength of purpose carried them forward to the formation of the State in times of great doubt and foreboding are those to whom we now pay honor. We come not so much to recount our achievements and to enjoy the sense of satisfaction they impart as to do deference to those who made possible the occasion of our pride. They builded better than they knew by bringing into being a State which, unlike themselves, lives on, and gathers strength as the years multiply, and yet while they live has grown greater than they anticipated, richer than they prophesied, stronger than they imagined, and more than fulfilled their brightest hopes.

"The physical features and natural riches of West Virginia have always been attractive and elusive. . . . The peaks and pinnacles and terraced mountainsides divide and distribute her waters with impartial favor. They give birth to the Potomac, which broadens into service for the capital of the nation, and mingle in the Chesapeake with those which have gone down through the historic James; to the north by the Cheat and Mo-

nongahela they reach at Pittsburgh the Ohio, and soon
join with the waters from the southwest of the Little
Kanawha. Nature has furnished the lines of a great
portion of the boundaries of the State in mountains
and streams, the Ohio River alone serving her well for
nearly three hundred miles along her border. The people of the State have inherited from its rugged nature a
spirit of freedom and self-reliance. They have cared
rather for the independence of its hills and valleys than
the interdependence of cities and towns.

"In 1860, about the time of the formation of the State,
the population was 376,000, or about fifteen persons to
each square mile. In 1870 it had grown to 420,000, and
in 1910 it reached 1,221,000, or an average of fifty persons to each square mile. It had a little more than
three times the population of fifty years ago."

After reviewing the agricultural and mineral wealth
of the State and the manufactures, Mr. Davis closed his
half-hour speech with this sentiment:

"Statistics of great variety could be produced to show
the health and prosperity of West Virginia, her present
high position, her rapid advance in all the material and
moral affairs of life, the happiness and ambitions of her
people; but facts are for moments of greater care. To-
day we put aside the sterner realities of life and lend
our thoughts and feelings to the spirit of the occasion.
We join with our neighbors and friends in making
merry, that we can with light hearts and cheerful mien
fittingly observe the day we celebrate. The State was
born in sentiment, and in sentiment let us remember
its birth. In our felicitations on West Virginia's fiftieth
birthday, an occasion fraught with pride in the accom-
plishments of the past, let us take advantage of the

golden opportunity and inaugurate to higher hopes and
greater aims the second half century of the State's history."

At night there was a banquet, which, notwithstanding
the fatigues of the day, Mr. Davis attended. He made
a brief speech expressing appreciation for the coöperation of Wheeling in the preparation and management of
the celebration. No one who listened to him on that
occasion could realize that he was in his ninetieth year.
He had all the energy and interest in his surroundings
of a man of fifty.

Among all the tributes to West Virginia and to the
men who had builded the new commonwealth, morally
and materially, who had molded its civic development
and laid the foundation for its educational institutions,
none reflected more truly the part which Henry G. Davis
had taken than that by Herbert Putnam in his poem,
"West Virginia," which was one of the features of the
celebration. These verses of Mr. Putnam's in particular
reflect the achievements and the aspirations of Mr.
Davis:

> To-day we celebrate
> The ripe achievements of our fifty years:—
> The mastery
> Of forest, field, and mine, the mill which rears
> Its bulk o'er many a stream, the forge and factory's
> Incessant hum,
> The railways linking mart to mart and home to home,
> The growth of trade in each emporium,
> And other wealth material that has come
> To bless
> Our subjugation of a wilderness,
> And mien undaunted in a time of stress:—
> All these we proudly sum.

The pride is just; but let it not ignore
Our progress in the things that count for more
  In strengthening a State
  Than wealth material won.
  Let it relate what we have done
To further Education, and promote
An understanding near of things remote.
  What may we claim
Of those fine civic traits which earn the name
  Of a great commonwealth,
And are the tokens of sound civic health?
Respect for law, to each his equal chance,
  For variant opinion, tolerance;
  Yet in the issues real
  That touch the common weal
Conscience implacable, that alike defies
The bribe, the threat, or coward compromise.

The more than fourscore years and ten of Mr. Davis's life prevented one tribute which West Virginia undoubtedly would have delighted to pay him as one of her foremost sons. This was a place in the Hall of Statuary in the Capitol at Washington. During his lifetime the two niches that are reserved for each State were filled by the statues of other citizens. It therefore remains for the State he loved so well to find some other means of showing her appreciation, perhaps by a statue at the Capitol in Charleston.

CHAPTER XIV

BENEFACTIONS AND PHILANTHROPIES

The habit of giving—Interest in free schools—Sentiment inspired by higher education—Permanent endowment for Davis and Elkins College—Contributions to religious objects—A home missionary's illuminating letter—Filial sentiment given expression in church edifice—Family affection exemplified in a Memorial hospital—Failure of plans for girls' industrial school—Realization of similar idea in Child's Shelter—Mr. Davis's deep personal interest in the homeless little ones—Belief in organized Christianity—Substantial support of Young Men's Christian Association—Eulogy of its methods.

THE pages that form this record might be called a chapter in practical philanthropy.

The habit of giving was with Mr. Davis a lifelong one, and the gifts in the earlier years were not always out of abundance. It was his practice to devote some part of his income to worthy purposes, religious, educational, and philanthropic. As his means increased he was able to make more ample provision, but it was never done indiscriminately. Professional charity-seekers found that when his aid was sought they must be able to show a reason for it, and also they must be able to make a satisfactory accounting. The careful business habits that found application in his private affairs were applied to benevolent purposes, and demoralizing and pauperizing effects of indiscriminate giving received no encouragement from him.

As his fortune grew he was able to make permanent

provision for several objects that appealed most deeply to him and awakened sentiments that rarely found expression in words. He did not believe in waiting until after death for his purposes to be realized, but rather preferred to lay the foundation himself and to contribute toward the current obligations, while at the same time making provision through endowment for carrying on the objects that had enlisted his sympathy. The principal ones were found recorded in his will, which provided endowments for them.

No subject appealed to Mr. Davis with greater force than that of education. The circumstances that had denied him the opportunities for schooling left a deep impress on him, and, in the numerous appeals that came to him for aid, a school in some remote section where the State agencies were difficult to be invoked seldom failed to obtain a response. Among his papers a letter here and there from some out-of-the-way corner conveying thanks for aid extended is the only record of some of his quiet benefactions. Here, for example, is one received from a hamlet in West Virginia a few months before his death, in which the writer says:

I received your check and letter last evening. Words fail to express my appreciation of the contribution you have made, but I say thank you with all my heart. Only God can reward such liberality to our country schools.

The sentiment that drew him to the communities in which he had lived found expression in an entry in his journal relating to Piedmont:

January 8, 1886. I have bought ground on which old Presbyterian Church stood. My intention is to build a free school building, to cost about $10,000, to be given to Piedmont as a high school; hope to commence the building this year.

Five years later a brief entry refers to a newspaper clipping in which is recited the set of resolutions adopted by the Board of Education of Piedmont accepting the deed of the school property and expressing the thanks of the Board and the citizens of Piedmont for the gift. This was the Davis free school.

When he was building railways and opening to settlement towns and villages, these grew faster than provision could be made under the school laws, and consequently he met the need of schooling in his usual practical way. At Henry, a mining town on the West Virginia Central Railroad, he built and gave to the people a brick schoolhouse, and at Davis he provided the larger part of the expense for a school building. When he was constructing the Coal and Coke Railway, and the new town of Gassaway sprang up, one of his first activities was to provide a schoolhouse. These cases illustrate in a quiet way his belief in the common schools, and his desire that the children of the people in the communities that developed from his mining and railway enterprises should be assured of educational privileges.

Higher education inspired Mr. Davis with the same sentiment that common-school education inspired. After the town of Elkins had been established the College Board of the Northern Presbyterian Church decided that this was an eligible place for a denominational institution of learning under the control of the Lexington Presbytery. They found Mr. Davis very sympathetic to the idea, and ready to provide for a substantial institution. Senator Elkins also took a deep interest in the plan and bore half the expense.

The two men gave the site for the campus, thirty acres, helped to make provision for the buildings, and contributed to the running expenses. In this manner Davis and Elkins College was established. The only condition made by Mr. Davis and Senator Elkins was that the Church should raise a like amount to the sum contributed by them. Mr. Davis also built a home for the president of the College.

The corner-stone of the principal building was laid in August, 1903, and in a few months the college itself was opened. From the beginning, Mr. Davis was its principal supporter. In 1911 he supplemented his previous gifts by an endowment of $100,000, conditioned on the college obtaining a similar sum. In his will the endowment was provided as a fund to be held perpetually in trust.

When the corner-stone was laid, Mr. Davis in a brief address declared his faith in higher education, especially Christian education, and this motive found expression in the inscription, "Erected for the advancement of Christian education. A. D., 1903."

A man of deep religious nature, it was natural that Mr. Davis should be a liberal contributor to religious objects, and in particular to the denomination with which he was all his life identified. But his benefactions were not bounded by denominational or sectarian lines. As in the case of schools, letters from out-of-the-way places, found among his papers, give evidence of his unostentatious gifts. One from the village of Granite, Maryland, back in 1880, incloses resolutions of the church and congregation thanking him for his munificent contribution.

There is a more significant letter which illustrates his ideas of practical Christianity. Apparently it was written in response to a communication received from him. The text follows:

The American Baptist Home Mission Society,
Rev. W. E. Powell, District Secretary, Kanawha District,
916 Swan Street,
Parkersburg, W. Va., January 11, 1898.

Hon. Henry G. Davis.
Washington, D. C.

My dear Sir and Brother:

After my kindest regards to you, I wish to say that the last
three months have been prolific in opportunities of doing good
with small sums of money ; and, following your advice, I have been
on the alert to help the worthy needy ones.

I found a student, a Christian young man, who had but one
hand, working his way through college, in great need of books.
Also two other young men, who had both graduated and are now
entering the ministry, both without means, and in great need of
books. I have bought $84.75 worth of good books and distributed
among these worthy young men.

I found a little church which had built a nice chapel at a cost
of $5,000. A debt of $500 has annoyed them much for several
years. They are making a heroic effort to pay off that debt, and
came to me for help, so I have promised them $50.

I found an old man, 3 years old, a true Christian, a Democrat,
who is proud of the fact that for over 70 years he has voted the
Democratic ticket. The old man was much troubled by a debt
of $10. I paid it for him, and he is happy as a child over this
help.

I found an aged Minister, seriously afflicted, and unable to pay
a debt of only $25. I paid this for him, and some smaller sums
have gone to help some orphan children.

The whole amount I have been able to appropriate by your
generosity during the last three months, is $184.60. These cases
were so urgent that I have advanced nearly all of this amount
out of my own funds.

I hope you will not feel that I have abused your kindness by
appropriating the $184.60. If you could have heard the earnest
words of thanks and seen the tears of joy as I have seen them, I
know your own heart would have been touched. There are so
many of these cases that I have not dared to attempt to help but
a few of the most needy. When convenient for you, I shall be

glad to receive your check for this amount, $184.60. Praying that the Lord may spare you many years yet to bless mankind by your kindly benefactions, I am,

Yours very truly,

W. E. POWELL.

Across the back of this letter is written in Mr. Davis's handwriting: "Check for the $184.60 sent to Mr. Powell."

The erection of church buildings was something that Mr. Davis liked to see in the new and growing communities along with schoolhouses. He rarely failed to respond to requests for aid for this purpose, regardless of denominational lines. At Gassaway he erected at his own expense a fine stone church for the Presbyterians. At Elkins he provided the colored Baptists with a commodious frame church. Other towns that owed their existence to his railway enterprises were aided in the same way.

Filial sentiment found expression in the erection at Elkins of a memorial church to his parents. In 1894, in conjunction with his brother, Thomas B. Davis, he determined to provide a memorial with the special thought of their mother, who had died in July, 1868, after having lived to see her children honored and respected in the communities in which they lived and well advanced on the road to success and prosperity. No monument to her memory could have been more fitting than that which her sons decided to erect—a church dedicated to the services to which she had been so much attached during her life. The handsome stone building was completed and dedicated in September, 1895.

The church was built of native light pink sandstone quarried near where it was erected. Stained Gothic windows setting forth subjects bearing upon the life of

Christ light the body of the edifice. A large triple window in the front, of stained glass set in lead, was the gift of Senator and Mrs. Elkins.

In his journal Mr. Davis tells very briefly of the event that was so full of meaning to him:

September 29, 1895. To-day Reverend Moses D. Hoge, of Richmond, dedicated the new stone church and Sunday-school at Elkins, donated by my brother Thomas and myself to Presbyterians in memory of our parents, especially mother.

Some newspaper clippings giving an account of the dedication ceremonies are attached to the journal entry. Sixteen years later, in October, 1911, the formal presentation of the church to the Presbyterians of Elkins was made by Mr. Davis as a part of special dedicatory services. In presenting the deed and keys, Mr. Davis paid a beautiful tribute to the memory of his wife, saying the church was a slight tribute to the memory of one whom he loved dearly, and with whom he lived happily for nearly fifty years. He also paid a tender tribute to his mother, to whose teachings he gave the credit for anything he might have accomplished.

The deepest family affection often found expression with Mr. Davis in some form of practical philanthropy. An illustration of this was the hospital erected at Elkins as a memorial to the eldest son, Henry G. Davis, Jr., who was lost at sea. It was the joint tribute of Mrs. Davis and himself. It represented their idea of doing good in an enduring way.

The hospital was begun in the winter of 1902. A handsome building of stone and brick, roofed with red slate, was constructed. It consists of a central octagonal building, with two wings so arranged as to receive the greatest possible amount of sunlight. The hospital throughout is fitted with the most modern appliances and conveniences. Mrs. Davis did not live to see it completed, and after her death special memorial services were held for her in the building.

In his will Mr. Davis provided a permanent endowment for the maintenance of the hospital, to be supplemented by such income and contributions as it may receive from other sources. It serves a wide region in which are railway shops, coal-mines, and factories, and provides facilities for the sick and injured which otherwise would be unavailable except at Baltimore or other large cities. Its location in a section that otherwise would have been left without the advantages of modern medical researches and their application was one of many instances of Mr. Davis's thoughtfulness in his charities.

Recalling his own struggles in early youth, and the cares that fell upon his mother and her children, Mr. Davis's sympathies always went out strongly to orphans and dependent children, and particularly to girls who lacked the means of obtaining a practical education. A cherished intention of his was to provide an industrial school for girls. This feeling found utterance in a letter addressed to Governor MacCorkle in January, 1895. In this letter he said:

I feel a deep interest in the education and training of young girls, especially in West Virginia, whose circumstances and surroundings would prevent them from securing such advantages. We ought to have a State institution where girls could, at small expense, be able to receive such education and industrial training as would better fit them for the affairs of life and enable them to become teachers, clerks, telegraph operators, &c. thus making them self-supporting and of greater benefit to the State.

He followed this suggestion by a proposition that if the State would establish an institution for the purpose named, and make an annual appropriation sufficient for its support, he would give $50,000 and suitable grounds. Governor MacCorkle, in acknowledging the proposition, spoke of it as magnificent, and promptly submitted it to the Legislature. Mr. Davis expected that the institution would be located at Davis or Elkins, and some opposition was manifested on that account. Other causes also prevented the Legislature from taking action; but, though he was not able to carry out the idea in this form, he gave substantial expression to it in another manner which reflected his deep human sympathies and the trend of his charitable impulses. This was by the creation of the Child's Shelter.

The Children's Society of West Virginia was doing the best it could with limited means to rescue children from unfortunate surroundings and find suitable homes for them. Mr. Davis met the emergency in his usual practical way. In the winter of 1899–1900, he bought property in the city of Charleston, consisting of a large brick building with sufficient grounds, and presented it to the society. This gift he supplemented by a monthly contribution for the maintenance of the Home, and this contribution continued regularly through a period of seventeen years, to the end of his life.

The Home was dedicated with appropriate ceremonies over which Governor Atkinson presided. The Governor paid a fitting tribute to Mr. Davis and the impetus that his generosity would give to carrying on the work of the Society. Hon. George E. Price, as trustee and representative of Mr. Davis, formally presented the keys to the Child's Shelter to Governor Atkinson, which the Governor in turn presented to the superintendent, Dr.

Thomas Comstock. The gift, Mr. Price said, was a deed of kindness that would live forever.

Mr. Davis's own account of his interest in the Home is given with customary brevity in several entries in his journal, most of which are explanatory of newspaper clippings that are attached. He recites:

March 1, 1900. I to-day paid draft for $9,500, to pay for what is known as Bodkin property on Washington Street, about one and one half squares from State Capitol, for use of Children's Home for helpless children. I am to expend $1,000 to $1,500 in improvements and repairs, and also contribute $1,000 per annum to support the Home.

The canceled draft is attached to this entry. It is one of the few instances in which Mr. Davis kept a souvenir of his benefactions. The permanent endowment for the Home or Child's Shelter, provided in his will, assured it a definite monthly income to supplement what it obtains from other sources. When in Charleston he never failed to visit the Shelter, and the hundreds of little ones were a constant reminder of the good he had been able to do. During the years in which he lived to direct his own benefaction to it, a thousand homeless children were received and cared for while they were growing into useful men and women under its fostering care. That its usefulness should be continuous was his guiding thought in the provision for permanent endowment.

There were many gifts and benefactions which received only passing comment in the entries he made in his journal from time to time, and these were usually explanatory of newspaper clippings that were attached. To the town of Elkins he and Senator Elkins presented a park.

The Odd Fellows' Lodges received during his lifetime various gifts, and these were supplemented in his will by endowments that insured some income for the Grand Lodge of the State and the Elkins Lodge. A similar provision was made for the Masonic Order at Elkins.

Mr. Davis believed in organized Christianity, or Christianity at work. It was perhaps for that reason that his journal shows numerous evidences of both his sentimental and his substantial interest in the work of the Young Men's Christian Association. He occasionally delivered addresses to the members of the Association in different parts of the State. In an address at Parkersburg in October, 1905, he commended especially the erection of a Y. M. C. A. building, the first to be put up in the State, as a good example for other towns. "The Sunday-school, the Y. M. C. A., and the church," he said, "are the three great agencies for good." And he concluded, "You can depend upon me for personal and financial aid." It need hardly be stated that the aid was quickly forthcoming.

The permanent form in which Mr. Davis showed his faith in working Christianity is to be found at the capital of the State. In 1906 he bought the property adjoining the park that he previously had presented to the city of Charleston, and presented this to the Association, which erected on it a commodious building. He supplemented this gift by further contributions, and he took the greatest interest in the work. In October, 1911, writing to Mr. W. B. Mathews, chairman of the program committee, he gave this analysis of the aspirations and the functions of the Young Men's Christian Association:

"The planning and erection of this splendid building was an undertaking worthy of any community, and its completion reflects great credit upon the citizens of

Charleston. It is essentially a tangible expression of the best impulses, of the highest attributes, and of the most ennobling traits of the good people of your city. It is a monument to unselfishness and an inspiration to the highest and best motives of mankind. With an administration building so commodious and complete in all its appointments, much should be accomplished by the Association in bringing within its fold the young men of Charleston, upon whom, more than upon all else, depends its future material and moral welfare.

"The youth of to-day is the citizen of to-morrow, and he will be helpful or helpless according to the light he has and the path he treads. No better beacon to guide his footsteps than the controlling influences of the Y. M. C. A. At the capital of the State it is most fitting that this, perhaps the greatest in its sphere of the moral agencies of the present time, should be appropriately, even liberally, represented, and I congratulate the people of Charleston upon the successful issue of a campaign undivided in sentiment and compact in result. My earnest prayers go out for those engaged in the great work of fortifying young men against the temptation of evil ways, and of strengthening them in the mental, physical, and spiritual relations of life."

Instances of the sentiment that was mingled with his practical suggestions could be multiplied, but enough has been recited to show the character of his benefactions and philanthropies. They were wide embracing.

CHAPTER XV

FAMILY AND KINDRED

Deeply rooted affections of Mr. Davis—Sentiment for the ancestral home Goodfellowship—Recalling the children of Caleb Davis and Louisa Brown—The four brothers—The tie between Henry and Thomas—A brother's tribute—Friendship for his cousin, Arthur P. Gorman—Warm eulogy of Senator Elkins, his son-in-law—Children of Henry G. Davis and Kate Bantz—Marriages, births, and deaths—Loss of eldest son at sea—Fifty years of ideal married life—Death of Mrs. Davis—The final resting-place.

FAMILY affection was deeply rooted in the nature of Henry G. Davis. It found expression in a hundred ways. His reverence for his mother was one of the most attractive traits of a strong character. She lived with him until her death, and there is nothing more beautiful than the many tokens of devotion that appear in all his acts during that period and afterward. To her he attributed many of the qualities that made him a successful man. After he built the hospital at Elkins, he directed that a portrait of his mother be hung in one of the hallways, and he never visited the institution without pausing before it.

This love for his mother was interwoven with the deep sentiment that he felt for the place which had been her home and the home of her ancestors, as well as of his father's ancestors.

The old homestead in Woodstock and the Goodfellowship estate were cherished memories with him which he sought to perpetuate. His journal contains several accounts of visits to it. In the summer of 1879 he records:

I meet brother John in Baltimore, and he and I drive out Frederick pike through Ellicott's Mills to Uncle John's and Sam's. We make a visit to our old homestead and father's grave. Many of the old landmarks are there, and many gone. The visit brings back recollections of old. We visit Woodstock. Things look small to us. We meet Cousin Arthur Gorman and Dr. Watkins at Uncle John's, and Kitty Hood Faithful meets us. We return same day, John to Richmond, I to Washington.

Again, in November, 1886, he writes:

Grace, Harry, and John, my children and I, went out to Woodstock, our old home; look over the ground where I used to play when a boy. Dined with Uncle John Brown, and returned to Baltimore same evening.

The sentiment attaching to the home of his mother and his father, and the yearning to make it a perpetual family possession, finds expression in the journal entry of March 15, 1904:

My brother Thomas and I have bought grandmother's old farm, Goodfellowship, near Woodstock, Maryland, 170 acres. We deed it to our cousin, William Howard Brown, in fee, with provision in deed that it is to always remain in name of Brown of our blood. The old place has been in mother's family, Brown, since the days of Lord Baltimore, and we wish it to stay for all time.

Unfortunately for this aspiration, a court decision after Mr. Davis's death declared against the provision of family ownership in perpetuity. Yet it is not likely that Goodfellowship ever will be allowed to pass to strangers.

Memories of Goodfellowship naturally carry the mind back to the family of Caleb Davis. There was a child by the first marriage, Nathan by name, who died in infancy, and this was the only step-brother of Henry G. Davis. A full sister, Elizabeth, also died in infancy. Another sister, Eliza, grew to womanhood, married Upton Buxton, and after she became a widow lived with her bachelor brother, Thomas, at Keyser. Mr. Davis was exceedingly fond of her, and there are many evidences of the warm feeling of kinship between them.

The youngest of the four sons of Caleb Davis and Louisa Brown was William R. Davis, who was the first to pass away. It has been told in an earlier chapter how the brothers Henry and Thomas aided him in his education and then took him into the firm of H. G. Davis & Brothers. He was identified with the mercantile activities of the firm and with the development enterprises in the upper Potomac for nearly twenty years. He died at Deer Park in March, 1879.

John B. Davis, the eldest brother, was a very successful business man, but he did not become identified with the coal and timber and railway projects of his brothers. In early life he went to Richmond, established himself in business, and became identified as a banker with the chief city of the Old Dominion. He died in 1889. Mr. Davis, with Mrs. Davis and Thomas B. Davis, was summoned to Richmond, but did not reach there until after his death. An entry in Mr. Davis's journal gives a kindly impression of the bond that existed between the brothers, although they had not been closely associated after they left the paternal home at Woodstock:

February 14, 1889. Mrs. Davis and I returned late last night from Richmond. We went down Tuesday morning. My brother Tom was with us. John died Monday morning about three o'clock. He was one of the best and kindest of men. All who knew him thought well of him. I feel the death deeply.

The affection between the two brothers, Henry and Thomas, was one of extraordinary depth. Thomas was younger by only five years, so that their lives ran almost evenly together. Both had shared the privations following the loss of the family fortune; both had worked on the Baltimore and Ohio Railroad, and together they had started in business in the upper Potomac country. Their business relations continued until the end, but Thomas always referred to Henry as the leader in their enterprises, which was the fact. Together they cleared the timberlands, developed coal-mines, and opened railways.

Their interest in public affairs also ran parallel. During the public life of Henry G., Colonel Tom, as he was called, who had less liking for politics, took the most intense personal interest in the elder's career. When Henry ceased to hold public position, Colonel Tom, largely through his urging, occasionally ran for office, sometimes successfully, sometimes unsuccessfully. He served as a member of the West Virginia Legislature for one term, and later was elected to the House of Representatives. In acknowledging a telegram from Henry congratulating him on his election to Congress, Colonel Tom responded: "Thank you, Henry; I owe it principally to you." This was true.

Colonel Tom maintained his home at Keyser, and the elder brother spent much time there. During one of his winters in Congress they took rooms together at a Washington hotel. Their business relations naturally kept them in close touch each with the other, but this intercourse was not enough to satisfy them. When they were apart daily letters were exchanged.

Thomas B. Davis died at Keyser on November 26, 1911, in his eighty-third year. The elder brother went at once to Keyser and arranged for the burial at Elkins, "near where I expect to be buried." And it was at Elkins that Thomas B. Davis was buried. A brother's tribute to a brother is found in an unusual document, that is, in the will of Henry G. Davis. It is thus given in his own language:

> When we were all young men my brothers Thomas B. Davis and William R. Davis and myself entered into business together under the name of H. G. Davis & Co., which continued until the death of my brother William, when the firm became H. G. Davis & Bro., and so remained until the death of my brother Thomas on November 26, 1911, leaving me the surviving partner of the firm, although the eldest born of the three original members thereof. During all this long period of partnership my brothers and I were in full accord in all our dealings; all our relations both business and personal were always harmonious and pleasant; and I wish to record here especially my appreciation of the generous and sympathetic coöperation of my brother Thomas, who long survived William, in all our business affairs extending over fifty years, and to speak of the affection and regard in which I held him and which endured and increased during this long association.

For his cousin, Arthur Pue Gorman, Mr. Davis entertained a friendship that was profound. Mr. Gorman was the son of his mother's younger sister, Elizabeth A. Brown, and Peter Gorman. He was born at Woodstock, and, though younger than Henry G. Davis, they were thrown much together in their early life. Later they came to be intimately associated in politics and business. This intimate relation was one of unbounded trust and confidence on the part of both.

Davis had a keen appreciation of Gorman's political acumen, and thought very highly also of his business qualities. Gorman, on his part, understood the character of Henry G. Davis as few men did, and probably possessed a greater influence over him than did anybody with whom he was associated throughout his long life. He knew the roots of that strong individuality; but, like others, he usually preferred to accept Senator Davis as the leader and regarded himself as a follower.

The letters interchanged between the two men show how strong was the bond between them. Usually they were signed "Your friend and cousin." There were many communications of this kind of a purely personal character, but there were also some of a political nature. In the account given of his public life it is shown how highly Senator Davis regarded Gorman, even to the hope of helping to make him President. The intimate personal relation has more human interest. In September, 1899, Mr. Davis's journal entry records a visit of two days "to my cousin and friend Hon. A. P. Gorman at his home near Laurel, Maryland," and there were numerous other visits of this kind.

When Senator Gorman died in June, 1906, Mr. Davis, in recording the event, gives some indication of his own feelings:

Received several telegrams telling me of death of Senator Gorman. Our mothers were sisters. The Senator was serving his fifth term in Senate, and was one of the leaders in Senate and country. A trusted Democrat. He leaves many, very many friends.

For another man who filled a large place in his day and generation, not of kin by blood, but by marriage, Mr. Davis conceived a friendship that was deep and strong. This was Stephen B. Elkins. Both were men of marked individuality, but in many respects their characters were directly contrary. They were opposed in politics, and each filled high positions of trust and honor bestowed on him when his party was in power. Naturally, this brought them into conflict during heated political campaigns, yet it never was allowed to alienate them even temporarily.   In business they were associated for more than thirty years and they worked harmoniously together.   In their family relations there was the warmest sympathy.   When Senator Elkins died in Washington, early in January, 1911, Mr. Davis, in his journal entry, put in a single striking sentence his estimate of his son-in-law:

Elkins was a noble, generous, brainy, and talented man.

Marriages, births, deaths—these are the records of every life.   The marriage of Henry G. Davis and Kate Bantz at Frederick, in 1853, has been told in preceding pages.   Eight children were born of this marriage, three of whom died in infancy.   Those who grew to womanhood and manhood were Hallie, Henry, Kate, Grace, and John.   Hallie was married to Hon. Stephen B. Elkins at Baltimore, in April, 1875.   Kate was married to Lieutenant M. R. G. Brown of the Navy at Washington, in 1886.   John was married to Bessie J. Armstead of Brooklyn, New York, at Brooklyn, in November, 1897.   Grace was married to Arthur Lee of Richmond at Elkins, in September, 1898.   From these unions sprang the group of grandchildren, the delight of Senator Davis in his advancing years, for whom he showed his fondness in a thousand ways.

Of the children who grew up, the first shadow came when Henry, the eldest son, was lost at sea.   Possessed of a wandering disposition, he showed an inclination for the sailor's life.   In 1892 he made a voyage to Libau, Russia, on the *Missouri,* a big ship loaded with grain for the relief of the sufferers from the great famine which at that time gripped with starvation the population of one section of the Czar's empire. Some years later he embarked on a voyage on a sailing vessel to South Africa, in the hope of regaining failing health. He took passage on the *Monkeston* from New York for Cape Colony, and started to return on the same vessel. This was in April, 1896. Early in May the family received a cablegram from Mt. Vincent, West Africa, saying that the son had been drowned. When the full particulars were received later it was learned that he had been swept overboard during a storm. He was twenty-six years old at the time of his death. The blow was a severe one for his father and mother, but it was accepted with Christian fortitude.

Kate, the second daughter, died in Washington in January, 1903, after a brief illness. Her husband, Lieutenant Commander Brown, died four years later. A bright page in his naval record was his heroic service on the *Trenton* at Samoa during the hurricane in 1889.

The record of the life comradeship of Mr. Davis and his wife is too sacred to be written in its intimate character. Mrs. Davis was a woman of keen intellect and of sprightly disposition. Temperamentally, in many respects she was the opposite of her husband. She was, nevertheless, in full sympathy with his aspirations and his ambitions. She cared less for the social side of public life than for her own family circle, but she never failed to maintain herself in a manner fitting the public responsibilities of Mr. Davis. The men and women with whom they were associated during his terms in the United States Senate and afterward always found the hospitality of the Davis home made the more congenial by the hostess.

Mrs. Davis was her husband's companion on many of his trips, both at home and abroad. She maintained the

family homestead at Piedmont during the early years
of his business career, but her greatest delight was in
the summer home at Deer Park. An entry in the journal of Mr. Davis gives the story of an anniversary in
their married life:

February 22, 1878. This is the twenty-fifth or our silver-wed-
ding-day. Time has passed so rapidly that it appears but a short
time since our marriage, yet we have two grandchildren.

We celebrate our twenty-fifth anniversary of marriage by giving a dinner at our rented house and home for the winter; dinner
at six o'clock. Present, Judge and Mrs. A. G. Thurman of Ohio;
Mr. and Mrs. William Keyser and Mr. and Mrs. Alex. G. Shaw
of Baltimore; Governor Mathews of West Virginia; Hon. A. P.
Gorman; Mr. C. F. Mayer, Baltimore; T. S. Bantz (Mrs. Davis's
brother); Mr. and Mrs. Elkins (our family); Katie, daughter,
and ourselves, making in all fifteen persons.

After the lapse of nearly a quarter of a century they
were looking forward to the celebration of another anniversary, their golden wedding; but this happiness was
denied them. Mrs. Davis was taken ill in the early winter of 1902, at the family home in Elkins. Her illness
was alarming, and in a few days hope was abandoned.
She died on the morning of December 10, surrounded by
the family. The tribute paid her by her husband in his
journal may be transcribed only in part, a sentence which
illustrates a strong man's ideal of married life:

We loved and honored each other dearly, and tried to so live
and act as to make each happy.

That family and kindred might be together in death
as in life was a deeply fixed sentiment with Mr. Davis.
This sentiment found expression in the mausoleum he
provided in Maplewood Cemetery at Elkins. He caused
to be erected there a granite monument to the memory of
his father and mother, with the dates and names of their

children.   The monument adjoins that of Stephen B. Elkins' family.   The remains of his mother were removed to this cemetery.   His brother Thomas was buried there, as was Lieutenant Commander Brown, beside his wife, Kate, the Davises' second daughter.   Of his own wife, Mr. Davis recorded in his journal:

Buried at Maplewood Cemetery near Elkins, W. Va., which is to be our family's final resting-place.

CHAPTER XVI

THE names of public men after they are gone float swiftly down the stream of oblivion. Later generations recall few of them. Yet in certain periods there are groups of these men whose memories do not so quickly vanish. Great events produce them. Mr. Davis served in the Senate of the United States at a time when there were many giants among his contemporaries. The names of some of these and the parts they played in the drama of national life begin to fade. The story of that period as told in previous chapters may be retold only to show his own intimate relation with some of them.

Allen G. Thurman of Ohio was the sturdy oak of the National Democratic party in the era following the Civil War. For ten years the two were colleagues in the

Davis Memorial Church at Elkins

Davis Memorial Hospital at Elkins

Senate and their associations were of the most intimate character. Davis admired and revered Senator Thurman's intellect. Thurman had the greatest confidence in the judgment of Senator Davis, leaned on him in matters of party tactics and in personal affairs, and always called him affectionately by his first name. What "Henry" thought about some question of political strategy, and where "Henry" was when Thurman himself was under some great personal strain, was always the inquiry of the Ohio leader of the Democracy.

Carl Schurz was another figure of note when Mr. Davis first entered the Senate. The cold analytic intellect and the German mind of Mr. Schurz with its destructive criticism would not appear to have attraction for the matter-of-fact intellect and the constructive mind of Senator Davis; but, while there was no intimacy between the two men, there was a mutual respect which brought them into friendly relations and continued after Mr. Schurz entered the Cabinet of President Hayes.

John Sherman had a genuine liking for Senator Davis. While they quarreled in the Senate over Treasury bookkeeping and over financial questions, Sherman had great respect for Davis's opinions and frequently consulted him on fiscal subjects, sometimes writing for his views and sometimes seeking the opportunity of a personal talk. He was occasionally the guest of Senator Davis at Deer Park, and on those occasions other guests observed a warmth of sympathy that seemed to be drawn out by Mr. Davis himself.

Among all the men who were in the Senate as his colleagues, Senator Davis was drawn to William Windom of Minnesota as to few others. They served together on the same committees, and were of kindred minds in the fiscal and other subjects of legislation which required knowledge of economics in the broadest sense. Senator Windom was associated with Mr. Davis in his business enterprises, and there was no one on whose judgment Mr. Davis was willing to defer so much as to him. When Mr. Windom was Secretary of the Treasury under President Harrison they were frequently together, and Mr. Davis probably had more to do than was generally known with shaping certain Treasury policies. Mr. Davis's estimate of his former colleague is given in two entries in his journal:

January 30, 1891. This morning the country was shocked and surprised at the sudden death of Secretary of the Treasury, Hon. William Windom. He had just delivered a speech at annual dinner of New York Board of Trade, and in five minutes after finishing was dead. He was a good, valuable man, and my close friend. He was four years my junior. I served in Senate with him and had respect and affection for him. I attended funeral as one of the family.

A newspaper clipping, accompanying a picture of Secretary Windom, gave occasion for this comment:

This is very good of my friend Windom; he was a noble and good man. The world is better that Windom lived in it.

The friendship between James G. Blaine and Henry G. Davis has been shown in many paragraphs in these pages. Mr. Davis felt the magnetic qualities of Mr. Blaine, as he had felt those of Henry Clay, but there was something beyond these personal qualities. It was not, on Mr. Davis's part, based entirely on respect for Mr. Blaine's knowledge of public questions, for he did not hesitate to criticize the great Republican leader. Though he had a great admiration for Mr. Blaine's intellect, he was distrustful of his brilliancy. Their friendship began when they were colleagues in the Senate.

Sometimes sharply differing on public questions from his party colleagues, Mr. Blaine was not without sympathy with attacks made by Senator Davis on the position maintained by them, and it is more than tradition that on one occasion he helped Senator Davis "round out" a speech that was somewhat disturbing to several of the Republican leaders in the Senate. The social intimacy of the two men was cemented by close business associations. It was, however, as a contemporary of Senator Davis, who to Mr. Blaine represented the embodiment of common sense, that in his "Twenty Years of Congress" he summed up the salient traits of Mr. Davis's character as a public man.

Thomas F. Bayard of Delaware was a contemporary who filled a large space in public life during the periods when Mr. Davis also was prominent. The scholarly Senator from Delaware was strongly drawn to the rugged Senator from West Virginia. Yet, though belonging to the same political organization, they frequently held strongly divergent views on public questions. Senator Bayard, in his association with Mr. Davis in railway enterprises, relied entirely on the latter's judgment. While Secretary of State during President Cleveland's first administration and Ambassador to Great Britain during the second administration, he never failed to keep in touch with his former colleagues.

William B. Allison of Iowa, who for a quarter of a century dominated the expenditures of the National Government through his chairmanship a part of the time of the powerful Appropriations Committee, and the remainder of the time through his general knowledge and his personality, was one of the contemporaries to whom Senator Davis was closely drawn. They had much in common. Senator Allison, as a legislator with a very practical mind, could appreciate and did appreciate the same qualities in Senator Davis. They worked together harmoniously in committee, and on the floor of the Senate they usually were found in complete sympathy in whatever related to the expenditures of the Government. Until the close of his life, Senator Allison always welcomed a visit from Mr. Davis after the latter had ceased to be a Senator.

William A. Wheeler, in his day an influential member of Congress who left his impress on the period in which he served, was another contemporary for whom Mr. Davis cherished a warm regard. Few now recall that he was Vice-President when Rutherford B. Hayes was President, and presided over the Senate with a grace and impartiality that disarmed partizan hostility. A hint of their friendship is given in the journal entries of Senator Davis when he records that Vice-President Wheeler frequently called him to the chair.

Vice-President Thomas A. Hendricks was a contemporary of his own political faith with whom his relations, while not intimate, were friendly, although he was not in the Senate during the brief period that Mr. Hendricks served as Vice-President before death called him. They had met at Democratic National Conventions and had had some association in campaign management. When Grover Cleveland was nominated for President and the selection for Vice-President lay between Mr. Hendricks and Mr. Davis, he had advised the selection of Hendricks. Mr. Davis had a warm admiration for Hendricks as one of the principal intellectual forces of the Democratic party. His personal regard was shown when he named one of the stations on his railway, Hendricks.

President Benjamin Harrison was the contemporary who of all public men received from Mr. Davis the greatest meed of respect for his intellectual qualities and his capacity as a political leader. Their service in the Senate did not run parallel for a long period, since General Harrison entered it when Senator Davis was closing his term. But the two men were attracted to each other from their first meeting. That the friendship between them developed into the closest kind of social intimacy has been shown in the chapters on Deer Park and on the political activities of Mr. Davis. He often commented on the grasp that President Harrison had on governmental affairs and the clearness with which he formulated political principles.

General Harrison, on his part, confessed a definite lack of ability when it came to his own business affairs, and he would turn to Mr. Davis for advice regarding private investments. He also had great respect for the judgment of Mr. Davis in public matters, and he did not hesitate to seek it, regardless of party differences, even to the composition of his Cabinet. It gave him much satisfaction when in a non-political appointment he was able to honor the Senator by designating him as one of the delegates to the First International American Conference. When new issues arose, growing out of the Spanish-American War, the two men found themselves in sympathy. General Harrison was among the elder statesmen of the Republican party who were not in accord with the Philippine policy and who distrusted the possibility of imperialism. Mr. Davis was also distrustful of the Philippines and of the imperialistic tendencies. They corresponded on the subject.

In the field of international affairs there was one contemporary of whom Mr. Davis was intensely appreciative. This was Porfirio Diaz of Mexico. When he visited Mexico in 1895 he was already known for his identification with the Pan-American Railway project. He had helped to initiate it in the International American Conference and had been active in the Intercontinental Survey. Mexico, as one of the countries on the intercontinental trunk line route, was interested in the general subject. It was also interested in railway construction as a means of internal development and political stability. Something was known by President Diaz of Henry G. Davis as a railway builder and as the exponent of an idea. They had several interviews, and through the President of Mexico Mr. Davis learned something of the Diaz policy.

Seven years later, when, as the chairman of the American Delegation to the Mexican Conference, he was enabled to give more definite shape to the Pan-American Railway project, Mr. Davis received the heartiest cooperation from President Diaz, who took a personal interest in furthering his plans. After Mr. Davis's return to the United States, President Diaz never failed to make inquiries regarding his activities, and occasionally he transmitted personal messages.

Mr. Davis found occasion to give his estimate of Porfirio Diaz in a book that was published a short time before the revolutionary storm broke over Mexico. He wrote in 1910:

General Diaz is a striking and commanding figure in modern times. Probably no country during the past century has felt the influence of any one man more than Mexico has of General Diaz. Although a soldier both by profession and nature, whose military services had been of the highest order, yet his greatest victo-

ries have been in the direction of peace and tranquillity. . . .
Under his forcible and effective administration of affairs the
people have advanced in all lines of domestic and commercial
welfare, and the Republic has been brought to a much higher
plane in the sisterhood of nations.   His personal character and executive strength have been a guaranty of the safety of foreign
capital, the introduction of which has done so much to aid in the
development of the country's wonderful mineral and other resources.   One may speak of almost any country of the world
without anyone predominating therein, but Mexico and Diaz are
inseparable.   He has built so well that I am sure the foundation
he has laid will endure, and that Mexico will continue under his
successors in the march of progress in which he has so masterfully
led it.

Events showed that Mr. Davis's judgment was at fault
regarding stable conditions in Mexico.   He lived to see
President Diaz, a contemporary whose life ran almost
parallel with his own, driven into exile and death.
Sometimes he commented on this tragic occurrence, but
it did not change his estimate of Porfirio Diaz and the
good that Diaz had wrought for Mexico.

Contemporary events as well as contemporary men
were recorded by Mr. Davis.   What more vivid picture
of a momentous episode in the history of the United
States than this page from his journal:

March 31, 1898.   For about a month the country has been in
an excited state about the U. S. and Spain question, Cuban independence, and the blowing up of the *Maine* in Havana harbor.
Best informed men think probabilities of war about equal.   President McKinley, Speaker Reed, Senator Elkins, are what is termed
peace men.

April 13, 1898.   Much excitement in the country generally
about war between U. S. and Spain in regard to independence of
Cuba.   Chances of war and peace about equal.

April 20, 1898.   War has commenced between U. S. and Spain.
War caused by Spain's brutal war on the Cubans, who are fight-

ing for their liberty and right of self-government. Also, blowing up of U. S. war vessel *Maine* in harbor of Havana. Official date of war is April 21, 1898.

May 10, 1898. On 1st inst Com. Dewey's great naval victory at Manila. Country in great enthusiasm over Dewey victory. 125,000 volunteers for war called, 600,000 offer. Com. Sampson gone with ships to Porto Rico, expect news of fighting soon.

May 16, 1898. U. S. and Spain war preparations going on rapidly. Naval battle daily expected off Cuba.

August 12, 1898. Protocol of peace between U. S. and Spain signed by French Minister Cambon for Spain and Secretary Day for U. S. President McKinley issued proclamation of peace.

Among Mr. Davis's contemporaries, entirely outside of the list of public men and political leaders, was W. W. Corcoran, the Washington banker and philanthropist. Mr. Corcoran was a few years older, but his life covered nearly the same period in its earlier activities as did that of Mr. Davis. The foundation of his fortune was laid during the Mexican War in the loan negotiated for the Government, and he rarely ventured beyond this field of financing; but he was sympathetic with the constructive enterprises of Mr. Davis. Their social relations were of the closest character, and when one of Mr. Corcoran's most notable charities, the Louise Home for indigent gentlewomen, was dedicated, he insisted on the presence of Mrs. Davis as a special guest.

Andrew Carnegie was a contemporary whom Mr. Davis looked up to with something akin to reverence, and on his part Mr. Carnegie regarded Mr. Davis as a distinctive figure in national history. Their constructive work and industry may have been the sympathetic bond on which their friendship was based. Their real kindredship found expression in their mutual interest in the Pan-American countries, and in particular in the

Pan-American Railway project. They worked together for this project at the First International American Conference, and when the Second Conference at Mexico provided for the permanent Pan-American Railway Committee, with Mr. Davis as its chairman, his first request was that Mr. Carnegie serve on the Committee with him. This Mr. Carnegie did.

Whenever he was in Washington he took time to call on "The Senator," as he always designated Mr. Davis. Many letters were interchanged between them. A characteristic letter related to the Pan-American Railway project. It was written at a time when Mr. Davis felt that governmental agencies in furthering this project were somewhat too slow and might be hastened by the aid of private enterprise:

My dear Mr. Chairman:

Yours of January 31st received. I can only repeat that the railway extension proposed is a wise missionary effort and I shall be glad to join your syndicate. You cannot engage in a nobler work and we youngsters all take heart when we see the old veteran with his coat off.

With best wishes,

Always very truly yours,
Andrew Carnegie.

Much of the life and times of Henry G. Davis, as it has been written, relates to his work as a railway builder. A supplemental chapter might be written on his relations with his railway contemporaries, the leading men of two generations, and of his observations on events that formed important periods in railway history. Nothing is more vivid than the brief description in his journal of the greatest railway strike in the history of the country. The whole story is found in these entries, which form a contemporary account:

July 16, 1877. The other trunk lines having made a reduction of ten per cent. of all employees, the Baltimore & Ohio gives notice they will do the same, taking effect to-day. The brakemen and firemen strike, commencing at Baltimore and Martinsburg. It soon extends all over the road, and no freight trains are allowed to run by the strikers; mail and passenger trains run as usual.

July 18, 1877. Governor Mathews of West Va. resisted calling on Federal Government for troops as long as safety to property would allow. He called on 18th. At Baltimore there were a number of lives lost. Mob stoned military when called out and on way to Camden depot. The troops fired on mob, killing about twenty.

July 22, 1877. Strike on B. & O. continues. All is quiet on this road, only passenger trains are run. Strike commences on Pa. Central road at Pittsburgh on 20th. It is becoming very alarming. Many persons are killed. Some of the military are among the killed.

July 21, 1877. Mob, including railroad strikers and many others (women and children included), have complete possession of Pittsburgh. Nearly all the property of Pa. Central Railroad is destroyed, among which is nearly three or four thousand cars and contents, 120 or 130 engines, shops, roundhouses, depots, etc., estimated loss $8,000,000.

July 22, 1877. Strike has become nearly general on railroads in the country. Only day passenger trains now run on B. & O., and most of the other roads.

July 23, 1877. Strike continues and is now general all over the country. There has been a great deal of property destroyed, especially at Pittsburgh.

Some of his experiences, however, were not recorded in his journal, but were told on the rare occasions when he was in a reminiscent vein. One incident, which it always pleased him to recall, related to the era when the railway president usually was the man whose individuality and force had made him such and who consequently dominated the policy of the company. It was the age of the railway autocrats. One of these who left a large impress on the history of the country was John W. Garrett, president of the Baltimore and Ohio.

Long after Mr. Davis had left the employ of this company, and when he had important lumber and coal contracts with it, he went to Baltimore to see about a new contract involving some important operations. With his customary business forethought he had the document drawn up in legal form with a view to saving time. He went over the provisions with President Garrett, who was satisfied with them, and then suggested that when the Board of Directors held their next meeting they should approve it and enable him to go forward with the work.

"Davis," said President Garrett, "when I am here the Board of Directors is always in session. Here's your contract"; and he affixed his signature.

In February, 1884, when he was at the height of his West Virginia projects, Mr. Davis gave a dinner to President Garrett at the Arlington Hotel in Washington. "There were present," he records, "besides the host and his guest, Secretary Folger, Postmaster-General Howe, Senators Bayard, Sherman, Windom, Pendleton, Gorman, and Camden, Representatives Hoge, Kenna, Wilson, McLane, and Flower." The friendship between President Garrett and Mr. Davis was a very intimate one. When Mr. Garrett died at Deer Park in the autumn of the same year, Mr. Davis was one of the honorary pall-bearers and accompanied the remains to Baltimore.

In January, 1887, he gave a dinner at Baltimore to Senator Gorman concerning which he made this entry:

Guests, President Roberts and Vice-President Thomson of Pennsylvania R. R., President Robert Garrett and Vice-President

Samuel Spencer of B. &. O., President Barnum of Hoosatonic R. R. and director in West Virginia Central, President Baughman of Chesapeake & Ohio Canal, Enoch Pratt, the philanthropist, and Mr. Burns, chairman of B. & O. Finance Committee, and S. B. Elkins, president of Piedmont & Cumberland Railroad.

Mr. Davis was always a welcome guest at the social entertainments given by the high officials of the Pennsylvania Railroad. In February, 1890, he recorded that he had been to a number of dinners, among them that of Mr. G. B. Roberts, president of the Pennsylvania Road, at Philadelphia. "I sat on Mr. R's left. Many noted gentlemen present, among them G. W. Childs, A. J. Drexel, &c." Two years later he went over to Philadelphia to dine with Mr. Frank Thomson. "The dinner was a noted one—Messrs. Roberts, Depew, Hill, Pugh, Whitney, Bristow, &c. Pierpont Morgan sat on right and I the left of Frank Thomson."

The following year, and in subsequent years, he was again the guest of Mr. Roberts. Railway men will read with special interest his characteristic comment on that great figure in the railway world. It occurs in his journal under date of February 2, 1897, attached to a newspaper clipping and picture of Mr. Roberts:

Mr. Roberts, president of Penna. Road, died a few days ago. He was a great and noble man; he was my friend. Among railway men he was generally conceded to be the first and ablest in the country. Died at sixty-five, old by overwork. Pennsylvania road is longest in the world. Revenue about $140,000,000.

For Alexander J. Cassatt, who became the head of the Pennsylvania system after Mr. Roberts's death, Mr. Davis entertained the greatest admiration. There was a sympathetic bond between them because Mr. Cassatt, like Mr. Davis himself, was a believer in the Pan-American Railway project, and lent the weight not only of his name but of his experience to it, since he served as the head of the Intercontinental Railway Survey Commission. A newspaper clipping pasted in his journal, under date of January 18, 1900, gives an account of a dinner to Mr. Cassatt:

Ex-Senator Henry G. Davis of West Virginia gave an elegantly appointed dinner to-day in honor of President Cassatt of the Pennsylvania Railroad Company, the guests being all men of note in the railway world. The dinner was entirely a social affair and had no connection with any railroad consolidation or other business matters. Guests—A. J. Cassatt, president of the Pennsylvania Railroad; John K. Cowen, president of the Baltimore and Ohio Railroad; Oscar Murray, of the Baltimore and Ohio; Samuel Spencer, president of the Southern; M. E. Ingalls, president of the Big Four; Chauncey M. Depew, president of the New York Central; J. S. Harris, president of the Reading; George F. Baer, vice-president of the Reading; W. L. Elkins, of the Widener-Elkins syndicate; Senator Gorman; Mr. Green.

To the newspaper clipping Mr. Davis added this comment:

It is believed that $1,000,000,000 of railway property was represented at above table. Never before so many great railway presidents at same table.

Mr. George F. Baer of the Reading, a conspicuous and combative figure in his day, was a warm friend of Mr. Davis and was his guest sometimes in Washington and sometimes at the summer home in Elkins. Mr. Davis entertained Mr. Baer in Washington in the midwinter of 1907.

President Oscar G. Murray of the Baltimore and Ohio was the guest of honor at a dinner given a year later, which included, among the guests other than railway officials, Chairman M. A. Knapp of the Interstate Commerce Commission, James Speyer, the banker, and several leading public men. The dinner the following year was a notable one. Mr. Davis was then in his eighty-fourth year. His account of it follows:

> I gave a dinner to railway presidents and vice-presidents. Twenty-four present. All went off well. Nearly all east of Ohio present.

The feeling entertained toward Mr. Davis by the high railway officials who were in the habit of meeting at his board found permanent expression, at the suggestion of President Frederick D. Underwood of the Erie system, at the dinner given in February, 1908. On that occasion an urn was presented to Mr. Davis which told the story of the respect in which he was held in these words:

The Honorable

HENRY GASSAWAY DAVIS

A TOKEN OF LOVE AND ESTEEM

From his associates in the Railroad Service

Washington, D. C., February 1st, 1908

Edward B. Bacon	Charles Edmund Pugh
William Abner Garrett	Charles L. Potter
Oscar George Murray	Alexander Robertson
William Nelson Page	George F. Randolph

James M. Schoonmaker
Henry Benning Spencer
Frederick D. Underwood
Daniel Willard

The last of these railway dinners was given on March 4, 1914, in Washington, when Mr. Davis was in his ninetieth year. It was in honor of Daniel Willard, president of the Baltimore and Ohio Railroad, for whom Mr. Davis entertained the highest respect as the best type of the younger generation of railway presidents who were grappling with the new conditions, economic and political, that were developing. How deeply this sentiment was reciprocated by Mr. Willard is apparent from an autograph under a photograph of himself which hung in the Senator's office: "From the youngest to the oldest railway president."

Mr. Davis's modest account of the dinner appears in this entry:

March 4, 1914. My railway dinner to President Willard last night was a success; adjourn about twelve o'clock. President Willard, Senator Owen, Hon. Oscar Underwood, President Schoonmaker, Judge Parker, and President Rea spoke.

The newspapers published a fuller story, mentioning the presence in particular of Judge Parker at the board of the man who had been his running mate on the Presidential ticket ten years earlier, and giving the complete list of the guests. These included the leading railway officials of the country, many of them born after Mr. Davis had reached middle age. Yet they were his contemporaries.

CHAPTER XVII

A SHEAF OF LETTERS

Gleanings from many contemporaries—Political history unfolded in correspondence—Senator Thurman's expectations in the famous Ohio campaign of 1875—George H. Pendleton on factional politics—Many communications from William Windom—Hopes and fears in the tragedy of Garfield's life—Comment from Paris on parties and candidates in 1884—European travel—Indignation over Blaine caricatures—Lines from Samuel J. Randall and Augustus H. Garland—West Virginia correspondents—Appreciation from the two Goffs—W. L. Wilson's ambition.

CHAPTERS of political history, momentous events, are illumined vividly in letters written to Mr. Davis by men of the generations with which he was identified. More than a thousand of these communications show how close were his relations with leading men for more than half a century. The most interesting are those that were penned before the typewriter had come to be the mechanical means of facilitating correspondence. It was rarely, too, even in the days before the typewriter, that amanuenses were resorted to by his correspondents. Statesmen in those days were not so pressed for time that they were unable to write their own letters to those who enjoyed their confidence.

Examination of these contemporary documents—for such they are—give many glimpses of political occurrences behind the scenes. They cast sidelights on eventful episodes of national history, but they also cover many subjects unrelated to politics and public affairs. They

The Tygart River at Elkins

are evidences of the deep attachment felt for Mr. Davis, and they also exhibit the personal qualities of the writers.

Political correspondence naturally fills a large space in this volume of epistolary literature. Some of it relates to Mr. Davis's own career both in his State and in the nation, but the larger part covers a wider field. The reliance placed on his common sense and his shrewd judgment is evidenced in numerous communications. There is also a sheaf of letters bearing witness to the frequent appeals made to a man of wealth who is in public life and who is ready to forward the political cause he espouses.

The close political and personal relations between Senator Allen G. Thurman and Senator Davis have been described in previous chapters. Some of the letters afford further illustrations of this intimacy, while at the same time they illuminate the politics of the period.

A brief letter from Senator Thurman gives a concise forecast of one of the most interesting episodes in American political history and one that was a determining factor in nominating a President. This relates to the famous Ohio campaign of 1875, when the soft money issue was fought out in a contest that absorbed the country from end to end. Judge Thurman's uncle, William Allen, who had served in the Senate, had been elected Governor of Ohio by the Democrats in the political reaction of 1873. This came to him after a long retirement to private life. His opponents had characterized his reappearance by designating him as "Rise-Up William Allen."

Governor Allen had espoused the greenback cause and made it the leading issue in his canvass for reëlection. Senator Thurman, while not fully in sympathy with the greenback issue, had adapted his views to his party's

stand, and was preparing to support the ticket.   Before
the campaign was under way, replying to an invitation
to visit West Virginia, he wrote to Senator Davis from
Columbus in May as follows:

My dear Senator:
Thanks for your invitation.   The trip would give me much
pleasure could I take it.   But I am engaged to speak next week
and probably longer in Cincinnati and must keep my promise.
We had a glorious meeting of the leading Democrats of Ohio here
last Thursday, and it will have a good effect.   We will have a
hard fight, but we are confident of carrying the State.   The very
best feeling prevails in the State.

In a letter just a few days before the election, that is,
on October 4, Senator Thurman wrote:

I think that Allen will be elected. . . . . There never has been
such a political campaign in the U. S.   The Rads are desperate
and it looks as if they will stop at nothing.

Senator Thurman's judgment proved to be wrong.
After a notable campaign Rutherford B. Hayes was
elected over Governor Allen, and his election as Governor of Ohio opened the way for the Presidential nomination the following year which brought him to the
White House.

In 1878 it was well understood that Senator Thurman
would be a candidate for the Presidential nomination
two years later.   Senator Davis had returned from his
European trip and already was interesting himself in
his friend's prospects.   Judge Thurman wrote from
Columbus under date of August 19:

I have just received yours of 16th, and am rejoiced that you
have reached home and are well.   I hope that you enjoyed your
trip to the Old World.   I fear that I will not be able to visit Deer
Park.   I do long to make you a visit, but the Democracy of Ohio

are inexorable. They have no mercy on me; so I have to take the stump. We have some doubtful Congressional districts that ought not to be doubtful. But they are, and the Democrats all say that my services in them are necessary. I think that we will carry the State, but the fight will be a hard one. Our State Convention *was all I could wish*. There is no dissension here now. As to my speech, be assured it is right. But we will talk on that when we meet. Give my love to your family and the Elkinses.

The social ties of the two families was evidenced in a letter from Columbus in June, 1883:

My dear Davis:

We are heartily rejoiced to know that we are to have a visit from Mrs. Davis and yourself. Don't fail to come and make us a good stay.

In later years there were other letters indicating both the social and the political intimacy of the two men.

Senator George H. Pendleton, who entered the Senate in 1878, was also a friend of Senator Davis, and while the relations were not so intimate as had been those between Senator Thurman and Senator Davis, they were close enough to be confidential. Senator Davis, knowing from his own experience the importance of a good seat in the Senate chamber, had taken care to provide his own for the new Ohio Senator, he himself, following the custom, having taken one vacated by an outgoing Senator. Senator Pendleton, in acknowledging the courtesy, added:

One of the pleasures I feel in being elected to the Senate is the opportunity it will afford of association with men whom I have known well and have learned to admire, and with none more than yourself.

A passing view of Ohio factional politics is given in a

letter several years later referring to a newspaper article. The substance of this article was that John R. McLean, who controlled the powerful *Cincinnati Enquirer,* had made a bargain to save Ohio for Governor Cleveland in return for the entire State patronage. Senator Pendleton was deeply concerned over this rumor, as appears from a letter addressed to Mr. Davis at Deer Park and written from Cincinnati on September 5, 1884:

> I cut the inclosed from the *Commercial Gazette* of this city purporting to be copy of an article in the *New York Star.* What truth is there in the reported "dicker" between McLean and Cleveland? What foundation for the rumor? You know why I feel an interest in the matter, and how closely I would guard any information you might give me.
>
> Present me kindly to the ladies.

One of President Cleveland's first official acts was to nominate ex-Senator Pendleton as Minister to Germany, so that it was clear that there had been no dicker with Editor McLean over the Ohio patronage.

The warm friendship and the congenial tastes of William Windom and Henry G. Davis are shown in numerous letters from Mr. Windom. They cover every subject—politics, business and personal affairs. Usually on political questions when one or the other was absent from the Senate they were paired. When Senator Davis was a candidate before the West Virginia Legislature for reëlection and there was no prospect of electing a Republican, Senator Windom wrote him from the Senate chamber, January 24, 1877, this letter:

> *My dear Davis:*
>
> As there seems to be little hope of our getting a straight Republican Senator from West Va., I do most heartily hope you may be successful. If I was a Rep. member, I would, under the circumstances, be most happy to give you my vote. Your services

to the State in the matter of internal improvements alone ought to commend you to both parties, and for my part, thoroughly sympathizing with your views on that subject, I feel a great anxiety for your reëlection. Hoping that the telegraph to-day will announce the pleasant intelligence that we are to have you with us six years longer, I remain,

Sincerely your friend,

WILLIAM WINDOM.

After Senator Windom entered President Garfield's Cabinet as Secretary of the Treasury many letters were exchanged with Senator Davis. In several of these communications the overshadowing national gloom caused by the assassin's bullet is reflected, although at times there is a cheerful note due to the temporary favorable condition of the patient. In reply to an invitation from Senator Davis to come to Deer Park with his family, Secretary Windom on August 10, 1881, wrote:

It would be exceedingly pleasant to do so, but I think it will be impossible to get away. The President's condition compels me to remain here. . . . I am not pleased with the President's recent condition, though the doctors seem to think that there is.in it no cause for serious anxiety. They report that he is doing very well to-day, and I am still hopeful of his continued improvement.

Two weeks later the growing hope that President Garfield was past the danger point was indicated in a letter from Secretary Windom saying:

I am happy to inform you that the President's condition is still very favorable. He has not gained much strength and not made any very great apparent progress, but he is holding his own, and the doctors think that in a few days he will begin to show a marked change for the better. We are all now very hopeful.

It was the opinion of Senator Davis that if the stricken President could be removed to the bracing mountain air of Deer Park his chances of recovery would be improved.

John W. Garrett, of the Baltimore and Ohio Railroad, was of the same opinion. They arranged to provide every comfort possible to facilitate the railway journey and to care for the distinguished patient after he should arrive at Deer Park. Their plan was communicated to Secretary Windom in a letter from Senator Davis mailed on September 2. Replying on the following day, Secretary Windom wrote:

> I will take pleasure in presenting the very kind offer of yourself and Mr. Garrett to the President's surgeons for their consideration. I think it is undecided yet to what place they will move him, or when it will be done. My impression is that they intend to make the change as soon as his condition permits, but fear that at present he is too weak. There has been but little change in him during the last two or three days, though the doctors still speak cheerfully of the prospect.

The doctors ultimately decided that the seashore would be better than the mountains, and President Garfield's removal to Elberon was accomplished. Later it was known that neither mountain air nor ocean air could have saved him.

Secretary Windom's temporary retirement from public life did not lessen his interest in political affairs. He wrote to Senator Davis from his home at Winona in Minnesota on September 22, 1882:

My dear Davis:

It seems an age since I have heard from you. How are you? How are the political elements shaping? Shall you come back to the Senate? How is our West Virginia Central enterprise showing up? Is there anything new about the Coal and Iron? Tell me all you know about everything, and especially about yourself and family.

I am having a disagreeable political contest in my own party, aided by a few of the Satanic class in the Democratic party. The respectable portion of your party is friendly. Dunnell and the Devil let loose all the liars who are not otherwise employed on me, but I shall beat them unless I am greatly mistaken in the temper of my own people. . . . How I should enjoy a week or two with you in the mountains of West Virginia!

Mr. Windom with his family visited Europe in the spring of 1884. He corresponded with Mr. Davis about many subjects, sometimes also giving his impressions of life abroad. In a long letter from Paris, dated April 2, 1884, he wrote:

My dear Davis:

I am inclined to think you are even a worse correspondent than myself, as I wrote you about three months ago and have received no reply. I presume you are very busy, as usual, but you must not be permitted to forget your old friends and I will therefore write again. We returned to Paris last Saturday from our Italian trip in excellent health and spirits. I need not say we had a grand good time, for no one can visit southern Italy without enjoying it, always providing that the fever doesn't get hold of him.

We spent two weeks in Naples and about the same time in Rome, and two more industrious people you never saw. We penetrated the depths of the catacombs, and climbed to the very edge of the crater of Vesuvius, and did all sorts of things which travelers are expected to do in that country. The weather was delightful during the entire two months—only one rainy day, and even that did not keep us indoors.

I feel now that my mission as a "tourist" is substantially ended, and I want to go home and be at work again. I shall go to London in about a week or ten days, and probably remain in England during the month of May.

I saw our friend Gov. Hendricks day before yesterday. He sails to-morrow for New York. He seems to be laboring under what my old colleague, Col. Aldrich, used to call "a mental hallucination of the mind" which inspires him with a belief that the Democracy will win at the next election. Are you afflicted in the same way still?

Who are *you* going to *nominate,* and who are *we* going to *elect?* These may be hard questions, but you are good at conundrums. From all I can see in the papers I should say that Blaine's friends are most active in our party. Logan's boom does not seem to have a very healthy growth. Your people keep very quiet, but I suspect there is a good deal going on beneath the surface. The tariff seems to be troubling the Democracy a little just now, but I have great faith in their combining capacity.

I have seen about enough of the Old World for the present, and shall be very happy to get back to a live country where the people speak the English language even if they do not always tell the truth in political matters. I am thoroughly rested and feel a good deal more like working than playing, but I have no desire to reënter the political field. . . .

I would give all my interest in Europe for a chat with you to-day. The fact is, when I think of you and a few others of my good friends, I am homesick.

A letter from Mr. Davis seems to have crossed the one from Mr. Windom. Writing again from Paris under date of May 12, Mr. Windom acknowledged this letter, and, after discussing business matters of mutual interest, referred to the business uncertainty in the United States and the effect in England. He also wrote with his customary freedom regarding politics:

The recent conspicuous failures in America have so alarmed everybody on this side that it is quite impossible just now to do anything with American enterprises. Money is very plenty and very cheap, but confidence seems to be entirely destroyed. I know of a large loan in London at the rate of one half of one per cent. per annum simply because no one is willing to invest in anything. What are we coming to at home? Is the bottom falling out entirely? From this distance it looks as if we are to have a grand smash-up.

I read the New York newspapers quite regularly, but I do not see the way out of the present tangle in either political party. The abuse of our friend Blaine is outrageous and ought to make him hosts of friends. When I saw the caricature in *Puck* posted on the Strand in London the other day, I felt like taking the next steamer for home to go to work for Blaine. I refer to the "Dime

Show," in which B. is represented as the "tatooed man." I hope
he will prosecute the scoundrels who got it up.

I do not venture any prophecy as to who will be the nominees
on our side. Blaine seems to be the strongest, as usual, but the
rest will probably combine against him. I believe your party will
nominate Tilden if he can be "held together" until the convention
meets.

Incidental glimpses of political affairs are afforded in
various letters from public men with whom Mr. Davis
was on friendly terms without their relations being intimate. Samuel J. Randall wrote him from his home in
Pennsylvania during the Congressional campaign of
1882, referring apparently to the necessity of getting two
candidates to forego their rival candidacies within the
party:

You can do more than any other man to bring peace. Excuse
my troubling you; it is for our cause. . . . I had a visit a day
or two ago from Honorable James Hagerman of Keokuk, Iowa,
who gives an encouraging account of that State as to Congressional candidates in five or six districts. He needed and asked
only encouragement. I favor such an invasion where our enemy
does not expect us. Atkins' speech is able and ought to be circu-
lated, and also to be in the hands of every speaker. Read it.

Augustus H. Garland of Arkansas, who became Attorney-General in President Cleveland's administration,
had served with Mr. Davis in the Senate and had been
in sympathy with his conservative views on various subjects. After the Chicago Convention in July, 1884, he
wrote a brief note:

Dear Uncle Henry:

After the good glorious work at Chicago in which you cut no
small figure, I feel compelled to drop you a word or two. When
I saw your name on the Committee on Platform I was satisfied
we would have a liberal, conservative document, and I was not

disappointed. Everything starts admirably and I feel satisfied we will win. If we do not now I fear we never will.

Mr. Davis's position as the political chief of his party in West Virginia for so many years naturally resulted in a very large volume of correspondence with political leaders and lieutenants in the State. But not all of it was of a partizan character or came from members of his own party. Nathan Goff, Jr., with whom he had served in the Legislature, on retiring from the office of United States District Attorney, in June, 1882, wrote him:

I desire to thank you for your uniform and continued kindness to me in official, business, and social matters. . . . It is hard to sever pleasant official relations, and it has been hard for me to conclude to do so; but my personal affairs and the business interests of my family require it, and to it and them I yield.

Will you hand this to Senator Camden to read, and assure him that I remember and appreciate his kindness to me. Both of you have been kind to me at times and under circumstances when it was not only pleasant but most beneficial to me, and I shall ever treasure the memory of it and be grateful.

A year later, when Senator Davis had announced his intention to retire from the United States Senate, the news was received with regret by another Goff, a political opponent, but also a personal friend. This was the venerable Nathan Goff, Sr., the uncle of the foregoing writer, who had been Mr. Davis's mentor when he first entered the West Virginia Assembly. Writing from Clarksburg, under date of January 10, 1883, in a trembling hand, and addressing Senator Davis as my "old friend," Nathan Goff, Sr., said:

I am very desirous that you shall again be elected U. S. Senator to succeed yourself. I much prefer you to any of the candidates mentioned, and I think the good of the State and a majority of its people wish and desire that you shall again be their representative. So I hope you will pardon an old friend for the liberty of making a suggestion to you. I would say step squarely out and say to our Legislature that you will serve them. I am quite feeble; some three years ago I had a slight stroke of paralysis and have never entirely recovered from it.

Though in the later years of the career of William L. Wilson his path diverged from that of Mr. Davis, they had worked together in their party activities, and Mr. Wilson was an occasional correspondent of Senator Davis. He wrote the Senator from Charlestown, under date of September 13, 1880, regarding some rumors that were afloat:

The result at Berkeley Springs explodes the rumor to which I called your attention. . . . I do not know how things will turn out to-morrow; it will at least show whether there was any bargain at the Senatorial convention. I shall have the solid support of this county if there is no foul play, and am not greatly exercised over result anyway. If I am not nominated and the prospects are not too encouraging, I hope to do some campaigning with you.

Nearly a year later, on June 28, 1881, Mr. Wilson wrote:

Dear Senator:

I see from the *Baltimore Sun* of yesterday that your little railroad is about to enter upon a very wide and ambitious career, and I judge from the men enlisted in the enterprise that it means business and is something more than the newspaper railroads now springing up over our State. I am a firm believer in the undeveloped resources of West Virginia, and that those who have the money and sagacity to develop them will not fail of immense returns; and so ever since reading the notice in the *Sun* I have been thinking that perhaps in your projected enterprise I might somewhere find an opening to better my fortunes and at the same time serve some useful purpose in the work.

When Mr. Wilson became president of the West Virginia University at Morgantown, Senator Davis wrote asking him to recommend a young man who could serve as a secretary and instructor.   This Mr. Wilson did in a most kindly letter, explaining that the young man he recommended was one of the many at the University who were struggling to get a good education through difficulties and to whom the compensation would be a great lift.

In the campaign of 1886 a number of letters were exchanged between Mr. Davis and Mr. Wilson, who was then in the House of Representatives.   From Charlestown, under date of September 30, Mr. Wilson wrote:

My dear Senator:

I am just about to start for Moorefield by buggy; am sorry you cannot be with me.   I am anxious for you to make your speech and *publish it* as a campaign document.   Berkeley court is October 12th, and I have written Parks, chairman of the County Committee, suggesting that he have you there on that day.   Possibly also Kenna will be there, or send someone from Washington. You can be of great service to me in Tucker County, I expect.   I want to visit both Elk Garden and Davis before the election.   We must have you at Charlestown during the canvass.

Memorial Church at Gassaway

CHAPTER XVIII

MORE LETTERS

Benjamin Harrison's request for advice on investments—Grover Cleveland's explanation of a misunderstanding—Senator Gorman on prospects and results in 1904—Thomas F. Bayard's illuminating correspondence—Spoils system responsible for Garfield's assassination—Views on his own campaign for the nomination in 1884—Tilden and the rise of the literary bureau—Maintenance of principles—Manly comment on the Chicago Convention—Abhorrence of Benjamin F. Butler's labor movement—Tribute to Mr. Davis's work in developing West Virginia's resources—The last letter—Some piquant notes from Andrew Carnegie.

BENJAMIN HARRISON was an occasional correspondent of Mr. Davis. He, however, preferred personal conference to letter-writing when public affairs were to be considered, although in a few instances after his retirement from the Presidency he wrote his views confidentially on current topics with considerable freedom. But the majority of the letters relate to personal or business affairs. A characteristic note was one sent from Indianapolis in June, 1883, in relation to an expected visit from Senator and Mrs. Davis. It exhibits the warm side of General Harrison's nature:

Yours of the 8th instant came this morning. We are all very pleased to hear that you and Mrs. D. can give us the long-promised visit. We are all at home; have got through house-cleaning and are in an attitude of *waiting* for you. So come and bring Katie along too;—plenty of room. Let me know when you will arrive.

261

General Harrison's confidence in the business judgment of Mr. Davis was profound, and he sought the Senator's advice on investments of which he confessed himself a poor judge. It was at his own insistence that the investment was made for him in Senator Davis's principal railway enterprise. From the correspondence, Mr. Davis apparently hesitated to take the responsibility of suggesting his own properties, and a check forwarded from Indianapolis by General Harrison was returned; but ultimately the investment was made as requested. Writing from Indianapolis on January 19, 1895, General Harrison said:

My dear Senator:

I wrote to Elkins some time ago asking him whether the new railroad was making any progress and when you would have your securities ready, but have not heard from him. I suppose he has been so much absorbed in the Senatorial contest—which I see is practically ended in his favor—that he has not had time to write. A paragraph which came to my notice indicates that your organization has been effected, and that the older companies have indorsed the bonds of the new company. I have something more than twenty thousand dollars on hand, and have been seeking an investment for it. If your securities are not to be issued soon I will make some temporary use of the money so as to get some interest on it, but if they are I will be glad to take the thirty thousand dollars' worth of your bonds as you suggested. The balance of the money I can probably pay before long.

General Harrison's satisfaction with the transaction as arranged for him by Mr. Davis was indicated in another letter from Indianapolis under date of January 26:

My dear Senator:

Your letter of the 22d came last week, and was forwarded to me at Richmond, where I have been engaged for a month in the trial of an important will case, which promises to hold on for another month, much to my dismay; as I did not contemplate a trial that would last over a month. I have concluded to take the West Virginia bonds which you offer, and inclose you S. A. Fletcher & Co.'s draft on N. Y. to my order, indorsed to you, for twenty thousand ($20,000) dollars.

I can arrange with you the matter of any accumulated interest on the bonds, if you will state the account to me. This check represents all that I can spare from my account just now; and while it does not pay for an even number of bonds at the price you name—107—you can so keep the account as to show what my investment is. You may just put the bonds up in an envelope with an indorsement that they belong to me, and keep them in your safety deposit vault. It will hardly be worth while to send them out here, if they are likely to be exchanged in the spring for the securities of the new road.

We were all glad to see that Mr. Elkins' election went off so harmoniously and unanimously.

I envy you and the rest your trip to Mexico, as we are having extremely changeable weather; from mildness to zero in less than twenty-four hours being a frequent occurrence in the last two weeks. When you come to add to this living for two months at a poor hotel and spending seven hours and a half a day in the court-room, you have a partial picture of my sufferings.

Mrs. McKee and the children fortunately continue well, and join me in kind regards to Mrs. Davis, Kate, and Grace.

Very sincerely yours,

BENJ. HARRRISON.

President Cleveland occasionally wrote Mr. Davis on political matters. A misunderstanding on one occasion, when apparently Mr. Davis went to the White House to keep an appointment with President Cleveland about some political matter and was not received, was cleared away in Mr. Davis's usual direct manner by asking for an explanation. The incident is indicated in an autograph letter from Mr. Cleveland:

Executive Mansion, Washington,
June 4, 1887.

My dear Sir:

Colonel Lamont surprised me very much to-day by telling me the purport of your conversation with him. I think it is the first instance of the kind ever presented to me, and I feel especially annoyed that it should relate to you, whose kindness and friendship has been so marked and constant.

I am often perplexed and often overwhelmed with visitors, sometimes engaged with public business which cannot be postponed or interrupted, but the circumstances would be very unusual which would prevent me from seeing you. I am afraid the matter to which you have referred has occurred through my oversight or inadvertence at a time when I was unusually vexed and troubled with other matters. I certainly have no remembrance of the occasion.

I hope I need not say to you that I am at all times glad to see you, and that I should be very much grieved if you should think otherwise.

I hope you will call the next time you are in the city. We often recalled our stay at Deer Park during the anniversary time of our marriage, and with it we recalled your kindness too.

Yours sincerely,
GROVER CLEVELAND.

Hon. Henry G. Davis,
Baltimore, Md.

A penciled memorandum on Mr. Cleveland's letter in the handwriting of Mr. Davis notes that he answered saying he highly appreciated the communication.

Among the hundreds of letters from his kinsman, Arthur Pue Gorman, two may be quoted which relate to comparatively recent political events. They give a contemporary view of the national campaign in which Mr. Davis was the candidate for Vice-President. One was written just before the election and the other just after it.

Fifth Avenue Hotel,
Madison Square, New York.

Nov. 2, 1904.

My dear Friend:

I received your letter upon my arrival here last night and note all you say about West Virginia. . . . You have no idea as to the confidence of Judge Parker and Mr. Sheahan in the outcome. They have absolutely no question about New York, and New Jersey, but they think Connecticut can also be carried. Altogether they are in a very hopeful mood, and we certainly have the Republicans on the defensive, the current running strongly in our favor. My own judgment is that we will poll our full vote, and it looks as if we will be great gainers by the dissatisfaction in the Republican party.

I want to congratulate you upon the wonderful contest you have made. I hear from mutual friends you have not overtaxed yourself and are quite well. I trust you will come out of it in the best condition.

Writing a week later, Senator Gorman said:

I confess the result is a very great surprise to me, as it is to everybody who watched the contest.

However, it is all over, and the immense majority against us all along the line shows the American people have determined that the President shall have another term. On the surface it looked as if our party were united, but it is evident it is not so with the rank and file.

Disagreeable as the result is, I know you well enough to know you will accept it without worry, as you do everything. You made a grand, indeed memorable, fight for our party, but the odds were too great to be overcome.

Something of the intimacy between Henry G. Davis and Thomas F. Bayard has been told in the preceding pages. The correspondence extending through more than a quarter of a century is further evidence of it. Mr. Bayard wrote freely on business and on personal and political matters. Some of his letters are vitally illus⸗

trative of his own high character and his lofty convictions. Writing on July 3, 1881, concerning a proposed visit to West Virginia, and referring to a previous letter, Mr. Bayard said:

> I write under the shock and depression caused by the wild and wicked attempt to murder the President. . . . This assault upon Garfield shocks me, and it really appears to be the natural results of the demoralizing and corrupting influence of the "spoils" system of machine politics. The letters of the assassin are like those of a Russian nihilist, and something heretofore unheard of in America.
> May Heaven avert the evil results which the death of Garfield would expose our country to. The consequences of turning over the executive powers to the wing of the party who have been at such bitter variance with the administration loom up darkly on every side.
> As I write (3 P. M. Sunday) bulletins are more encouraging.

A sensational political episode was briefly adverted to by Mr. Bayard in a letter from Wilmington dated April 22, 1883. The occasion was a dinner given by the Iroquois Club of Chicago, the leading Democratic organization of the West, at which Mr. Bayard was the principal speaker. In the morning hours Mayor Carter Harrison, in responding to a toast, took occasion to controvert the tariff views which Mr. Bayard had expressed and to declare the Democratic party could not carry the country on such a platform. Mayor Harrison was a very forceful personality with an unexcelled faculty for securing publicity. At that period he filled as much space in the newspapers as did the President of the United States. Mr. Bayard wrote of this incident to Senator Davis:

> I had hoped to have seen you and told you about Chicago. I think the Iroquois Club dinner was a success, although it seems to have disagreed with our Republican friends and their news-

papers. In fact, we can hardly be said to have any general Democratic press in the United States. Here and there is a Democratic newspaper, but in Chicago, for instance, there is *none*. The *Chicago Times,* which is not a Republican organ, is as little a Democratic organ, and perhaps injures us more than if it was an avowed Republican. Carter Harrison, the Mayor, made a silly and very uncivil harangue at the end of the dinner, which mystified our hosts. It was seized upon by the Republican press and published as a "bombshell," etc., but it amounted to nothing.

Senator Bayard was an active candidate for the Presidential nomination in 1884. His friends were well organized, but the Tilden influence was hostile. A reverse in the preliminary campaign in West Virginia brought forth a notable letter on political methods—the literary bureau—that have since become common.

Referring to the inability of Mr. Davis to secure the West Virginia delegation for him, Senator Bayard wrote from the Senate chamber under date of April 9, 1884:

My dear Davis:

I have your note of yesterday informing me that the local conventions in West Virginia had declared in favor of Mr. Tilden's nomination at Chicago. I had seen the statement in the *New York Times* a day or two previous.

Do not, my good friend, let this action disturb you—at least not on *my* account. We ought, as sensible men, to accept the situation, and if, from any cause or number of causes, a genuine sentiment pervades our party in favor of nominating the "old ticket"; it will control the convention, and *I* for one shall not obstruct it.

It is perfectly clear also that Mr. Tilden has *not* as yet objected to it, whatever he may have done to promote it. No such personal organization ever existed in this country as that which he carefully and elaborately has built up since his canvass for the office of Governor of New York until now. His "literary bureau" I believe is still maintained, and I do not care to give an accurate definition of that, but it results in a purchased and paid-for expression in favor of the owner of the bureau.

Now, my good friend, you know how entirely outside of my capacity or personal methods is such a system. I have no reliance upon anything to give me high office but the belief of my countrymen that I have the wish and the ability to serve them intelligently and faithfully.

To represent a party animated and controlled by such beliefs and such objects would be an honor that no man would value more highly than I, and even in defeat there would be the solace of self-respect. Really I do not want, nor can I logically or reasonably expect, to receive a nomination at the hands of a set of delegates who, looking the facts of the present and the history of the near past squarely in the face, approve of the nomination of Mr. Tilden, or to place the nomination subject to his wishes either to accept it for himself or control it in favor of anyone he desires.

I am unable to believe that Mr. Tilden's physical condition renders it possible for him even to contemplate the assumption of the labor of a canvass, much less the duties of the Chief Magistrate. Unless I am wholly mistaken, he is too feeble in health to undertake labor of any kind.

Therefore, the movement to send delegates to nominate *him* is in fact a mere cover to nominate someone to be approved by him. It would be a Tilden convention, and it seems to me that logically none but Tilden men ought to have their names placed before it.

For one, I am sure I do not and would not justly represent such a convention in the wishes and opinion of those who selected and sent them there, and therefore my name ought not to be placed before them.

Profession, promises, and platform all depend in the end upon the personal character of the individual chosen to represent and carry them into execution.

I expect to go along as you have heretofore seen me, trying hard to find out the paths of honor and prosperity to our country and to point them out to our countrymen. This has gained me the confidence and good will of men like you, and as I value that I shall endeavor to retain it.

As the Democratic National Convention drew near, Senator Bayard wrote to Mr. Davis freely and frequently concerning his prospects. From the Senate chamber on June 19 he wrote:

On Monday we will meet at my house at dinner and have a free conference. I have written to Travers, and McPherson goes to New York to-day and will learn how matters stand there. What the result of the Saratoga Convention really is I do not presume to know, but I can see a restoration of ancient forces in the presence of Belmont, Travers, and Kelly to delegateships. Hewitt met me to-day (he is a delegate) and told me he would make me President of the United States in preference to any living man. (Whether he would say so an hour hence is doubtful.)

Gorman is coming on Monday.

Writing under date of June 27, Senator Bayard said:

Gorman told me all about New York, which is a curious pool for me to be fishing in, and I feel it quite impossible to prognosticate anything of the results.

I confess it made my flesh creep to know that you and McPherson had been in consultation with Butler, of whom I entertain the most profound distrust and constant apprehension. Of course, I know a great party must contain all kind of elements, and there is no use in driving those you disapprove into opposition, but the fact remains that *principles must be maintained* and not departed from under the name of pretense of an alliance with the foes of principle.

Now as to the selection of a delegate to present name to the convention. You suggest Judge Thurman, and I need not say how delighted and honored I would be to have him do it, but I can scarcely think it practicable under the circumstances, nor do I suppose with his relations to McDonald he would be disposed to go for an "eastern man," nor do I know how my old friend regards my promotion to a position which perhaps he still may himself aspire. Now, let me say that it had been suggested to me that Governor Leon Abbett of New Jersey would be a proper person to present my name. Jersey is a northern State and a tariff State, and one of the doubtful States. Think this over, and write me at once your views.

Senator Bayard's comment on the result at Chicago, while tinged with some asperity, was a manly recognition of the loyalty of those who had supported him. He wrote to Mr. Davis from Wilmington on July 18, 1884:

My dear Davis:

Our "beaten troops" have all returned from Chicago, and I have many accounts of the incidents and workings of that strange body of our countrymen called the Democratic Convention. Like all such assemblies, there was a great deal to make me think better and *some* things to make me think worse of human nature.

To *me* there was a great deal to gratify in the conduct of my friends, those upon whom I relied and who have only endeared themselves more than ever to me by their staunch and generous advocacy, and among them *you* stand. I am quite conscious that my share of praise is beyond my merits, and my ambition is to be really worthy of the place assigned me in our party councils and the estimation of the country. Some day when we are quietly together you will explain to me some things about the Maryland delegation, and Gorman will also, I doubt not. I had come to regard Maryland the same as Delaware—perhaps without warrant—and yet I believe that before the people of both States I have the same position.

I hope we will prove to have been mistaken in our estimate of the defection from Cleveland in New York. It is too early yet to descry the movement of the currents of popular feeling. Some strange novelties appear, and to find *Harper's Weekly,* the *New York Times,* the *Evening Post,* the *New York Herald,* etc., all aiding the Democratic nominee is enough to make a man stare.

Certain it is that new political forces are at work, and some of them *dangerous.* Butler's organization of the "labor vote" is a dangerous and demagogical movement, for the laboring classes (so-called) have surely no such wrongs as yet in this country as to justify a *separate* organization. How many Presidents have we had who were men of inherited fortune? How many Cabinet ministers, how many men in the Senate to-day, have worked with their hands for a living! How many millionaires have we who did not spring from poverty? You see how unjust in *this* country is the *separate* and hostile array of laboring men.

The man for whom I feel just now is our friend McDonald.
I do not think Indiana was faithful to him—but, but—when we
meet we will talk it all over.

During the progress of the campaign Senator Bayard
frequently wrote Mr. Davis. One of the letters is especially interesting as reiterating his views of General
Benjamin F. Butler. On August 27 he wrote from Wilmington:

There are so many new elements in the canvass that it is hard
to foretell their relative force. My judgment of Butler and the
danger of having anything to do with him—except to put him to
death—has had ample confirmation.

The canvass *drags* on both sides, but will be hot enough ere
long. I think I will speak in Brooklyn on the 15th of September.

What may happen in New York I cannot say, but elsewhere
I do not think Blaine will make any serious inroad in the Irish
vote and will lose heavily with the German vote. The Independ-
ents attack him with a bitterness quite unknown to the Democrats.
Regards to Gorman.

The intimate personal correspondence of the two
friends would make a large volume. Innumerable letters are filled with graceful tributes from Senator Bayard to the lifework of Mr. Davis. After one of his
many trips through the region traversed by the West
Virginia Central Railway he wrote from Wilmington,
under date of June 23, 1890:

My dear Davis:

I enjoyed the trip over your road immensely, and feel well
satisfied with my small pecuniary interest in that region of industry and growing wealth. I must congratulate you upon the
monument to your energy and far-sighted enterprise and intelligence which the West Virginia Central and the whole region
it penetrates constitute.

It is a just cause of pride to you, and will be to your children,
that you have let the sunlight of civilization and prosperity in upon

a region so secluded by its rugged natural features. May you fully enjoy the fruition of your labors.

When the autumn comes I shall try to let Mrs. Bayard see the West Virginia Central in the glory of the change of leaves, and will write you.

A New Year's letter from Mr. Bayard, penned a few months before his own death, is a fitting tribute with which to close the story of the deep friendship of these two men:

Wilmington, Del.,
January 1, 1898.

My dear Henry Davis:

I was very glad to get your kind note of yesterday with a pass over the lines of the West Va. Central for 1898 for me and Mrs. Bayard.

I have always been desirous that she should see the beautiful region your enterprise has so developed, and I am personally desirous of noting your progress since I was last in your territories.

The death of a dear sister clouds the entry of the New Year, and just now I am a prisoner in the house with a bad cold.

I hope you are a little more conservative of your fine physical powers and are learning a little how to play.

As a Christmas card I send you a verse by one of our countrymen, Whittier, which will please Mrs. Davis quite as much as you.

When I am next in Washington I shall hope to see you, provided you hold still long enough.

Wishing you a Happy New Year.

Sincerely yours,
T. F. BAYARD.

Hon. Henry G. Davis,
Washington.

Andrew Carnegie was a regular correspondent of Mr. Davis, not only in connection with the Pan-American Railway, but also in reference to other subjects. His crisp and concise letters would make a vest pocket edition of piquant comment. When he was appointed a delegate

Graceland, Mr. Davis's home at Elkins

to the Second Pan-American Conference at Mexico, in sequence to his membership in the First Conference at Washington in which he and Mr. Davis had been colleagues, under date of March 8, 1902, he wrote from New York:

My dear Mr. Davis:

Notice of my appointment duly received and acceptance mailed. Shall be glad to be of service with you in the great work. Sorry that I am so busy these days that I am not able to accept your kind invitation to visit Washington. We are sailing soon for our summer holiday. Tell Senator Elkins hope to see him and his at Skibo this summer.

In later years came a crisp note from Dungenness:

Dear Mr. Chairman:

Here on Lister Island three generations of Carnegies and I head the family.

We leave to-day for Hot Springs, Arkansas. Madam has need to take the cure for the first time. Shall reach New York say April 1st and let you know when I can get to meeting.

Long life to you, grand old man.

It was well known that Mr. Carnegie in his benefactions excluded gifts to denominational institutions. This, however, did not prevent Mr. Davis from laying before him the claims of the West Virginia Institution to which he and Senator Elkins had contributed so liberally and which he had endowed. The answer was characteristically brief and frank. Mr. Carnegie wrote from New York on December 4, 1911:

My dear Friend:

I am so glad to hear from you, venerable sage.

I must give you the rare opportunity of taking that Presbyterian College under your sole control. I would not rob you of the privilege for the world.

It is a rule which I shall never break; *viz.,* I will support no educational institution which favors one sect or discriminates against other sects. Education should be undenominational, all religions and creeds on equal footing.

Happy to see you in Washington when I am there for a few days.

Very truly yours,
ANDREW CARNEGIE.

CHAPTER XIX

PERSONAL CHARACTERISTICS

Mr. Davis's journal as an illustration of his character—Intimate record of half a century—The observant traveler at home and abroad—European trip—Shrewd reflections on the Southern States—Mexico and California—Personal thrift and business liberality—Passion for order and detail—Faculty of concentration —Making a bargain—High standard of integrity—Dislike of speculation—In all things an individualist—Austere home life mellowed—Favorite documents of American history—Fondness for biography—Material for speeches—Nature's physical endowment—Horseback rider at ninety—Capacity for sleep—Religious convictions.

THE intimate story of Henry G. Davis's life for half a century has been told by himself. This is not in the form of an autobiography or of a sketch prepared by him, nor was the story told for a moralizing purpose. It contains no meditations with sly thoughts of posterity's comment. It simply grew out of one of his leading characteristics, which was the love of order and the desire to have before him the record of current events and of his own activities. For nearly fifty years he kept a journal in which he entered the things that most concerned him or that at the time made the strongest impression on him.

This journal in reality is the record of his associations as well as of his own work from year to year. It is comprised in a single volume, a large business ledger bound in sheepskin and filled from beginning to end with his notes.   It commences in the spring of 1867, when he moved to Deer Park for the summer, and it ends a short time before his death in Washington, in February, 1916. There are some scattering records of his earlier years, but the memorandum books of those years, to which he sometimes refers, unfortunately have been lost.

Much that has been written in the account of his life and times that this volume comprises is drawn from the journal, as has been made clear by the frequent quotations from it, but it has to be studied from cover to cover to exhibit fully the qualities that made him a successful railway builder and organizer of industry as well as man of public affairs.

The entries relate to his prospecting trips among coal and timber lands, to family matters of an intimate character, to social intercourse, to political events, to interviews with railway officials and financiers of his own type, with occasional comment, never of an unkindly nature, on his contemporaries.   In the later years there are numerous newspaper clippings, especially in connection with politics and the business enterprises in which he was concerned.   His impressions are recorded spontaneously, but with many shrewd reflections.   The weather is frequently noted, but the notation is that of the farmer, the lumberman, the railway builder, or the contractor, for whom meteorological conditions have a definite meaning.

The faculty of observation that Mr. Davis possessed doubtless has been apparent to the reader of these pages. It helped to supply the deficiency of his early education. His was the schooling that comes from observation, from association with workingmen, men of business, statesmen, and diplomatists, and from meeting and overcoming difficulties.   It was an education that made his judgment sought and respected in great business enterprises, in political management, and in public affairs.

The faculty of seeing intelligently was especially shown in his various journeys. He was the observant traveler in whatever place he found himself, on horseback or on foot in the primeval forests of the Alleghanies; in Europe; making a hasty trip to Cuba or Bermuda or Mexico; crossing the continent; journeying as a member of a senatorial committee or traveling with his family for recreation. Wherever he was he saw all that the ordinary traveler saw and much more.

In the spring of 1873, when Senator Davis went to California with his daughter Hallie, after noting the many buffalo, antelope, and prairie-dogs on the plains, he also notes seeing "one wolf." Denver he found a promising place, but he was "only tolerably well pleased" with San Francisco and the country around it. The same observation was made about Salt Lake City. Like all travelers, he went to the Mormon Tabernacle on Sunday. His visit was before the enactment of anti-polygamy laws, and he remarks that some Mormons have twenty wives, others one, two, three, and so on.

In the summer of 1878, as a relief from senatorial duties, he made a trip to Europe in company with his daughter Kate, his colleague Senator Camden, and Senator Camden's daughters, Annie and Jessie. The party spent four days in Ireland visiting Blarney Castle, Killarney, and Dublin. Then they went to Scotland and London, and from London to Paris, where they visited the Exposition. Switzerland, the Rhine, and Belgium also were visited. This itinerary is recorded in his journal with an occasional observation but apparently he was taking full notes all the time, for he remarks: "For full account of trip see memorandum books."

When the Senate Committee on Transportation visited various parts of the country he made copious entries in his journal, most of them relating to the subject of the inquiry and therefore including observations of trade and industry.   While in New Orleans he recorded this impression:

I am pleased with the country in Louisiana, but much of the southern country and States are going to waste.   Taxes in New Orleans are $5.12 on the $100, and in the county $4.75.   No people can stand this long.

In the midwinter of 1884, with Mrs. Davis, he took a trip to Florida and Louisiana.   His impressions of the towns and of the country were given in brief entries in the journal.   He found Charleston, South Carolina, "quite an old town, fairly built, and looking tolerably prosperous."   The many cotton-fields on the road from Charleston to Jacksonville were noted, with the observation also that the oranges were still hanging upon the trees.   Proceeding to New Orleans by way of Tallahassee, he remarked that the country was mostly sandy and poor.   Of New Orleans on this second visit he briefly remarks: "City has a business appearance.   Theaters and many stores are open on Sunday."   Returning North, he commented on the coal and iron in Alabama, and added that Birmingham was a very thriving place which had grown very rapidly.   Nashville, Tennessee, he described as a growing town with a fine country around it, and the country between Nashville and Louisville was also referred to as "fine."

Mr. Davis, accompanied by members of his family, visited the World's Fair in Chicago in midsummer, 1893.   His comment was brief but comprehensive: "The Fair is very large, and is a wonderful exhibit of the United States and the world."

In the early spring of 1894, with Mrs. Davis and other members of the family, he made a flying trip to Havana by way of Florida, but he did not record his impressions of Cuba under Spanish rule, as it then was.

In the spring of 1895 he visited Mexico City and California, chiefly for business purposes. While in Mexico he was received by President Diaz, who treated him with much consideration. He expressed some annoyance at the attention shown him. The President had detailed an army officer to accompany their party, and this officer performed his duty with military fidelity, while Mr. Davis wanted to get away by himself at times and take a look around, as he phrased it.

In 1897 he went to Bermuda from New York, recording that the trip was rough and that he was seasick all the way. The visit, however, was an enjoyable one. The attractiveness of Bermuda was thus summed up: "Climate in March about our early June. Nearly everything is white."

In his other travels, sometimes for recreation, sometimes for business, and not infrequently combining both, he never failed to make notes; but it would be difficult to trace in these notes anything that could be attributed to the standard guide-books. His observations were as original as they were pointed.

Mr. Davis had few idiosyncrasies or peculiarities, but such as they were they bore the impress of a strong personality. The hardships of his early life, and the privations that followed the reversion of the family from comfort and wealth to poverty, left a deep impression on his character. Besides this there was an innate aversion to waste and an appreciation of the real meaning of economy. He had learned to practise thrift from necessity, but he would have been saving in any circumstances because thriftiness was the basis on which to build.

In his personal habits through all his long life he was simplicity itself. His wants were few and were easily satisfied. In making a small purchase or providing for some slight need, he would exercise the same care that he had found it necessary to bestow when dollars were very scarce and hard to get. These habits were not eccentricities; they were simply the reflex of a principle. Some of them were too superficial to be worthy of mention. If there were good reason for being generous he did not hesitate to show liberality, but the liberality that is quite distinct from prodigality.

In the same way, while all his life he exhorted to economy, he distinguished it from parsimony. His subordinates in the management of his properties were frequently told, sometimes sharply, that they must exercise greater economy, but where there was a real need of liberal expenditures they had only to show it and they were allowed to go ahead. In public affairs, and the administration of government, economy naturally was one of Mr. Davis's favorite themes, and in particular he held the opposition party to strict account for expenditures. But when he came to exercise his functions as a legislator he never was parsimonious toward the Government.

In his business affairs he would weigh every expense carefully, even to the cost of a short trip, but he would not hesitate to close a million-dollar transaction overnight as the result of such a journey. In his private and family life there was no trace of undue economy, yet there was no extravagance. Disliking display and ostentation, he always maintained his household on a scale befitting his own position and his hospitable inclinations. It was a generous hospitality, for he was not ashamed to be known as a rich man.

Witness an illustration of his activities when he was in his seventy-fifth year as given in his journal:

Sept. 10, 1898. I am quite busy arranging to open mine at Simpson. Call New York Coal Co.

Also building or extending road (W. Va. Central) from Beverly to Huttonsville.

An important element in Mr. Davis's character which had much to do with his success was the faculty of concentrating his energies upon the work in hand and his ability to dismiss business cares from his mind when the time came for recreation. Whatever he had to do, whether it was working on a farm, running a railway train, framing an appropriation bill, drawing up a report for an international conference, or managing a railway or a coal company, he always was able to concentrate his attention and his energies on the one subject. He always wanted to have as much as possible of his work carried out under his own eyes.

A leading trait in Mr. Davis's business methods was his love of order. This was inherent. In his personal habits the practices of his early boyhood, which had been taught him by his mother, were followed, even to carefully laying out his towel to dry. Everything he did was methodical. His explorations of lumber and coal lands were never taken at haphazard. The full details of these inspections and investigations, written down by himself at the time and afterward entered in his journal, always could be used to refresh his mind and undoubtedly were of great value to him. Having made a thorough study of the resources of a given region, having gone over it on foot or on horseback, he was then in a position to go forward with his plans. It was confidence in his knowledge that enabled him to interest other capitalists in his railway projects. It was sufficient for them that "H. G. D." had gone over the ground and satisfied himself that there was traffic to be developed.

In dealing with others he always dealt on a business basis, and there were few who could excel him in making a bargain; yet no one could complain of unfairness. He knew the value of what he had to sell, or of what he wanted to buy, and knowing it he laid the foundation for the prospective transaction. An incident shows his method. Along toward the end of his life he decided to dispose of certain timber and coal holdings. The operation was a somewhat complicated one. He formulated the plan himself, and in giving the outline to his lawyers to be put into legal form he remarked: "This is about what it will have to be. There may be a few changes from what I have put down, but they won't be important."

The prospective buyers thought otherwise, but after months of negotiations the transaction was consummated on the lines laid down by Mr. Davis. In concluding it there came a business letter from the head of the corporation, who years previously had been associated with him. The business letter, notwithstanding the rigid terms, closed with a word congratulating the writer's old principal that his eye had not lost its clearness nor his hand its cunning. Mr. Davis was a little doubtful about the compliment, but his associates knew it for what it was intended, a tribute to sagacity. His correspondence was the essence of clearness and conciseness.

Mr. Davis's business morality was of the highest standard. He never speculated in his own properties, although his enterprises were carried forward during a period when this was not considered unethical. Closely in touch all his life with Wall Street, its methods made no appeal to him, and its standards as practised by some of its leaders never received the sanction of his coöperation. He dealt with the reputable financial leaders and was content.

Every dollar of his fortune which grew out of timber and coal lands and railroads was the result of investments made after thorough investigation, and for every dollar he created for himself wealth was created for entire communities. While some of his enterprises seemed hazardous and doubtless were so, considered as speculations, there was no hazard in them when considered as investments. To him it was simply a question of working and waiting, and his foresight and conservatism were demonstrated in the comparative ease with which he passed through the unsettled conditions. His long business career covered several periods of national panics and also of local depressions. Yet there is no evidence that he was ever seriously affected by them.

The panic of 1873 found him engaged in many important enterprises requiring considerable capital, but it did not find him over-extended. He was able to speak from his place in the Senate against inflation during this panic, although some of his colleagues, who were men of large business affairs, were advocating "more circulation medium" doubtless as the unconscious reflection of their own difficulties.

Mr. Davis's fondness for detail was a passion, yet it was a part of his success. Where he knew everything so thoroughly, he was the better able to carry out his own ideas. Long before the railways had been compelled by the Interstate Commerce Commission to adopt a uniform system of bookkeeping, the accounts of his lines were thoroughly systematized. Long before manufacturers and mining companies had realized that they ought to know the cost of production, he had worked out his own system under which he knew what it cost him to mine and sell coal and coke. Some of the most interesting exhibits among his papers in the latter period of his business activities are the cost sheets of his railways and his mines.

It sometimes was a question with the railway leaders of the country, "Why Davis confined himself to one little corner?" Knowing his constructive capacity and his grasp of large operations, they wondered that he was content to occupy what they looked on as so small a field when a whole continent stretched before him. His passion for detail doubtless was one reason, since the railway projector who seeks to span a continent cannot be a man of detail. Mr. Davis may have had this feeling himself, but back of it was his sense of responsibility. He did not, with his high standard of integrity, want to be identified with any enterprises that were too big for his personal supervision, and he wanted to be unhampered in carrying out his own ideas. He was essentially an individualist.

In business conferences it was usually remarked by his associates that "Davis sat at the head of the table." Some of these associates were men of great adroitness who would seek results by indirect methods. Sometimes, too, they would enter a conference with somewhat cloudy ideas of what they wanted to accomplish. They found that Davis could not be convinced by these methods. He must know just what they were aiming at and how they were going to achieve their end.

His own views were always clear. His directness was really the reflection of his mental honesty. Because he could think only straight he could do things only in a straight manner. His judgment was not infallible, but usually it was good and deference was paid to it. Like all men of native force, he was positive, even obstinate, in his opinions, and when he allowed his obstinacy to influence his course of action and paid for it, as sometimes happened, he did not complain or seek to hold others responsible for his own mistakes.

One of the sources of his success was the confidence he inspired in his associates and the loyalty he inspired among his employees. Few young men who entered his employment and showed their worthiness failed to have the opportunity of bettering themselves. But it was always on the basis of self-help. The young man who had enjoyed some responsibility, and who had shown both capacity and fidelity, and who could exhibit the results of money saved, rarely failed to get the opportunity to make a profitable investment.

In his home life Henry G. Davis was seen at his best. Yet until a comparatively late period it was an austere home life. He long practised faithfully the Covenanter's Sunday. No work that possibly could be done on week-days was allowed to be performed on the Sabbath. Even the food was cooked, as far as possible, on Saturday. For many years the horses belonging to the family carriage were turned loose Saturday night, not to feel the harness again until Monday. Children of the family grown to womanhood and manhood recalled how the swings were tied Saturday night, not to be released until

Monday. In later years these strict observances gradually relaxed, and the head of the family even allowed
himself the recreation of whist and euchre and other entertainments on week-day evenings.

Mr. Davis was not a man given to much book reading,
but he had a very wide fund of information. He read
the newspapers and magazines discriminately and there
was seldom a current topic of interest on which he was
not fully informed. Fiction never appealed to him, because he knew it was fiction. "The people in the stories
are not real," he would sometimes say when urged to interest himself in a popular novel. "Everything there
is made up by the folks who write those books." This
indifference to fiction continued to the end of his life, and
it is doubtful if he ever read a novel.

American history to him unrolled in a few leading
events and he was never tired of reading them. The
Declaration of Independence and the Constitution were
two of the favored documents, but there were other State
papers. A little volume containing half a dozen of these
so appealed to him that he presented copies of it to his
friends. Among them were Washington's Farewell
Address, the Missouri Compromise and the Compro-
mises of 1850, the Monroe Doctrine, the Emancipation
Proclamation, and Lincoln's Gettysburg Address.

Mr. Davis was very fond of ancient history and of
biography. In middle life he read much literature of
this character himself, but in later years he was wont to
have some member of the family read to him. Like so
many men of constructive natures who are educated by
observation and experience, the great characters in history stood out before him as the exemplars of deeds
rather than of abstract ideas. In his speeches and addresses he frequently drew on his knowledge of history.

When he made his speech on agriculture in the Senate
in 1879, his copious historical introduction was the fruit
of his own reading, and in later speeches on the same
subject he amplified his observations.

A neat typewritten outline of a speech he made on
agriculture at Parkersburg in November, 1910, when he
was in his eighty-second year, illustrates in a few para-
graphic quotations his mode of historical thought:

History informs us that a nation or people that neglects agriculture decays.

In support of this under the wise policy of Philip of Macedonia
the country gave great attention to agriculture, and grew rich,
powerful, and prosperous.

Alexander neglected agriculture and commenced his conquest
of the world, and the nation decayed. Carthage grew great and
happy by attention to agriculture and commerce.

Hannibal, the great General, abandoned agriculture and commenced a war to conquer other nations, and his country went to
pieces.

Rome in the early days, following the example of such farmers
as Cato, Cincinnatus, and others, gave great attention to agriculture, and grew to be the greatest and most powerful nation in the
history of the world. Cæsar, Antony, and others caused agriculture to be neglected and went to war to conquer other nations, and
Rome declined and was finally blotted out.

Seventy-five per cent. of the signers of the Declaration of Independence were agriculturists.

Four of our great Presidents were farmers—Washington, Jefferson, Jackson, and Lincoln.

In his reading of history Mr. Davis sometimes found
illustrations to serve a polemic purpose. In his support
of Mr. Bryan for President in 1896, he spoke of the
charge against Bryan on account of his youth, and cited
these illustrations of young men:

"Pitt, perhaps the greatest Minister England has ever
had, was at the head of the English Government before

he was thirty. Alexander Hamilton, one of the ablest men of this or any other country, was aid and companion to Washington at twenty-two, was made Secretary of the Treasury at thirty-two. Jefferson wrote the Virginia Bill of Rights at thirty, and the Declaration of Independence at thirty-three. Alexander the Great conquered the world at twenty-five. Napoleon, the greatest of European generals, ruled France and most of Europe at thirty."

In the preparation of his speeches and addresses, Mr. Davis followed the methodical habit that he applied in business affairs. Everything was carefully thought out in advance, given its proper sequence, and thus noted. The outlines of several of these speeches show him as a clear thinker and as a shrewd special advocate. Sometimes the notes served as the basis for remarks of an extemporaneous character, later to be embodied in more formal language. He was always sure of his facts and his statistics were carefully verified.

An interesting reminder of political activities is an outline in his own handwriting of a speech he made in 1878. Since he was speaking as a Democrat, it might be taken for granted that he would vigorously attack the Republicans. Among his indictments of the party in power is the great increase in the number of office-holders. He does not deal in generalities, but gives the figures: Buchanan, 44,527; Lincoln, 46,146; Andrew Johnson, 56,113; Grant, 102,350.

Nature had endowed him with a strong constitution. Life in the open air, hard work in youth and early manhood, had developed his physical powers. Simple habits of living had preserved the stamina with which nature endowed him. His vigor was the wonder of his family and friends, who had many opportunities of noting his

Mr. Davis on horseback

powers of endurance. His fondness for horseback riding dated from his boyhood. In the frequent citations from his journal the horseback journeys through the wilderness are noted. He would spend twelve hours in the saddle, and at night, while his young companions would be wearied to the point of exhaustion, he would show no signs of fatigue.

At his summer home in Elkins almost daily he would mount his favorite horse and ride over the farm and the surrounding country. In Washington it was not unusual for those who took their early morning exercise on horseback to meet him riding through Rock Creek Park. Sometimes his ride was taken later in the day, and the chance observer who saw him was apt to remark how well he sat his horse. If the same observer saw him dismount easily and walk off with a springy step, he could hardly be made to believe that the horseman was ninety years old.

There was no secret about the physical vigor he maintained in his later years, but the retention of his extraordinary powers of body and mind undoubtedly was in a measure due to his ability to sleep, though, reasoning in a circle, it might be said that his ability to sleep was due to his physical attributes. He was accustomed to take a nap after luncheon, and in the closing years the length of this nap gradually lengthened. All his life he had the faculty of securing a short sleep in the daytime, but the real source of his strength was due to sleep during the hours that nature has prescribed for it. Regularly he went to bed at eleven o'clock, and he was wont to say that within five minutes he would be in a sound sleep from which he would not wake till morning.

Once he took part in a railway conference in which not only much money but other considerations equally important were involved. Men of large affairs were there. Their interests were conflicting and the antagonisms that developed became sharply personal. The conference broke up without coming to any agreement. Mr. Davis, as one of the principals, himself had been lifted out of his usual self-possession and exhibited some annoyance. The next day, when he came to his office, he spoke of the matter complainingly, which was unusual with him. "I was much upset by that dispute," he said. "Last night I couldn't get to sleep for half an hour after I went to bed." The probability was very strong that the majority of his associates had not been able to sleep at all.

Mr. Davis's religious faith was deep and unquestioning. It was conviction and not simply belief. He was a Presbyterian and his Calvinistic faith was part of his Scotch-Irish inheritance. All his life he was a member of the Presbyterian Church, but he was tolerant of all creeds. After his death, among his papers was found a newspaper clipping quoting J. Pierpont Morgan's confession of faith:

I commit my soul unto the hands of my Saviour, in full confidence that, having redeemed it and washed it in his most precious blood, He will present it faultless before the throne of my Heavenly Father; and I entreat my children to maintain and defend, at all hazards, and at any cost of personal sacrifice, the blessed doctrine of the complete atonement for sin through the blood of Jesus Christ, once offered, and through that alone.

Mr. Davis himself subscribed to that deep sentiment. Another newspaper clipping gave in parallel columns the old and new Presbyterian catechism; that is, the Westminster catechism and the new catechism. This was three years before his death, and bore his initials. His own confession of faith appears in the most sacred and intimate form that the words of man can express. It is in the entry in his journal describing the illness and death of his wife, paying her the tender tribute that is meant only for a life companion, and concluding: "I hope and believe in Heaven."

CHAPTER XX

THE CLOSING YEARS

Tranquil activities of Mr. Davis to the end—Slowing up in business affairs not marked—Fraternal associations—Memories of the Order of Odd Fellows—The commemorative jewel—No Ciceronian reflections on Old Age—Reforesting the wilderness for future generations—Anecdotes of contemporaries—Health strategy—Comment on public affairs—Anniversary tributes to his life and work—At ninety-two—Last summer at Elkins— Meditations for the Railway Builder—Winter in Washington— Journal entries—Illness and death—Retrospect of a long life.

THE time when a long and active life drew to an end has been anticipated in the previous chapters. Yet until the very last there remained much of that remarkable life to be told. The closing years might be thought by those of his own age to begin at threescore and ten, but that was the period in which his activities were too manifold to think of their coming to an end. After it came the second decade of biblical old age, but he was then beginning and carrying through important railway and development enterprises. Perhaps the last decade might be taken as the closing period, and that included continuous if not incessant activities. Though these activities have been told in detail, some of them bear elaboration.

Mr. Davis's mode of living in the closing years was little different from that which it had been throughout the many previous years. In the early spring he would go to Elkins and remain till the late autumn or even till the frosts of winter appeared. The summers would be broken by visits to Bedford Springs in Pennsylvania or to Webster Springs in the heart of West Virginia, where he found the waters salutary. The winters were passed in Washington, sometimes at one of the hotels, but oftener with one of his daughters, either Mrs. Lee or Mrs. Elkins. After the death of Senator Elkins in 1911 he went to live at the home of Mrs. Elkins. During these winter stays at the national capital he spent several hours every day at his office, following his accustomed routine. Business trips to New York were not infrequent, while scarcely a week passed that he did not go over to Baltimore. Fortress Monroe usually provided a fortnight's recreation.

During the last years he "slowed up" somewhat, as he phrased it, in business affairs; yet the numerous entries in his journal throughout this period concerning the Coal and Coke Railway, the mines, and collateral matters afforded little outward indication of any lessening of his labors. He was wont, however, himself to remark that too much should not be expected of a man of his age, and that he did not feel that he was capable of carrying on alone the various enterprises with which he was so closely identified.

In the winter of 1912 a tacit admission on his part that he had been attempting too much was the arrangement under which his associates took more direct control of the railway and coal and timber properties. In noting the election of the new officers, he adds the comment: "I was eighty-nine." A year earlier he had relieved himself of some of the responsibilities of the financial institutions with which he was connected by resigning, and his comment on one of these resignations is equally brief: "I was a bank president for fifty years."

While relieving himself of responsibility for the properties with which he was identified, he took a greater interest than ever in trade and industry in their broader aspects. His activities in the West Virginia Board of Trade have been described in an earlier chapter. Something also has been said of his relation to the West Virginia Bankers' Association. This was largely of a personal character, and it gave him opportunity to discuss the general subject of financing and banking with a clearness which showed that his mental powers were unimpaired. The address he delivered when the State Association met at Elkins in the summer of 1913 illustrates his clear mental grasp. He was then in his eighty-eighth year. On neatly typewritten sheets the various topics are given in orderly and logical arrangement, and they are interspersed with numerous memoranda in his own handwriting.

Natural phenomena interested him in the same measure as current events. He watched with eagerness, like the rest of the world, the reappearance of Halley's comet in the spring of 1910 after its seventy-five years' absence, and confessed to some disappointment that when the comet did appear its transit was not up to his expectations as a spectacle of the skies. To the lad of twelve, three quarters of a century earlier, it had seemed more brilliant; "anyhow, folks made more fuss about it," he quaintly remarked. And he thought it had appeared in winter. His memory was not at fault. The transit of Halley's comet had been in mid-November, 1835.

In these later years his mind turned back to old fraternal associations and he renewed the memories of his membership in various orders. His journal recites that he became a Mason, a member of Hiram Lodge, at Wesernport, Maryland, in 1860. It was, however, the early associations with the Order of Odd Fellows that filled his mind and time most completely. His life literally was linked with the growth of this order in the United States, for his recollections went back to Thomas Wildey, who was one of the founders of the first lodge, organized at Baltimore in 1819, and who continued to be identified with it for forty years. Mr. Davis knew him, and had sat in the same lodge with him. He frequently attended the public functions of the Order.

In May, 1909, Randolph Lodge presented him with a jewel in commemoration of his having been a member sixty-four years. The jewel was of solid gold studded with diamonds. The presentation was intensely gratifying to him, but the account of the ceremony, including his own speech as given in his journal, is very modest, with a passing reference to newspaper clippings which give a full account of the ceremonies.

Through the remaining years of his life the various lodges of Maryland and West Virginia continued to honor him. On the ninety-second anniversary of the Order at Baltimore, in April, 1911, he was the principal guest. His own story of the celebration is characteristically concise:

April 26, 1911. By invitation of Maryland Grand Lodge I made about a half hour talk to a great crowd at Odd Fellows Temple in Baltimore; gave a short history of Odd Fellowship, referred to good done by the Order, including Rebekah Order.

Judge Alston G. Dayton in a reminiscent letter regarding the presentation of the jewel indicates the deep sentiment of Mr. Davis toward the Odd Fellows' Order:

It was the occasion when the Odd Fellows' organization presented to him the medal which it confers upon its members who have kept up their membership in good standing for fifty continuous years. The presentation was made the occasion for one of the largest gatherings ever held in the city of Elkins. It was my pleasant duty as a Past Grand Master of the Order to make an address on the occasion, and, speaking of the period of time covered by the Senator's life, the discoveries that had been made in it, the progress of civilization during it, I said the Senator had, by Divine Providence, been permitted in his nearly ninety years of life to see and have part in more important affairs than were embraced in any thousand-year period previous to that time. The thought struck him so forcibly that, in my deliberate judgment, he made one of the strongest, if not the strongest, most interesting, and really eloquent addresses of his life. It very greatly affected both the Senator and the very large audience of his Elkins neighbors and friends.

As the years grew on him Mr. Davis sometimes talked of his age, but always in a matter-of-fact way. Cicero's reflections on Old Age would have made no appeal to him, because he was not given to philosophizing or moralizing. He took the growing years, like everything else in his existence, as something that was part of life and therefore not to be set apart as a subject for consideration in itself. To him it was the simple and natural thing to keep on planning and working. His mind was habituated to looking forward. While he was constructing his last railway, some comment was made on a short-term bond, fifteen years, which he issued as part of the financing. When asked why the term was so short he merely replied: "Why, we may be able to get better interest rates in fifteen years, and we don't want to be tied up with our bonds too long."

When he built his beautiful home, "Graceland," at Elkins, the estate was lined with poplars. While these grew rapidly, they did not prove to be in keeping with the landscape, and he therefore had them taken down and replaced by maples. To a member of his family who gently reproached him, saying that he would be without shade the rest of his life, he replied: "Oh, no; I shall be enjoying the maples." And this proved to be true. He lived to enjoy their shade.

One day, in those closing years, a lawyer who had achieved a competency and was about to retire, was his companion on the train going over one of the Davis railway lines. Mr. Davis talked to him as the train sped along about the way the timber wilderness had been opened, lands cleared, and then reforested. The spruce used for pulp-making had been replanted. Later Mr. Davis showed him several tracts that had been cleared of hickory and replanted, commenting casually on the utility of this tree as one of the reasons that had impelled him to reforest those tracts.

"How long does it take hickory to grow?" inquired the lawyer. "About forty years," was the reply. "We can always use hickory, and it ought to be kept growing." The lawyer reflected that if a man in his eighties still found something to do replanting forests and providing for the needs of future generations, it was not quite the thing for him to retire in middle age from his own profession in which his career had been both honorable and useful. He at once telegraphed countermanding the sale of his law library and continued his practice. Innate abhorrence of waste had something to do with replanting the hickory and the spruce, but the striking thing was that Mr. Davis should keep on doing it in his old age.

Mr. Davis did not care to be called venerable or a patriarch, and even the title of Grand Old Man of West Virginia was not always pleasing to him. But he sometimes indulged in comparisons with other old men. A New England clergyman who was born on the same day of the same year used to write him annually, as the birth anniversary approached, and sign himself, "Your birthday brother." Mr. Davis enjoyed these letters, but they were somewhat too copious for him, and in dictating the reply he once remarked, "The minister has more time to write than I have. He doesn't have anything to do, while I am pretty busy."

When well along in the eighties, he had an interview on some business matter with former Vice-President Levi P. Morton in the latter's New York office. Mr. Morton, when a trifling difference of opinion arose, jokingly remarked that Davis ought to agree with him, as he was the older. Coming away from the interview, Mr. Davis told the story with much glee, remarking: "Morton doesn't seem to know that I am a year older than he is."

A Baltimore friend of early years in the casual meetings with Mr. Davis plumed himself on his greater age. Once Mr. Davis showed impatience at his friend's reminiscences, and after the prospective centenarian had left he said: "Blank is getting old; he has told that story before." Blank was then ninety-seven.

Occasionally Mr. Davis would be compelled to admit that, while his health was good for a man of his age, he was not entirely free from the possibility of illness. At times he suffered severely from lumbago, and he bore the pain with a stoicism that was the wonder of his family. It took indirect methods of persuasion to induce him to heed the doctor's orders and lessen his activities. On one occasion when he was badly run down, and the doctor advised him to drop business and go away for a rest, he obstinately refused, insisting that he knew more about his health than the physician did.

Strategy had to be employed. A member of his family approached him and said that the doctor wanted to talk with him about engineering and timber cruising and coal mining and running railways. "What does he want to talk about those things for?" was the inquiry. "Oh," was the reply, "he has concluded that he can do better mining coal and running a railway than in practising his profession of medicine." "May be he can," was the rejoinder. "May be he does know more about those things than about medicine and health. But you get my things ready and we'll start away to-morrow on that trip he told me to take."

Mr. Davis's interest in politics and public affairs was undimmed until the very end. West Virginia politics became involved in a turmoil and both parties were rent by factions. The way in which he followed the developments is attested by several large envelopes with clippings giving full accounts of the various manœuvers and of the politicians engaged in them.

Whenever he happened to be in Charleston during the meeting of the Legislature he would pay a visit to both branches. In the Senate, of which he had been a member for four years, he would be given a seat of honor by the presiding officer, and usually a recess would be taken in which members of all parties would show the warm regard in which they held him. Usually, too, on these visits to the State capital, he would give the local newspapers an interview in which, with his wonted frankness, his views would be expressed without regard to expediency.

While conservative in his political views and actions, Mr. Davis had nothing of the trimmer in him, and whenever he talked on politics it was known that he meant what he said. By his own example he had shown throughout his life the duty that he believed the citizen should take in public affairs, and this was not confined to the State and nation; the civic welfare of the town and the local community were also of concern to him. An inconvenient journey under unfavorable conditions of travel, undertaken at ninety in order to vote at a local election, was evidence of this concern.

Spending so much of his time at the national capital, Mr. Davis's interest in public affairs was the more keen. His visits to the Senate chamber were not frequent; but on one occasion, after meeting many of the Senators who had not even begun their public career when he retired from public life, he caused an inquiry to be made concerning those who had served with him when he entered the Senate and who were still alive. He himself was eighty-nine years old. Of his former colleagues who were then living, Cornelius Cole of California was ninety, William Pitt Kellogg of Louisiana, eighty-two; Adelbert Ames of Mississippi, seventy-seven; William Sprague of Rhode Island, seventy-nine; George F. Edmunds of Vermont, eighty-five; Alexander Caldwell of Kansas, eighty-three; and Powell Clayton of Arkansas, eighty. Of these Senatorial contemporaries, George F. Edmunds and W. P. Kellogg were the only ones who survived Mr. Davis.

These closing years brought to him many testimonials and tributes to his life-work. The anniversaries of his birth never failed to call forth articles in the newspapers. When he was ninety there was a whole sheaf of newspaper felicitations. Some of these reviewed his long and active career in business and in public affairs, while others contented themselves with an interpretation of his life. Said a Pittsburgh journal:

A man who is physically and mentally well and strong and active at ninety is an inspiration not merely to men of ripe years, but to young men—to young men, for example, who are beginning life as railroad brakemen, as he did, or in some similar occupation which does not appear to hold out large hope of after eminence and affluence.

A newspaper of his own State commented:

His has been a remarkable career; he has risen from the ranks, beginning life in humble circumstances and attaining many years ago a position of influence in the affairs of his State second to that of no man born or living within its borders. He has contributed probably more than any other one man to its development and growth. He has had confidence in it and in its people, and the people have had reciprocal faith in him. He has developed its resources, increased its wealth, built railroads and cities, and creditably represented the interests of its people in positions of trust and responsibility to which they have called him.

When he reached ninety-two the tributes and the testimonials were even more appreciative. One of the West Virginia newspapers made the ninety-second anniversary the theme for this comment:

Ninety-two years ago in the city of Baltimore a child was born who was destined to have more to do with the upbuilding of a sister State, then unborn, than perhaps any other man. That child was Henry Gassaway Davis. . . . Mr. Davis has been a prominent figure in the business, social, and political life of his adopted State. He has grown old in the service of his people, always devoting his time and energy to the upbuilding of their interest.

More than a score of years have passed since the Grand Old Man of West Virginia, as he has long been affectionately called, reached and passed the allotted threescore and ten. In the course of human life he cannot be expected to remain many more years, but it is the earnest hope of his thousands of friends throughout the State that he may at least be permitted to round out a full century of useful life. When the time for his passing does finally come it will leave a void in West Virginia such as the loss of no other resident of the State could cause.

A Wheeling journal, after summarizing some of the events of his life, concluded with this estimate:

His career is part of the history of the State. His enterprises have helped to build it up, and he has represented it in the highest legislative halls of the land as well as in the councils of the brainy, resourceful, and wealthy—the men who do things.

Mr. Davis's last summer at Elkins was an ideal one for a long life that was drawing to a serene close. A quarter of a century earlier he had selected for the site of his home a wooded hill to the north of the town, on which he erected a commodious residence of Norman architectureal design, which he named "Graceland" in honor of his daughter Grace. The house was built of pink sandstone taken from a near-by quarry. To the east of this residence on another hill was the summer home of Senator Elkins, named, in honor of Mrs. Elkins, "Halliehurst."

During this last summer Mr. Davis in the ordinary course of his business activities visited the towns that had grown up from the wilderness under his guiding hand—Thomas, Davis, Parsons, Hendricks, Bayard, Blaine and the others that marked the progress of the West Virginia Central Railway. He also visited Gassaway on the Coal and Coke Railway, and the other new communities that also owed their existence to his enterprise.

At Elkins he found his greatest enjoyment. He wandered over the farm, with all its modern improvements, just as he had wandered over the Woodstock farm as a boy eighty years earlier, and in a hundred ways he showed how keen was still his interest in rural life. His interest was even greater in the town of Elkins. From his room at "Graceland" he could look down on the smokestacks of the factories that owed their existence to him, and he could watch the locomotives as they were shunted in and out of the shops that had been built by him. Here was a thriving community of 8,000 busy, contented people, a railroad center, where a quarter of a century before had been a crossroads with a blacksmith shop. If he grew tired watching the industrial activities spread below him, his eyes could wander along the horizon of the mountains that inclosed the valley. It was a scene for the contemplation and the meditation of the Railway Builder.

In his journal, just before leaving Elkins, he recorded, under date of November 20, 1915: "This is a fine fall." His last journey to the national capital is thus described:

December 18, 1915. I left Elkins for Washington. Stopped overnight at Gassaway. Left Gassaway, spent day at Charleston, came to Washington on night of 19th; am at Hallie's (Mrs. Elkins's). While in Charleston called upon Gov. Hatfield, Secretary Reed, and Auditor Dent. Also at Davis Children's Home; about forty little ones there. They have found homes for 845 children.

This was the Child's Shelter which he supported. On reaching Washington the following morning he went to church with Mrs. Elkins.

The winter in Washington was after his usual routine. He spent several hours every day at his office. Social intercourse claimed much of his attention. He attended a few formal functions, but he enjoyed much more informal dinners and luncheons at the Elkins home. He especially enjoyed being a guest at a luncheon given to ladies, he being the only man permitted to be present.

"The women's talk is much more interesting," he used to say, and then would add quaintly: "They are all so attentive when there's only one man."

His own observations on the winter season were recorded in two entries in his journal:

December 25, 1915. Christmas. Weather good. Country generally is prosperous, and looks good.

February 15, 1916. Weather cold. Railway and coal mines doing fairly well. I am in Washington, staying with Hallie.

A few days after this entry was made he took a bad cold which developed into a case of the grippe. He did not himself consider it as serious, although he realized that his powers of recuperation were getting feebler. Until the last he was well enough to see the members of the family, and it was rarely that some of them were not in the sickroom. He talked of current matters with his usual conciseness and deprecated the family taking too much trouble about him.

There was a pause in the progress of his illness which appeared to indicate a temporary improvement. So favorable seemed the change that on the night of March 10 his daughter, Mrs. Elkins, was bidden by the physicians to go to her own room for a good night's sleep, while the other members of the family were also told that there was likely to be no change for the worse. Accordingly they retired. Shortly after midnight the change came unexpectedly, and an hour later Mr. Davis passed away almost as in a quiet sleep. Funeral services were held at the Elkins home in Washington, and then the remains were taken to Elkins and interred in the beautiful Maplewood Cemetery beside his wife and among the kindred for whom he had prepared this final resting-place.

Eulogies of his career, interpretations of his life and work, filled the journals after his death. The estimate of what he had wrought for his own State was crystallized in this paragraph in the *Wheeling Intelligencer:*

Day-dreams of the Piedmont station agent transformed into perpetual realities. . . . Towns, mills, railroads, villages, cities, churches, schools, stand monuments to meet the quiet gaze of the man who brought them to a thriving existence.

Reviews of the period covered by this remarkable life were not confined to local achievements. Nor should they be. The times in which he lived, the events of which Henry G. Davis was a part, covered almost a century of history. He was a babe of a fortnight when President James Monroe enunciated the Doctrine with which he himself three quarters of a century later was to become identified through his participation as a member of International American Conferences. He was a year old when Lafayette visited the United States and revived the memories of France's contribution to the Revolution. He was in advancing childhood when John Quincy Adams was President, and was an observant, growing boy during the administration of Andrew Jackson. A child old enough to see the venerable and imposing Charles Carroll of Carrollton lay the corner-stone for the first railway in the United States, he lived to see in operation a quarter of a million miles of railroad to the building of which he had contributed his share.

His first vote, that for Henry Clay, was cast in the year when the first telegraphic message was transmitted between Baltimore and Washington. That was the year, too, in which Rutherford B. Hayes, whose term as President was to run parallel with his career in the United States Senate, was born. He was in vigorous young manhood, demonstrating his abilities for railway management, when Alton B. Parker, who was to head the ticket fifty-two years later for President with Henry G. Davis as the candidate for Vice-President, was born. He was thirty-five years of age, the period that Dante marks as the arch of life, when Theodore Roosevelt was born, and the pony express, the forerunner of the transcontinental railways, was established between St. Louis and San Francisco.

Looking beyond the boundaries of his own country, he was a lad of twelve when Queen Victoria ascended the throne of England, and he lived through that reign, and more than a score of years after the Golden Jubilee. He was in public life and political leadership in his own State, and at the threshold of his career as a Senator of the United States, when Sedan fell, Paris capitulated, and victorious Prussia established the German Empire over the body of prostrate France. He lived to see the Empire thus established plunge Europe into a war that was to become a world war without parallel and to involve his own country at the period most critical for the cause of civilization.

He lived through the War with Mexico, the Civil War, and the Spanish-American War, and as a citizen and a public man, discharging official duties, he had his part in all the national responsibilities growing out of those wars. In every phase of his career—as a railway builder, in the development of the natural resources of his own State, as a guiding force in the building of the commonwealth with which his public life was identified, as a factor in the affairs of the Western Hemisphere on their international side, as a Senator of the United States, and as a trusted political leader—the constructive character of his mind was always manifest. And throughout his long and varied career he was always in touch with his own kind. He literally worked as if he were to live forever, and lived as if he were to die tomorrow.

THE END

INDEX

309